ENCYCLOPEDIA OF
NORTH AMERICAN
BIRDS

ENCYCLOPEDIA OF
NORTH AMERICAN
BIRDS

David Alderton

Bath · New York · Singapore · Hong Kong · Cologne · Delhi · Melbourne

First published by Parragon in 2008

Parragon
Queen Street House
4 Queen Street
Bath BA1 1HE, UK

Created and produced by

studio **cactus** ⊙

13 SOUTHGATE STREET WINCHESTER HAMPSHIRE SO23 9DZ

DESIGN Sharon Cluett, Sharon Rudd, Laura Watson
EDITORIAL Jennifer Close, Jo Weeks

ISBN: 978-1-4075-2436-8

Printed in China

CONTENTS

ABOUT THIS BOOK

The way in which birds are grouped together is based on the same underlying principles that apply in other areas of the natural world. The classificatory system works through a series of ranks, which become increasingly more refined, allowing the individual birds to be recognized within this general framework.

BIRDS AND US

Attempts to evolve a classificatory system not just for birds but for all life forms began with the ancient Greeks, but the modern science of classification, called taxonomy, stems from the pioneering work of Swedish botanist and zoologist Carl Linnaeus in the 1800s. This is not a static field, however, and the scientific names given to birds have changed quite frequently in the past. A major shift in our understanding of bird groups is now starting to occur, thanks to DNA studies, and this will finally establish avian relationships from a genetic rather than an anatomical viewpoint.

DISTRIBUTION MAPS

The maps in this book give an indication of where a particular species is most likely to be seen in North America. Migrants may occur over a wider area as they are fly back and forth between their wintering and breeding grounds.

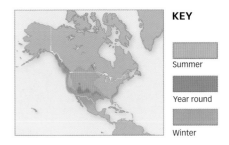

KEY

Summer

Year round

Winter

SYMBOLS IN THIS BOOK

The silhouettes give some indication of the profiles of the birds in particular Orders, although there can be marked divergences in a few cases, notably in the Piciformes, which embrace species ranging from woodpeckers to toucans. Each order consists of a number of families. Then below the family rank are the different genera. It is possible to orientate yourself within the classificatory tree by the way in which the names are written. Orders always end with -formes, as in the case of Columbiformes, while at Family level, the ending is -ae, as Columbidae. Genera are the the first rank to be written in an italicized form, as in *Columba*. The species is a binomial name, as in the case of *Columba livia*, and, again, is always written in italics. Where there is a subspecies recognized, there will be a third name, such as *Columba livia livia*, marking the lowest level in the classificatory tree.

SILHOUETTES

GAVIIFORMES

PODICIPEDIFORMES

PROCELLARIIFORMES

PELECANIFORMES

CICONIIFORMES

ANSERIFORMES

FALCONIFORMES

GALLIFORMES

GRUIFORMES

CHARADRIIFORMES

COLUMBIFORMES

CUCULIFORMES

STRIGIFORMES

CAPRIMULGIFORMES

APODIFORMES

TROGONIFORMES

CORACIIFORMES

PICIFORMES

PASSERIFORMES

THE WORLD OF BIRDS

Birds rank as the most conspicuous of the creatures that live alongside us. Whether in a city, out in the country or on a beach, you are likely to see them. This helps to explain our interest in birds because they feature so evidently in daily life, but equally, they are fascinating in their own right, thanks partly to their aerial abilities. There are about 8,800 different species of bird worldwide, and nearly 1,000 are to be found in North America. Sadly, among the significant extinctions over the course of the past century was the only naturally occurring member of the parrot family endemic to the United States, the Carolina Parakeet (*Conuropsis carolinensis*). Today, much is being done to aid the survival of endangered and vulnerable species. New threats such as pollution and climate change have emerged, however, and their often insidious effects may be harder to counter in order to ensure the survival of many species in the future.

AMERICAN ICON The Bald or White-headed Fish Eagle (*Haliaeetus leucocephalus*) is often sometimes described as the American Eagle, being the bird most closely identified with the United States, although its distribution is more widespread, extending down to Mexico and northward to Canada.

WHAT ARE BIRDS?

Perhaps the most obvious characteristic associated with birds—an ability to fly—is actually not one of the features that separate them from other vertebrate groups. In fact, a number of birds such as penguins, kiwis and ostriches cannot fly, while on the other hand, mammals such as bats have mastered the power of flight. A distinguishing characteristic of birds is, however, their body covering. Feathers, which help to protect the body and insulate it, as well as providing an ability to fly, are only seen in birds. Another trait of birds is the way in which they reproduce: all species lay eggs with a hard calcareous ("chalk-like") shell.

ANCESTOR This is a fossil of *Archaeopteryx*, which is currently the world's oldest known bird. The distinctive claws on the wing tips can be seen here.

BIG BEGINNINGS Quetzalcoatlus had a wingspan approaching 40 ft (12 m). This pterosaur is therefore the largest creature yet discovered that possessed the power of flight. It fed on small sea creatures, lacking any teeth in its narrow jaws.

THE ORIGINS OF BIRDS

Over the past decade, the origins of birds have become clearer, and many zoologists believe that they are descended from small dinosaurs, which evolved the ability to fly. They survived the mass extinction of their larger relatives that took place at the end of the Cretaceous era, some 65 million years ago, and soon became the dominant group of vertebrates possessing the power of flight. Birds rapidly diversified and spread around the world, replacing the pterosaurs, a reptilian group that had first taken to the skies about 130 million years previously.

Fossilized evidence of the early birds that would reveal the history of their development is sparse, compared with many dinosaurs. This is partly due to their much smaller size. Their bodies were more likely to be eaten by larger scavengers rather than being preserved in such a way that their remains would ultimately be fossilized. Nevertheless, a growing number of avian fossils have been unearthed over recent years, particularly in the area of present-day China, revealing more about how the group developed.

The earliest recognizable bird is still *Archaeopteryx*, whose remains were unearthed in a Bavarian slate quarry in Germany during 1861. Based on the age of the layer of rock in which the fossil was found, this bird died about 145 million years ago. *Archaeopteryx* had a similar appearance to modern birds, with recognizable feathers, and was able to fly rather than just glide from tree to tree.

It would appear that these early birds were far less agile on the wing than their descendants today. They were equipped with claws on their wing tips, which allowed them to clamber around on the branches. This characteristic is still evident in one species today—the South American Hoatzin (*Opisthocomus hoatzin*—see box).

OSTRICH The bulk of the Ostrich (*Struthio camelus*) means that these avian giants cannot fly, relying instead on their powerful legs to outrun potential predators.

Hoatzin chicks

Like early bird ancestors, Hoatzin chicks hatch with claws on the tips of their wings. The nest is often built above water, but, thanks partly to their claws, if they fall in they can anchor on to vegetation and then climb back up to the nest site. These claws are soon shed as the chicks grow older and are able to start flying.

Early birds such as *Archaeopteryx* also had sharp teeth in their jaws. These gradually disappeared as the bird's skeleton lightened, enhancing its flying abilities. Seabirds hunting fish were seemingly the last group to lose their teeth, reflecting the difficulties of grasping their slippery prey. Gradually, however, the shape of their bills became modified to undertake this task efficiently.

Many of the avian families that are now in existence had already evolved around 38 million years ago. Fossils cannot show the colors of these early birds, but it is likely that seabirds were relatively dull, with black and white coloration predominating in their plumage, while forest species were probably more brightly colored.

EXTINCT GIANTS

The African Ostrich is the biggest bird on earth today, but there used to be other, even larger and far more ferocious species. These birds were all too large to fly, but they made up for this by their long-legged gait, which enabled them to move fast on land. The most fearsome group were the phororhacids that roamed from the southern United States down across South America and lived and hunted in flocks. They could grow to about 10 ft (3 m) tall and had powerful bills as well as sharp talons on their feet that allowed them to overpower their quarry easily.

AVIAN MOVEMENTS

Birds have spread throughout the world, and are even able to survive along the northern coast of Alaska and Canada, well inside the Arctic Circle. Many of the species occurring here are sea birds, which obtain their food in the surrounding oceans, moving southward when the sea freezes. Other birds migrate to and from this region, taking advantage of the brief summer period in the far north. At this time of the year, the upper part of the ground thaws, while beneath, the deep soil remains frozen solid. The meltwater that forms is unable to drain away, and this provides a breeding ground for midges: a source of food for many birds. They head south as the Arctic winter closes in, and the ground freezes over again.

MIGRATION

It is not just species from the far north that may head southward in the fall. Barn Swallows (*Hirundo rustica*) are a relatively common sight across much of North America during the summer months. But the onset of colder weather severely curtails the swarms of flying insects that they feed upon, forcing the birds to leave the region or face starvation.

Aside from swallows, there are many other birds that undertake regular seasonal movements, with this behavior being described as migration. Further studies have revealed that virtually all birds, ranging from small passerines to large storks, share set flight paths when migrating. These may not be the shortest, most direct route because, just like aircraft, birds avoid crossing over large expanses of

On the move

The urge to migrate is driven by changing seasonal conditions, threatening the birds' supply of food. North American birds tend to follow set flight paths when migrating, not necessarily taking the most direct route. Those that overwinter in South America, for example, tend to fly down over Central America rather than crossing the Caribbean. On occasions, however, birds do get lost or blown off-course and then can be seen well-away from their usual area of distribution.

FAST MOVER The Greater Roadrunner lives in the deserts of New Mexico, United States. The lack of cover in this type of environment also means that these birds must pursue their prey at high speed across the ground, attaining speeds equivalent to nearly 16 mph (10 kph) over short distances.

sea, preferring to fly over land. Most Northern American migrants funnel down through Central America, although some from eastern areas cross via the isthmus of Florida and Caribbean islands to the south, in order to reach South America, taking the same route again when they head back north. Banding studies, and more recently, the use of radio telemetry have enabled scientists to track such movements in increasing detail.

Sometimes, however, things can go wrong and birds may end up being blown off-course, turning up in areas where they would not normally occur. They are described as vagrants. It is not uncommon for various North American birds, especially gulls from the eastern side of the continent, to be observed on occasions in western parts of Europe, having been blown here by strong winds. The Scilly Isles, off the southwest tip of the United Kingdom, is an area where vagrants are often reported, being the most westerly outpost of land here in the Atlantic.

Equally, birds that are usually observed in western parts of North America may occasionally turn up in Hawaii. There are also cases of mainland species being seen

in new areas. The Social Flycatcher (*Myiozetetes similis*), whose northerly range extended no further than Mexico, was observed in the United States for the first time in January 2005, in southern Texas. It may become more commonly seen in this region, expanding its range in a northerly direction.

PHYSICAL ADAPTATIONS

Instead of migrating, some birds modify their appearance in winter to disguise their presence more effectively in a snowy landscape. The Rock Ptarmigan (*Lagopus mutus*) molts its brown plumage at the end of the brief Arctic summer, to become pure white in appearance. Snowy Owls (*Nyctea scandiaca*), which are forced by lack of trees to spend much of the time near the ground, are also mainly white, which helps camouflage them when hunting.

At the other extreme, there are other birds well suited to living in arid areas of North America. One of the best known is the Greater Roadrunner (*Geococcyx californianus*), so-called because of its hunting habits, which confirm how it has adapted to its habitat. In desert areas, the temperature can plummet at night. In the morning, cold-blooded reptiles bask on roads, because the tarmac surface warms up more quickly than the surrounding land, enabling them to regain their body heat faster. This is where roadrunners hunt, ambushing small reptiles and scavenging roadkills.

COLOR CHANGE Rock Ptarmigan (*Lagopus mutus*) in summer plumage (*below*) and transformed to blend into the winter landscape (*left*). This color change is particularly vital in an area where there is little natural cover for the birds.

SEASONAL JOURNEY Flocks of Snow Geese (*Anser caerulescens*) fly considerable distances to and from their breeding grounds. Migratory birds often travel in large flocks, which can build up days before they depart.

AVIAN ENVIRONMENTS

The adaptability of certain species of bird has been shown by the way in which they can now be found living successfully in cities. Almost anywhere in North America, particularly in urban areas, there are feral pigeons to be found. These, however, are not true wild birds. They are descendants of the Rock Dove (*Columbia livia*), which is still to be found living on coastal cliffs of Europe.

FERAL PIGEONS These descendants of the Rock Dove (*Columba livia*) are widely found throughout the world's cities today, having adapted to living and breeding in this type of environment. They often scavenge on the streets rather than being regular bird-table visitors in the suburbs.

SUCCESS STORIES

About a millennium ago, Rock Doves started to be domesticated and kept in dovecotes as a source of food, particularly in the grounds of monastic communities. There could be hundreds of thousands of birds at some localities. Inevitably, some strayed and started breeding in the wild again. The early settlers brought these pigeons to North America, and the same process started again. The pigeons were drawn to towns and cities, and starting to breed in and on the sides of buildings, which offered a relatively safe refuge. Food, in the form of scraps, was readily obtainable in this environment.

The presence of pigeons has in turn attracted a natural predator, in the guise of the Peregrine Falcon (*Falco peregrinus*), to settle in various cities. Here, the highrise apartments are similar in terms of height and inaccessibility to the cliff faces on which these falcons

NEW HUNTING GROUNDS A large flock of starlings being harried by a hunting Peregrine Falcon (*Falco peregrinus*). Trained birds of prey are now being used by falconers to keep such flocks away from sites such as airports where they could be a danger.

Threats

The major threats facing birds today include:
■ Loss of habitat, including nesting sites
■ Declining food sources often linked with human activity, such as overfishing
■ Oil and other forms of environmental pollution
■ Hunting pressures
In most cases, it is a combination of these factors which brings a species to the verge of extinction.

will more commonly breed. They provide vantage points too, from which the falcons can hunt feral pigeons, just as they will naturally pursue Rock Doves elsewhere.

A temporary movement of birds, arising from a shortage of food, can be seen in the case of Snowy Owls (*Nyctea scandiaca*). In North America, they prey largely on lemmings, and roughly every seven years, the lemming population crashes. This forces the owls to wander over a wider area in search of other prey, heading further south into Canada and even the United States. Many species can be seen in the wild far away from their native haunts, often as the result of deliberate translocations by people in the past. Early European settlers brought a number of species to North America to remind them of home. Common Starlings (*Sturnus vulgaris*)

CLOSE WATCH Radio-tracking of a Californian Condor (*Gymnogyps californianus*) released in the Grand Canyon region of the state. This has helped to provide information about the habits of these birds, as well as ensuring that the captive bred offspring are adapting to life in the wild.

have advanced significantly, the ultimate challenge remains being able to recreate a viable population in the wild. The very pressures that brought the species to its imperiled state, however, almost inevitably involving loss of habitat, are particularly hard to reverse successfully. The most high profile and costly project of this type in the United States involves the California Condor (*Gymnogyps californianus*). This giant bird of prey—the largest of North America's raptors—was on the very verge of extinction when the last remaining wild condors were captured for a captive breeding program in 1987. Since then, however, the captive breeding population has grown to over 100 birds, with a similar number having been released back to the wild in areas of California and the Grand Canyon.

Not all conservation programs prove to be successful, however, for reasons that may not be immediately obvious. The Whooping Crane (*Grus americana*), once found as far south as central Mexico, no longer breeds in the United States, with its nesting grounds currently restricted to a small area in Alberta, Canada. Scientists tried to create a separate U.S. breeding population by placing Whooping Crane eggs under a more widely-distributed endemic North American species, the Sandhill Crane (*Grus canadensis*), but the attempt failed. Meanwhile, efforts are being made to reestablish a resident population of Whooping Cranes in Florida.

were released in Central Park, New York in 1890. They spread very rapidly across much of the continent, reaching the west coast by the 1950s. A decade later, these starlings were to be seen in Alaska for the first time, and they are still spreading, particularly in a southerly direction through Baja California and western Mexico.

STRUGGLES TO ADAPT

There is a growing number of endangered avian species in the world today. While captive breeding techniques

AVIAN ANATOMY

Birds' front limbs have evolved into wings, and cannot be used for walking. As a result, their center of gravity differs from that of mammals: their legs have been brought forward to support the weight of their bodies. A bird's wings are rather like those of an airplane, with flight being made possible by curvature over the upper surface. This lessens the air resistance here, compared with the underside, making it easier for the bird to take off and remain in the air.

BEATING WINGS The long feathers running along the back of the wing of this Bewick Swan (*Cygnus columbianus*) are the flight feathers, which provide the thrust that a bird needs to be able to become airborne.

Parts of a bird

Specific terms are used to describe the various areas of a bird's body, and assist in the identification of individual species by enabling differences in coloration or markings to be highlighted easily. These features can also help in terms of determining an individual's gender. More general descriptions may also be used, such as the underparts, which relates to the underside of the body, or the upperparts, running down over the back to the rump.

Crown
Forehead
Eye ring
Nape
Back
Throat
Wing bar
Rump (under wings)
Breast
Upper tail coverts
Flank
Belly
Tail
Under tail coverts

FLIGHT

Some birds such as condors use their wings to glide, relying on upward columns of warm air, known as thermals. This enables them to stay airborne without having to flap their wings frequently, providing an energy-efficient way of remaining airborne.

The angle of the wings affects the bird's movement, with flapping of the wings providing propulsive power. Well-developed chest muscles assist with this task. There are specialist flight feathers running along the back of each wing, whose position alters during the flight cycle. The most evident feathers are the flight feathers, running along the back edge of the bird's wings. The primary flight feathers, located toward the tips, are the longest, and provide thrust. They can move independently to adjust air resistance. The secondary flight feathers, closest to the body, are shorter, and help to give the bird lift in flight. With each downward thrust, the flight feathers are held together, helping the bird to climb. Once the bird wants to slow down, approaching a perch for example, then it simply glides down, ceasing to flap its wings, but adjusting their position to help to reach the branch. When it wants to slow down more quickly, the bird spreads its tail feathers, increasing air resistance and exerting a greater drag effect.

PLUMAGE

Birds rely on the body covering of feathers, described as their plumage, to keep warm as well as ensuring that they can fly. The body itself is covered in soft, smooth contour feathers that cover its surface. These are organized in distinctive feather tracts, called pterylae.

Beneath these feathers can be a layer of down feathering, which helps maintain body temperature, trapping warm air close to the skin. This insulation is important because birds' body temperature generally averages between 106–110 degrees F (41 and 43.5 degrees C), and they have no body fat beneath their skin, unlike mammals. Apart from flying, however, birds use their feathers for other purposes too. In some cases, as with Tricolored Blackbirds (*Agelaius tricolor*), males will use their breeding plumage as part of their courtship display. The coloration of the feathers helps to distinguish the sexes easily in some cases throughout the year and also enables young birds to be recognized.

The plumage is kept in good condition by preening, using bills and occasionally claws. There are various parasites such as feather lice that may nibble at the feathers, and some birds treat themselves with a natural insecticide, smearing the formic acid from ants that they catch over their feathers. The plumage is usually shed on an annual basis, enabling frayed or damaged feathers to be replaced. Some birds, such as the striking Indigo Bunting (*Passerina cyanea*), molt at the start of the breeding season as well, growing more colorful or elaborate plumage for display purposes. Birds keep their plumage waterproof by smearing oil over the feathering. This is produced from the preen gland at the base of the tail.

SWIMMING All birds that spend large amounts of time in or on the water have webbed feet for more efficient paddling. This allows them to swim faster and with less effort. Birds that often dive and swim underwater, such as auks and guillemots, use front limbs as flippers. Propulsive power underwater is generated by their legs rather than their wings.

Flight

While the basic structure of the wing remains broadly identical, birds display a range of wing shapes, and these can give important clues as to their lifestyles. Birds such as swallows that spend much of their time in flight have angular wings and can fly with relatively little effort, gliding if needed. Other long-distance migrants such as curlews may have a similar wing structure, while the wing shape of kestrels enables them to hover, while they scan the ground below for prey. The wings of hummingbirds can be extended back behind the body, with the wing beats helping the bird to remain airborne, while at the same time, enabling it to hover and feed. This allows the hummingbird to move in close to the flower without its wings getting in the way. Pheasants, in contrast, are heavy birds, and not well adapted to flight. It takes considerably muscular effort for them to become airborne. Nevertheless, the rounded shape of their wings enables them to glide down smoothly when they spot a suitable area of cover. Vultures have long wings so they can remain airborne for long periods with minimal effort, gliding on columns of warm air known as thermals.

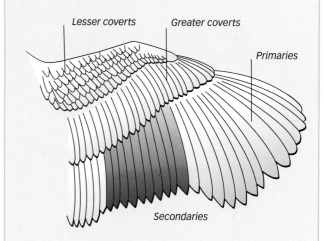

Lesser coverts   *Greater coverts*   *Primaries*   *Secondaries*

AN EXTENDED VIEW OF A BIRD'S WING, SEEN FROM ABOVE.

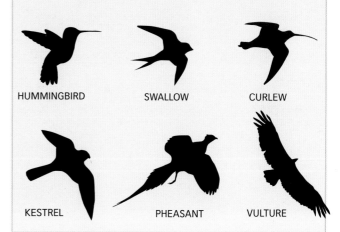

HUMMINGBIRD   SWALLOW   CURLEW

KESTREL   PHEASANT   VULTURE

FEEDING

Birds eat a wide variety of foodstuffs, with some species being carnivorous, while others are essentially herbivorous. The majority, however, will feed on a mixture of foods. Much can be learnt about the feeding habits of a particular species by the shape of its bill. Birds that feed on seeds, such as finches, tend to have a fairly sturdy, conical-shaped bill. This allows them to crack the outer casing of the seed and extract the kernel. Species that have narrow and relatively long bills are likely to feed largely on invertebrates, poking and probing to extract insects and spiders from their hiding places in bark, or using their bills to locate worms and oysters hidden in the sand at low tide.

Some birds have very specialized bills related to their method of feeding. Hummingbirds, which rely on flower nectar as a source of energy, have slender bills of varying shapes, to aid their ability to extract nectar from specific types of flowers growing in the areas where they occur.

Certain families of birds rely not just on their bills but also their feet to help feeding, holding food down on the perch and ripping off pieces that they can swallow easily. Such behavior is commonly seen in birds of prey, which also have sharp claws known as talons on their toes, enabling them to seize their quarry in the first instance.

INTERNAL ANATOMY

The internal organs of birds reflect the demands of flight, and so are adapted accordingly, so as to minimize body

SPECIALIZED HUNTERS Birds of prey have hooked bills, enabling them to rip their prey apart with relative ease. They also have strong feet, equipped with sharp, curved talons. This enables them to catch and carry heavy prey, such as the fish caught by this Osprey (*Pandion haliaetus*).

weight. In the case of the digestive system, there are no teeth in the mouth, which in turn lessens the need for strong jaw muscles. Food typically passes down into a storage organ called the crop, before moving on to the proventriculus, where the digestive process starts, before passing into the gizzard. Seed-eating birds have a powerful muscular wall to this organ, which grinds up food so that it can be digested more easily. It then continues along the intestinal tract, with nutrients being

FIT FOR PURPOSE The bird's bill serves as a specialist tool, having evolved primarily to obtain food, but also being used for other purposes. These include preening the feathers and helping to build the nest as appropriate, reflecting the lifestyle of the individual species.

GRANIVORE

RAPTOR

SPECIALIST SEED EATER

FISHING

FILTER FEEDER

NECTAR FEEDER

PROBING

INSECTIVORE

NETTING

SURFACE SKIMMING

absorbed mostly in the small intestine. Herbivorous birds have the most complex digestive system, with tubes called caeca connecting to the intestinal tract. Special beneficial microbes are present in these organs, helping the breakdown of plant matter.

THE KIDNEYS

The kidneys of birds produce a highly concentrated urine, and there is no potentially heavy, fluid-filled bladder that would affect their ability to fly. Instead, this semi-solid, whitish material merges with the darker feces at the end of the digestive tract in the cloaca, where the intestinal, renal and reproductive tracts all open, and then exits from the body via the vent.

BREATHING

The effort of flying means that birds require high levels of oxygen but, at the same time, their lungs are relatively compact, not moving in the same way during inspiration and expiration as those of mammals. Instead, the lungs connect to a series of air sacs, which act as air reservoirs and also contract like bellows, forcing air through the system. Adjacent air sacs link to the humerus in each wing, which is a pneumatic (hollow) bone. These bones act as further air reservoirs in the bird's body, with the avian skeleton being light overall, again as a way of lessening the energy and oxygen demands of flight.

The avian heart is a four-chambered structure, not dissimilar to that of a mammal, although it works at a much faster rate. Even at rest, the heartbeat of a domestic canary can be about 1,000 beats per minute. This will increase very significantly once the bird is airborne, pumping oxygen-rich blood to the flight muscles.

HUNTER AND HUNTED Its forward-facing eyes reveal that the Snowy Owl (*left*) is a predator, able to strike accurately. The Northern Bobwhite's eyes, on the sides of the head, offer better protective all-round vision.

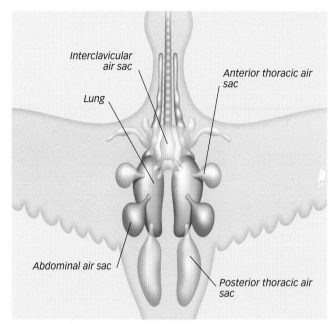

AIR SACS Birds have a different breathing system to mammals. Although they do have lungs, they also have air sacs. Very efficient gaseous uptake in the bird's body is essential, to give sufficient oxygen for the flight muscles.

Labels in figure:
Interclavicular air sac
Anterior thoracic air sac
Lung
Abdominal air sac
Posterior thoracic air sac

THE SENSES

Most birds have very keen eyesight, allowing them not just to detect the approach of would-be predators and take evasive action, but also to obtain food. The positioning of the eyes gives an indication of a bird's lifestyle. Predatory species such as owls have their eyes at the front of the face, pointing forward. This enables them to locate the position of would-be prey with great accuracy. In contrast, the eyes of game birds such as quail are located on the sides of their face, because here, they afford a much broader field of vision, making it much harder for a predator to creep up on the bird unnoticed. An owl must turn its head to see what is happening on either side.

Most birds do not possess a significant sense of smell, with the notable exception of vultures. This enables them to home in on a dead animal, aided by their keen sense of vision. Hearing is also not especially important to birds, although owls are an exception in this case. Hunting at night, their keen hearing helps these birds to detect the high-pitched, ultrasonic calls of rodents, being combined with excellent night-time vision. All birds do have ears, however, as openings covered by feathering on the sides of the head behind the eyes.

Petrels have special valves in their nasal passages. These provide information about the speed of the wind and potential changes in its direction, allowing them to adjust accordingly in flight as they swoop over the oceans, feeding from the surface.

THE AVIAN LIFECYCLE

The reproductive system of birds is effectively slimmed down, to reduce weight and so enable them to fly with less effort. Although hen birds have right and left ovaries and corresponding oviducts, they rely entirely on the left side of their reproductive tract for breeding purposes, with the right side normally never developing. In the case of the male, there is no actual penis either, although in a few groups such as waterfowl, there is a slight swelling that aids the transference of sperm during mating.

MATING GAME The plumage plays an important part in the courtship of many birds. Here a male Wild Turkey (*Meleagris gallopavo*) is displaying.

MATING

Successful fertilization of the female's eggs relies on sperm passing directly out from the male's cloaca into the female's vent, and then passing up the oviduct. Only one mating is normally required to fertilize a clutch of eggs, with sperm potentially remaining viable in the female's reproductive tract for three weeks or so afterward.

ONSET OF BREEDING BEHAVIOR

The changes in the birds' behavior and within the reproductive system of both sexes at the start of the breeding period are the result of hormones produced in the body. The most significant trigger for birds in temperate latitudes is increasing light exposure, caused by longer day length.

In the case of the hen, the resulting hormonal output acts on the ovary, triggering the development of ova, which will be released to form the eggs. Meanwhile, the male's testes increase in size, and behavioral changes take place. Cock birds start to sing loudly, laying claim to breeding territories and hoping to attract mates. Their behavior becomes more aggressive, and their appearance can change, with some cock birds molting into more colorful plumage.

EGG DEVELOPMENT

The hen's ovary is full of masses of immature ova. When she comes into breeding condition, several of these ova will swell up, and ultimately break away, a process called ovulation. The

FIGHT FOR THE NEST Birds become far more territorial at the start of the breeding season, and skirmishes at this stage, as shown by these Ospreys, are not uncommon. Even in the case of birds that breed communally, there are often disputes over nest sites at the outset.

male's sperm must unite with the ovum before the inner shell membranes are formed around it, followed by the shell, otherwise these will create an impenetrable barrier, preventing any sperm from reaching their target. It is not until perhaps a week after the egg is laid that it can be determined externally whether or not it was fertilized.

The passage of the egg down the oviduct is a lengthy process, lasting perhaps 30 hours. After fertilization, the ovum moves down into the magnum, where it joins with the egg white or albumen. This takes about three hours, before the barrier created by the rubbery shell membranes around the egg is formed in the isthmus. The shell is formed in the shell gland or uterus, and usually takes a day.

Generally, birds that lay their eggs in tree hollows and similar locations produce white eggs, whereas those that nest in the open, such as blackbirds, have colored or spotted eggs, which provide them with camouflage.

Many birds build nests for their eggs. These can take the form of loose platforms of sticks, as favored by pigeons, or they may be far more robust structures, as reflected by the nests of mud used by swallows. The birds laboriously scoop up mouthfuls of damp mud that then hardens to create the nest. Many birds abandon their nest after rearing their chicks, reducing the likelihood of parasites becoming established in the nest site, but others will return annually to the same nest site.

In many cases, the hen sits alone, although in some instances, as with pigeons, incubation duties are shared.

Egg shapes and sizes

Birds' eggs vary, both in terms of size and coloration, as shown by this selection of eggs from American species. Those such as ptarmigans that nest on the ground usually produce speckled eggs. Their random shell patterning helps to conceal them from predators.

| CAMOUFLAGED (WILLOW PTARMIGAN) | UNUSUAL SHAPE (COMMON MURRE) | TINY SIZE (RUFOUS HUMMINGBIRD) | LARGE SIZE (ANDEAN CONDOR) |

The incubation period itself varies, typically ranging from 10–30 days, depending on the species concerned, being generally longer in the case of bigger birds.

Some chicks hatch in an advanced state of development, being able to move instantly from hatching. This is common in the case of ground-nesting birds such as quails, helping them to escape predators. In contrast, those nesting in tree hollows where they are relatively well-concealed are usually helpless, with their eyes closed when they hatch.

NEWLY HATCHED FERAL PIGEON Such chicks are totally helpless at first, and entirely dependent on their parents to brood them, keeping them warm and providing their food. In due course, their eyes open and their feathers grow.

A BROOD OF YOUNG CANADA GEESE Waterfowl as a group have chicks that hatch in a more advanced state of development, able to see, feed and even swim soon after hatching, although they still have down plumage and cannot fly.

WATCHING BIRDS

Birdwatching is a very popular hobby, partly because it can be carried out almost anywhere. Although you may not need any special equipment, it will certainly help you to see birds at much closer quarters if you invest in a pair of binoculars. These will be useful even if you are simply watching garden birds, and quite essential if you hope to spot birds in localities where they are further away from you.

BASIC EQUIPMENT

The choice of binoculars will be influenced by the locality where you intend to go birdwatching. Clearly, if you are venturing near water then binoculars with features such as waterproofing and anti-fogging can be recommended. The minimum focusing distance is significant in all cases though, to allow you to bring the birds into focus easily. In most cases, this tends to be around 10–13 ft (3–4 m).

If you are unsure about buying binoculars, then visit a local shop that stocks them, and try out a number of models, to see which is best suited to your needs.

It is not just binoculars that are popular for birdwatching these days, with fieldscopes now gaining a greater share of the market. They have a single eye piece, and may be

MUTUAL BENEFIT
Backyard bird tables and feeders provide a great opportunity to observe birds from the comfort of your armchair. A large number of species may be drawn here, particularly when the weather is bad, and providing food aids their survival.

mounted on a tripod, rather than being held by hand, as is necessary with binoculars, making for ease of viewing.

BIRD PHOTOGRAPHY

Fieldscopes can also have the additional advantage of allowing you to take close up photographs of your bird-table visitors. This is achieved by means of a universal digital camera adaptor, which, as its name suggests, is fitted between the scope and the camera. You can also purchase a digital telephoto lens for digiscoping purposes, while, in some cases, you may be able to use a camcorder in place of a camera.

Once you've actually invested in this type of equipment, there is little further expenditure because, with a digital camera, there is no film to buy or associated costs in having a film developed, and camcorders with hard drives for recording purposes are now commonplace. This is a particular bonus for wildlife photography, since even professionals have to take large numbers of photographs to obtain just one or two good pictures, or record for relatively long periods.

As the technology has advanced rapidly over recent years, so has the ease with which it can be used. Even so, do not overlook the basics. If you decide to set up a feeder or bird table in your backyard specially to allow you to take photographs of the visiting birds, make sure that you check out the background view first through the camera. You can then ensure that there is nothing in the

Safety tips

Going birdwatching should be a safe pursuit, but you need to take sensible precautions, bearing in mind that you are likely to be heading off into areas where there will be few if any other people around. Take a suitable phone therefore, so that you can seek help in any emergency. Always wear suitable clothing and footwear, and pack a map, compass plus adequate drinking water if you are trekking off any distance.

Be very careful in boggy grounds, and also near cliff edges, which can crumble easily and unexpectedly, so do not venture too close to the edge. When birdwatching along the coast, be sure to check tide times, because the sea usually comes in very quickly over mud flats and you could end up being trapped. If you actually venture out to sea, then it will be advisable to wear a life jacket. Always check the weather forecast too, before setting off any distance—if only because birdwatching in heavy rain is not necessarily great fun!

shot that will distract from your final photographs, such as a neighbor's washing line!

LOCATION

There are some localities that are likely to be better for birdwatching than others and, on reserves, you can usually take advantage of special hides, which allow you to get close to the birds. As they are not harassed in such localities, the birds here are unlikely to be unduly worried by the presence of people concealed in the hide. Always take care not to disturb birds, however: this is particularly crucial near nests, as you may otherwise cause the adult birds to desert them.

When birdwatching outdoors, use whatever natural cover is available, crouching down behind a bush or tree. This helps to conceal your presence, and birds tend to be less frightened if they are not confronted by a standing figure. Move quietly and slowly at all times, as this is likely to give you the best view of the birds in due course, but always be prepared to be patient.

NATURE RESERVES On reserves where birds may congregate in significant numbers, hides are often constructed, allowing flocks to be viewed from the best vantage points. A hide allows birds to be observed in relative comfort, irrespective of the weather, without disturbing them.

PHOTOGRAPHY Modern camera technology means that photographing birds is now more straightforward than in the past. Always be sensitive about your position, however, and do not photograph breeding birds, as the disturbance may cause them to abandon their nest.

GALLERY OF BIRDS

The following pages reflect the wide diversity of birds found on the North American continent. Some are just summertime visitors, heading back to warmer climes in the late summer or early fall, whereas others are resident throughout the year. Certain species undergo seasonal movement within the continent itself, generally moving to localities where food will be more readily available, and the weather is likely to be less extreme over the winter period. A number have adapted, however, to thrive even under the most severe climatic conditions, remaining within the Arctic Circle throughout the year. Much depends on their diet. Distributions are not static and especially when migrating, birds may be spotted well away from their usual haunts.

NEED TO FEED Dietary needs are one of the strongest influences affecting avian movements. Insectivorous species will face a shortage of food over the course of the northern winter, and so withdraw further south over this period. The same applies to hummingbirds, which depend on flowers for nectar.

GAVIIFORMES

Divers

Members of this Order are often spotted on water, but can disappear very quickly from view, as they dive below the surface in search of food. They are often known collectively as "divers" for this reason. These birds have a very distinctive swimming style, tending to remain low in the water. Loons can also be easily distinguished from other waterfowl by the shape of their bills, which are relatively long, as well as being narrow and pointed. Depending partly on the species and time of year, they may be observed on both fresh and tidal waters. Their breeding grounds lie in the far north.

Common Loon

FAMILY Gaviidae
SPECIES *Gavia immer*
LENGTH 33 in (84 cm)
HABITAT Lakes/coasts
CLUTCH SIZE 1–3

DISTRIBUTION Breeds through most of Canada. Overwinters down the west and east coasts of North America, and in the southeastern United States.

THE BLACK BILL of the Common Loon distinguishes it from the similarly colored but larger Yellow-billed Loon (*Gavia adamsii*), which has a more restricted range in northern Canada. Its plumage over the winter months is much duller overall, with the throat area being white. When hunting fish, Common Loons may dive to depths of 150 ft (46 m).

FAMILY GROUP The chicks can swim soon after hatching, sometimes hitching a ride on the back of one of the adult birds.

Pacific Loon

FAMILY Gaviidae
SPECIES *Gavia pacifica*
LENGTH 26 in (66 cm)
HABITAT Lakes/coastal bays
CLUTCH SIZE 1–3

DISTRIBUTION Breeding range centered to the west of Hudson Bay. Overwinters on the western coast, from the Aleutians and southern Alaska to California.

THERE IS a characteristic purplish-green iridescent area on the throat of these loons when they are in breeding plumage, but it is hard to observe, tending to appear black from some distance away. The throat becomes white during the winter, with a thin brown area, referred to as a chin stripe, being apparent here.

LOW SLUNG The distinctive swimming style of loons means that their bodies are low in the water. They feed mainly on fish. This individual is in breeding plumage.

Red-throated Loon

FAMILY Gaviidae
SPECIES *Gavia stellata*
LENGTH 25 in (64 cm)
HABITAT Lakes/coastal bays
CLUTCH SIZE 1–3

DISTRIBUTION Breeds across northern areas, east to the west coast of Greenland. Winters along both coasts, from the Aleutian Islands down to California, and to Florida.

ALTHOUGH THE RED throat plumage of the male can only be seen during the breeding period, these loons can be identified easily by the absence of the checkered patterning that is apparent across the backs of related species. The throat and sides of the face are white when they are in winter plumage. Young birds are grayish-brown overall. When migrating to and from their breeding grounds, these loons may fly individually, or in small groups. Red-throated Loons are well suited to their aquatic lifestyle, but are not able to walk well on land. This species generally overwinters around the coast, but may also be seen on the Great Lakes at this stage.

NESTING BEHAVIOR A cock Red-throated Loon on its breeding grounds. The eggs are laid on a pile of vegetation, with both birds sharing the task of incubation.

PODICIPEDIFORMES

Grebes

Grebes are closely tied to areas of fresh water and also coastal areas where they are most likely to be observed over the winter. They will dive underwater in search of food. Perhaps the most obvious distinctive feature of these birds, however, which sets them apart from all other water birds, is their evident lack of tail feathers. Their bill shape varies quite markedly between species, with some having much longer bills than others. Although grebes often tend to be seen either singly or in small groups, larger species may sometimes be observed in much bigger aggregations consisting of hundreds of individuals.

Horned Grebe

FAMILY Podicipedidae
SPECIES *Podiceps auritus*
LENGTH 13½ in (34 cm)
HABITAT Lakes/coastal bays
CLUTCH SIZE 1–7

DISTRIBUTION Breeding range extends from Alaska southeastward across Canada, just across the United States border. Occurs along both coasts in winter, and over much of the southeastern United States.

IT IS THE BRIGHT golden plumage on each side of the head that has led to this species becoming known as the Horned Grebe. This feathering looks rather like horns from a distance, set against the surrounding black plumage. During the winter months, however, these grebes are far less colorful, as this feature is not obvious then. Pairs tend to nest on a stretch of water on their own, but in some areas, several pairs may congregate together. They rarely come ashore, spending most of their time on water. Even their nest is in the form of a raft, built from reeds and other vegetation, and anchored in place in a reedbed.

IDENTIFICATION The appearance of the Horned Grebe is unmistakable, especially in breeding plumage, but it is not possible to distinguish between the sexes by differences in their plumage.

Red-necked Grebe

FAMILY Podicipedidae
SPECIES *Podiceps grisegena*
LENGTH 20 in (51 cm)
HABITAT Lakes/coastal bays
CLUTCH SIZE 3–6

DISTRIBUTION Breeds from Alaska southeastward, to the north of the Great Lakes. Overwinters right down the west coast, and on the east coast to North Carolina.

THE CHARACTERISTIC chestnut-red plumage on the neck of these grebes is only apparent in the summer. Their coloration is duller over the winter, with their neck and face then being gray. Young birds display black-and-white striping on the sides of the face. Pairs breed in shallow areas of wetland, hunting not just fish but also amphibians including tadpoles at this stage. They then migrate to coastal areas for the winter, although sometimes they may be found on large lakes, which are unlikely to freeze over at this time of year.

PREDATOR Keen eyesight, a sharp bill and powerful neck muscles mean these grebes can catch prey with relative ease in marshland areas. They are primarily aquatic birds.

Eared Grebe

FAMILY Podicipedidae
SPECIES *Podiceps nigricollis*
LENGTH 12½ in (32 cm)
HABITAT Lakes/bays
CLUTCH SIZE 3–6

DISTRIBUTION Breeds from southern Canada down to parts of California and across to western Texas and Oklahoma. Resident in southwestern parts, and overwinters through the southern states.

THESE SMALL GREBES develop elegant gold-colored plumes on the sides of the head as they come into breeding condition. They are social by nature, nesting in groups. Pairs construct a floating raft of vegetation for their eggs, usually at the water's edge. Eared Grebes are normally found on shallow stretches of water, feeding on invertebrates including crustaceans, rather than fish. Tens of thousands congregate together each fall, attracting birdwatchers to their traditional molting grounds on Utah's Great Salt Lake and Mono Lake in California.

DISTINCTIVE The Eared Grebe is one of the species that has particularly striking red eyes. Both parents care for their young.

Clark's Grebe

FAMILY Podicipedidae

SPECIES *Aechmophorus clarkii*

LENGTH 25 in (64 cm)

HABITAT Lakes/coastal bays

CLUTCH SIZE 3–4

DISTRIBUTION Breeds from southern Alberta to Manitoba, east to western Minnesota. Resident in the southwest, overwinters on the coast and also in New Mexico and Texas.

AS WITH RELATED SPECIES, Clark's Grebes spend the summer on large freshwater lakes. These birds then migrate to the coast for the duration of the winter, often flying in small flocks. They favor relatively sheltered areas, such as bays and estuaries, where they can feed easily on crustaceans and other invertebrates, as well as catching fish. Once back on their breeding grounds, their courtship is striking to watch, as potentially hundreds of birds may be gathered here. Pairs undertake elaborate dances, mirroring the way in which their partner moves. When the young hatch, they are often carried for periods of time on the backs of their parents.

IDENTIFICATION The yellow-orange bill and the black area of plumage on the head, which does not extend down to the eyes, identify Clark's Grebe.

Western Grebe

FAMILY Podicipedidae

SPECIES *Aechmophorus occidentalis*

LENGTH 25 in (64 cm)

HABITAT Lakes/coastal bays

CLUTCH SIZE 3–4

DISTRIBUTION Breeds widely in the western half of the continent, from southern Canada to northern New Mexico. Resident in the southwest.

THE SIMILARITY in appearance between this species and Clark's Grebe means that for a period, they were regarded as the same species. The Western Grebe has a wider distribution, however, although their ranges do overlap and this can create identification difficulties. It has a paler, yellowish-green bill and the black plumage extends down to the eyes, being more extensive. Pairs breed in loose colonies but can be quite territorial, with both members of the pairs incubating the eggs and caring for the chicks.

COLORING In winter plumage, the area of black feathering around the eyes is less distinctive, being clearly whiter from a distance away.

Pied-billed Grebe

FAMILY Podicipedidae
SPECIES *Podilymbus podiceps*
LENGTH 13½ in (34 cm)
HABITAT Lakes/ponds
CLUTCH SIZE 3–4

DISTRIBUTION Wide summer range from central parts of Canada south down to Kansas and east to Nova Scotia. Resident throughout the rest of the United States.

THIS IS A SMALL, rather plainly colored grebe, predominantly brown in color, with a yellowish bill and white plumage under the throat, extending around the sides of the head. During the breeding period, birds of both sexes develop a distinctive black band on the bill, which is bluish-gray at this stage. Although generally common through their range, these grebes are rather hard to spot, retreating among vegetation such as reeds if they feel under threat. Individuals may even submerge themselves at this stage, so only their head is above the water level, or they can simply dive underwater. Pied Grebes spend most of their time swimming, rarely coming on to land.

HABITAT Pied Grebes will move to waters unlikely to freeze over the winter, allowing them to carry on feeding, but they do not congregate on the coast.

PROCELLARIIFORMES

Albatrosses, shearwaters, and petrels

Members of the Order Procellariiformes are often regarded as ocean travelers, spending much of their lives traversing the world's seas, making landfall simply for breeding purposes. Albatrosses are not normally seen in the northern oceans, however, remaining in southern latitudes, but both shearwaters and petrels are often sighted in the seas around North America. In common with other seabirds, their coloration tends to be rather subdued: Shades of brown and black, offset against white areas of plumage in some cases. It is not always easy to distinguish species accurately because of similarities in appearance.

Greater Shearwater

FAMILY Procellaridae
SPECIES *Puffinus gravis*
LENGTH 19 in (48 cm)
HABITAT Open sea
CLUTCH SIZE 1

DISTRIBUTION Throughout most of the western Atlantic, extending up to Greenland, and south into the Caribbean, and along the Gulf states.

LIKE OTHERS of its kind, the Greater Shearwater is an ocean wanderer, rarely seen closely into shore. It is an Atlantic species, breeding on islands in the southern ocean, but there are certain times of the year, such as the summer months off the Canadian coast, when it is more likely to be sighted, albeit from a boat rather than from the shoreline. Edible scraps thrown overboard from trawlers are most likely to attract these seabirds. Their feeding habits are unusual, because although in common with other related species Greater Shearwaters will seek food at the surface, they will also dive below the waves as well. They can be identified quite easily, in comparison with related species, thanks to the well-defined black area on the face and white underparts, broken by a darker plumage in the center of the belly. The upperparts are brown, with a white band at the base of the tail.

EFFORTLESS Aided by their large wingspan of 44 inches (112 cm), Greater Shearwaters glide over the sea, swooping down to the surface in search of food.

Pink-footed Shearwater

FAMILY Procellaridae
SPECIES *Puffinus creatopus*
LENGTH 19 in (48 cm)
HABITAT Open sea
CLUTCH SIZE 1

DISTRIBUTION Extends up the Pacific coast of North America to British Columbia, although it is not found as close to the coast here as further south.

AS ITS NAME suggests, this particular shearwater has pinkish feet. It is otherwise dull in coloration, with dark upperparts, which become paler on the sides of the body, merging with white feathering. It has a wingspan of 43 inches (109 cm). Sightings are common from spring onward, being most numerous in the fall.

RARE SIGHT These shearwaters are occasionally seen off the North American coast in their thousands.

Short-tailed Shearwater

FAMILY Procellaridae
SPECIES *Puffinus tenuirostris*
LENGTH 17 in (43 cm)
HABITAT Open sea
CLUTCH SIZE 1

DISTRIBUTION Summer range is centered around the Alaskan coast, extending out into the Pacific. Population moves south for the winter, to the western coast of the United States.

AS THEIR NAME indicates, Short-tailed Shearwaters have short tails. With a wingspan of 41 inches (104 cm), these birds fly huge distances through the year, being most likely to be sighted off the Canadian coast and Alaska during the fall. At this stage, they are even venture into coastal areas, which means that—unusually in the case of shearwaters—they can be observed from the shore.

DISTINGUISHING MARKS Dark coloration helps to identify the Short-tailed Shearwater, with grayish-brown coloration predominating in its plumage. The head is rounded, and the bill slender.

Black-vented Shearwater

FAMILY Procellaridae

SPECIES *Puffinus opisthomelas*

LENGTH 14 in (36 cm)

HABITAT Sea

CLUTCH SIZE 1

DISTRIBUTION Overwinters on the western coast of the United States, off southern California, with individuals occasionally being sighted as far north as British Columbia. Breeds off Baja California.

THE BLACK-VENTED SHEARWATER has dark markings on the undertail coverts, in the vicinity of the vent. Its upperparts too are dark brown, while the facial markings are quite individual, depending on the amount of dark mottling here, extending down the throat. The rest of the underparts are white. It has a wingspan of 34 inches (86 cm), but this species is not a great ocean wanderer, unlike other shearwaters. It does not stray very far from the coast, although temperature shifts do impact on its range. From the fall through until early summer, larger flocks are often seen in years when the weather is warm, splitting into small groups in less favorable years.

IDENTICAL The breeding grounds of the Black-vented Shearwater lie on islands in the vicinity of the Baja Peninsula. It is impossible to tell the sex of these birds visually.

Sooty Shearwater

FAMILY Procellaridae
SPECIES *Puffinus griseus*
LENGTH 18 in (46 cm)
HABITAT Open sea
CLUTCH SIZE 1

DISTRIBUTION Summer range extends up the Pacific coast to southern Alaska and the entire Atlantic coast, but absent from western Florida and the Gulf coast.

THE SOOTY SHEARWATER lives up to its name, being a dark sooty-brown shade overall, with white plumage under the wing becoming visible when these birds are in flight. Its forehead is quite narrow,

as is its bill. They nest in colonies in the southern hemisphere, seeking out remote islands for this purpose. Subsequently during the southern winter, corresponding to summer in the northern hemisphere, these shearwaters fly back across the equator. They are quite adept at utilizing the wind, taking advantage of air currents that allow them to fly with minimal effort. Their wingspan measures 41 inches (104 cm).

WIDESPREAD This is a widely distributed and common shearwater, whose worldwide population numbers millions of individuals.

Audubon's Shearwater

FAMILY Procellaridae
SPECIES *Puffinus lherminieri*
LENGTH 12 in (30 cm)
HABITAT Open sea
CLUTCH SIZE 1

DISTRIBUTION In summer found from New England southward through the Caribbean and Gulf of Mexico and eastward out into the Atlantic.

COMMEMORATING THE NAME of the famous avian artist, Audubon's Shearwater is the smallest representative of the family to be found in North American waters, where it is seen during the summer months. The breeding range of this species is to be found in the Caribbean. These birds nest communally here in what are often large colonies, with the young shearwaters being slow to develop. They rarely leave the nest until they are approximately three months of age. The adult wingspan is 28 inches (71 cm). This is a species with clearly defined coloration, having dark upperparts and white underparts. Like other shearwaters, it is very agile in flight, being capable of swooping down low over the waves in search of food.

DISTINCTIVE EYES The pale spot present in front of each of the Audubon Shearwater's eyes is clearly evident in this individual.

Wilson's Storm-petrel

FAMILY Hydrobatidae
SPECIES *Oceanites oceanicus*
LENGTH 7 in (18 cm)
HABITAT Open sea
CLUTCH SIZE 1

DISTRIBUTION Occurs in both the Atlantic and Pacific oceans over the summer, tending to come closer to the east coast, and also seen in the Caribbean.

SPENDING MOST of its time flying and feeding in the open ocean, Wilson's Storm-petrel is likely to be seen scavenging on edible scraps thrown overboard from boats. Although common visitors to the North Atlantic between May and September, these birds breed in the southern hemisphere.

NEST SITE Wilson's Storm-petrels lay in a bare rocky crevice. The species is less common off the Pacific coast. Their wingspan is 15 inches (38 cm).

Leach's Storm-petrel

FAMILY Hydrobatidae
SPECIES *Oceanodroma leuchroa*
LENGTH 8½ in (22 cm)
HABITAT Open sea
CLUTCH SIZE 1

DISTRIBUTION From the Aleutians down the west side of the continent, overwintering off Mexico. Seen off northeastern North America in summer.

THE APPEARANCE of Leach's Storm-petrel is quite similar to other species. It is relatively dark in color, with long, pointed wings, with a span of 18 inches (46 cm). There are variations, however, between birds found in the Atlantic, compared with the Pacific population. Away from their breeding grounds, they tend to be solitary.

FEEDING ON THE WING When feeding, these storm-petrels hover just above the surface of the sea, grabbing fish and crustaceans that come within reach.

Fork-tailed Storm-petrel

FAMILY Hydrobatidae

SPECIES *Oceanodroma furcata*

LENGTH 8½ in (22 cm)

HABITAT Open sea

CLUTCH SIZE 1

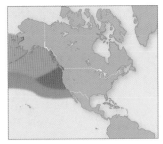

DISTRIBUTION Occurs from southwestern coast of Alaska westward across the Pacific, also southward down off northern Mexico, overwintering here. Resident further north off the United States coast.

THIS PARTICULAR storm-petrel differs in several respects from related species, perhaps most evidently in terms of its appearance. Although it has blackish areas of plumage, it tends to be of a silvery-gray color overall, with this silver coloration having a slightly bluish suffusion on its upperparts. As its name suggests, it also has a deeply forked tail. Its area of distribution tends to be much further north, and it is not uncommonly sighted to the northwest of Alaska during the summer. Small, remote islands serve as colonial breeding sanctuaries for Fork-tailed Storm-petrels, but remarkably, the birds only visit their nests under cover of darkness.

AEROBATIC Spending long periods in flight, these storm-petrels will actually glide on occasions, if wind conditions are favorable. They are very agile in flight, and have a wingspan of 18 inches (46 cm).

Northern Fulmar

FAMILY Procellariidae

SPECIES *Fulmarus glacialis*

LENGTH 19 in (48 cm)

HABITAT Open sea

CLUTCH SIZE 1

DISTRIBUTION Occurs in the far north during the summer, resident around the southwestern and southern coasts of Alaska in the Pacific, and Newfoundland in the east.

ALTHOUGH THESE SEABIRDS may initially look more like gulls, thanks in part to their white-and-gray color scheme, they are actually more closely related to shearwaters. Some individuals are of a considerably darker shade of gray than others. The average wingspan is 42 inches (107 cm). In common with other marine species, Northern Fulmars have a special gland in their nasal passageways that allows them to excrete salt from the body. They are therefore able to drink seawater safely, as a substitute for fresh water, without becoming increasingly dehydrated as a consequence.

NESTING Northern Fulmars only come ashore to breed, choosing remote cliffs in the far north.

RED-BILLED TROPICBIRD IN FLIGHT The long tail streamers that characterize these birds convey a sense of grace, and avoid any risk of confusion with terns. When at sea, tropicbirds rest with their tail streamers held upward.

PELECANIFORMES

Pelicans, tropicbirds, and their allies

Although the majority of members of this Order are seabirds, often ranging far from land, there are others, such as the American White Pelican and a number of cormorants, that also can be observed on lakes and other stretches of freshwater. All these birds tend to be either predominantly black or white in color, but they may undergo some dramatic changes in appearance at the start of the breeding season. They have also evolved a range of different yet highly effective fishing techniques. These range from diving down to pursue fish deep underwater through to trawling for them at the surface.

Red-billed Tropicbird

FAMILY Phaethontidae
SPECIES *Phaethon aethereus*
LENGTH 40 in (102 cm)
HABITAT Open sea
CLUTCH SIZE 1

DISTRIBUTION Summertime visitor off southwestern United States. Also off the northern and eastern coasts of South America and the Galapagos.

AS ITS NAME SUGGESTS, the Red-billed Tropicbird can be distinguished by the coloration of its bill. Its plumage is white in color, with black stripes running through the eyes and barring on the back and wings. It is much harder to distinguish their young from those of the White-tailed species, however, as both have yellow bills on fledging.

SILHOUETTE These birds appear able to fly almost effortlessly, thanks to the shallow beats of their 44 inch-wide (112 cm) wings.

White-tailed Tropicbird

FAMILY Phaethontidae
SPECIES *Phaethon lepturus*
LENGTH 30 in (76 cm)
HABITAT Open sea
CLUTCH SIZE 1

DISTRIBUTION Offshore from North Carolina in the summer to Florida and southeastern United States. Breeds on the Bahamas and Bermuda.

THIS SPECIES is significantly smaller than the Red-billed. It can also be identified by its yellow bill and prominent black areas on the wings. This species' incubation period lasts for about 40 days, and it will take up to nine weeks before the chick is ready to fledge. At this stage, it will display barring on its back. The eventual wingspan is 37 inches (94 cm).

NESTING Tropicbirds often nest in a cave or under a rock. The young will be reared on fish and other aquatic creatures such as squid.

Masked Booby

FAMILY Sulidae
SPECIES *Sula dactylatra*
LENGTH 32 in (81 cm)
HABITAT Open sea
CLUTCH SIZE 1–3

DISTRIBUTION From the coast of North Carolina, around the Gulf of Mexico and through the Caribbean in the east. Also occurs off western Central America.

THE BLACK AREA on the face of these boobies enables them to be identified easily. There is also black plumage evident under the tail and in the wings, which span 62 inches (157 cm). Young birds actually display more black plumage than adults, with a dark head and upperparts, aside from a white collar.

PARTNERS Both birds share incubation duties, with the eggs being laid on bare ground.

Brown Booby

FAMILY Sulidae
SPECIES *Sula leucogaster*
LENGTH 30 in (76 cm)
HABITAT Open sea
CLUTCH SIZE 1–3

DISTRIBUTION Resident off the southern end of Florida, across the Caribbean to northern South America. Also occurs in the Gulf of California, down to northwestern South America.

THE BROWN BOOBY spends much of its time out at sea, but may sometimes be seen closer inland perching on channel markers. It may also be observed diving down vertically into the ocean from a considerable height. Its wingspan is 57 inches (145 cm). The booby's powerful, webbed feet, along with its strong bill, aid the underwater pursuit of fish, which make up the bulk of its diet.

GENDER DIFFERENCES Males of this species have blue markings on the sides of the face, whereas hens can be distinguished by their yellowish coloration here.

Northern Gannet

FAMILY Sulidae

SPECIES *Morus bassanus*

LENGTH 37 in (94 cm)

HABITAT Coasts and cliffs

CLUTCH SIZE 1

DISTRIBUTION Occurs off northeast Canada, centered on Newfoundland, overwintering along the coast to the south, via Florida to Central America.

THIS IS THE LARGEST SEABIRD to be found on the Atlantic coast of North America, with individuals weighing up to 8 lb (3.6 kg), and an average wingspan of 72 inches (183 cm). Northern Gannets wander quite widely over the sea outside the breeding period, with their acute eyesight enabling them to identify the presence of a shoal of fish in the ocean below. They return to land to breed in the spring, forming large colonies in their traditional cliff nesting sites at this stage, with squabbling often taking place between neighboring pairs on the densely packed ground. In contrast to the adults, young Northern Gannets are grayish-brown and they mature slowly, acquiring adult plumage over successive molts over the course of up to four years.

AN ADULT NORTHERN GANNET Like many seabirds, they can be long lived, with their potential life expectancy measured in decades.

American White Pelican

FAMILY Pelecanidae

SPECIES *Pelecanus erythrorhynchos*

LENGTH 62 in (157 cm)

HABITAT Sea/large lakes

CLUTCH SIZE 2

DISTRIBUTION Summer breeding range centered on lakes in western and central Canada. Winters in central California southward and from Florida around the Gulf coast to Central America.

THESE PELICANS ARE UNMISTAKABLE, thanks to their size, with a wingspan measuring 108 inches (274 cm), and predominantly white plumage, as well as the greatly expandable pouch that forms part of the lower bill. American White Pelicans are very social birds by nature, and live in flocks. They also fish communally, so that a school of fish can find itself surrounded by these birds, with little scope for escape. Just prior to the nesting period, a fibrous plate develops on the upper bill, being shed soon after egg-laying occurs. A yellow crest also develops at this stage, but again this is only transitory, with the plumage on the head becoming blackish once the young have hatched.

SPECIALIST BILL The pelican's pouch can accommodate almost three gallons (11.5 liters) of water at full capacity, acting as a trawl net when the pelican is fishing.

Brown Pelican

FAMILY Pelecanidae
SPECIES *Pelecanus occidentalis*
LENGTH 50 in (127 cm)
HABITAT Open sea
CLUTCH SIZE 2–3

DISTRIBUTION From British Columbia on the Pacific coast, south to Central America. Eastward, extends from New Jersey around the Gulf coast. Northern range less in winter.

THE BROWN PELICAN, unlike its white cousin, is essentially a marine species. It lives in flocks and constructs a bulky nest of vegetation for its eggs. Adults are a variable shade of grayish-brown, with the back of the neck becoming darker and a yellow patch developing on the throat at the start of the breeding period. The change in Pacific Coast Brown Pelicans is even more marked at this stage, as their bill and pouch lose their gray tones and become red.

Being heavy birds by nature, with large wings measuring 84 inches (213 cm) in span, they appear cumbersome when taking off, particularly from the surface of the sea. Once airborne, however, they can fly quite effortlessly, frequently being seen flying as a flock in single-file formation.

SKYDIVERS Brown Pelicans frequently dive from heights of 30 ft (9 m) into the sea in order to catch fish.

Double-crested Cormorant

FAMILY Phalacrocoracidae

SPECIES *Phalacrocorax auritus*

LENGTH 32 in (81 cm)

HABITAT Coasts/
          freshwater

CLUTCH SIZE 2–9

DISTRIBUTION Breeds inland in freshwater areas across the continent, but with resident populations notably around the Gulf coast and south from British Columbia down to Central America.

THE DISTINCTIVE TUFTS of feathers that characterize the Double-crested Cormorant are only apparent during the breeding season. There is a distinctive variance in the separate populations at this stage, with birds from the southeastern race having black crests, whereas this area of plumage is whitish in the case of those occurring elsewhere. These cormorants are the most commonly encountered species in North America, often seen near inland waterways where there are adequate feeding opportunities. They hunt fish, with their hooked bill helping them to seize their quarry more effectively. In flight, these cormorants usually adopt a V-shaped formation, with their necks being held slightly raised. Their wingspan is 52 inches (132 cm).

COMMON SIGHT These birds are often seen close to water, alert to feeding opportunities.

Neotropic Cormorant

FAMILY Phalacrocoracidae

SPECIES *Phalacrocorax brasilianus*

LENGTH 26 in (66 cm)

HABITAT Coasts/
          freshwater

CLUTCH SIZE 3–6

DISTRIBUTION Resident on the coastline of Texas and western Louisiana, sometimes moving further inland to New Mexico.

ALTHOUGH IT WAS known for a period as the Olivaceous Cormorant, this species is actually black in color, aside from its yellow throat patch, which develops a white border at the start of the breeding season, but does not extend up to the eyes. The sexes are identical, although young birds can be distinguished by their brown coloration. Its distribution overlaps in part with that of the Double-crested Cormorant, but they can be distinguished quite easily in flight because the Neotropic Cormorant flies with its neck fully extended. Its wingspan is 40 inches (102 cm).

VARIED RANGE These cormorants may be seen both in coastal areas, and also further inland, in the vicinity of lakes.

Great Cormorant

FAMILY Phalacrocoracidae

SPECIES *Phalacrocorax carbo*

LENGTH 36 in (91 cm)

HABITAT Sea/coasts

CLUTCH SIZE 4–5

DISTRIBUTION Breeds along the coast of eastern Canada and western Newfoundland to Maine in the United States. Wintering range extends further south as far as South Carolina.

THE LARGE SIZE of this cormorant—it has a wingspan of 63 inches (160 cm)—aids its identification, but perhaps more significant are the white areas on the body. The black plumage of the adult birds is replaced by brown in the case of the youngsters, with the bare skin of the throat being dull yellow.

SEASONAL CHANGE White plumage is seen on the flanks as well as the throat in the breeding season.

Pelagic Cormorant

FAMILY Phalacrocoracidae

SPECIES *Phalacrocorax pelagicus*

LENGTH 26 in (66 cm)

HABITAT Sea/coasts

CLUTCH SIZE 3–7

DISTRIBUTION Breeding range centered on the western coast of Alaska, resident along the southern coast to California, moving south in winter.

THE PELAGIC IS THE SMALLEST of the cormorants occurring on the West Coast of North America. They are again predominantly black, but molt to gain white plumage on their flanks at the start of the breeding season. Their wingspan measures 39 inches (99 cm). This species is not as social as many cormorants, and individuals are more likely to be seen on their own. Pelagic Cormorants tend to swim quite low down in the water, like other members of the group, with their bodies almost hidden by the waves.

NESTING BEHAVIOR When breeding, Pelagic Cormorants build nests using seaweed, on very narrow cliff ledges that offer safety from predatory gulls.

Brandt's Cormorant

FAMILY Phalacrocoracidae

SPECIES *Phalacrocorax pencillatus*

LENGTH 35 in (89 cm)

HABITAT Open sea

CLUTCH SIZE 3–6

DISTRIBUTION Birds may disperse northward after the breeding period, as far as British Columbia, and southward too, from California. Main distribution from Oregon to Baja California.

BRANDT'S CORMORANTS spend much of their time out over the ocean, venturing further away from land than other species. They live in large groups, with birds fishing communally. When the breeding season is imminent, the throat pouch of these cormorants starts to turn cobalt-blue.

HABIT These birds return to the same breeding grounds each year, although they may have different partners. Their wingspan measures 48 inches (122 cm).

Red-faced Cormorant

FAMILY Phalacrocoracidae

SPECIES *Phalacrocorax urile*

LENGTH 79 in (31 cm)

HABITAT Sea/coasts

CLUTCH SIZE 3–4

DISTRIBUTION Resident from south Alaska westward, via the Pribilofs and Aleutian Islands across to Japan. Some birds may overwinter along the western coast of Canada.

THE RED-FACED CORMORANT is so-called because of the presence of the bare red skin surrounding its eyes. This contrasts with its glossy black feathering, although at the start of the breeding season, these birds acquire white areas of plumage on their flanks, and develop similarly colored plumes on their head and neck. They have an average wingspan of 46 inches (117 cm). Their toes are webbed, which aids their swimming abilities. Food is usually acquired by diving, with cormorants generally being well-equipped to fish under water. They may also catch crustaceans such as crabs.

TYPICAL LOCATION Pairs nest on cliffs and islands through their range in the far north, with both parents playing a part in rearing the young.

Anhinga

FAMILY Anhingidae
SPECIES *Anhinga anhinga*
LENGTH 35 in (89 cm)
HABITAT Swamps
CLUTCH SIZE 1–5

DISTRIBUTION Resident throughout Florida and along a narrow band of the Gulf coast into Central America. Breeding range extends further inland and north, to the Carolinas.

THE ANHINGA USES the reach provided by its long, muscular neck to lethal effect, spearing prey that includes frogs and fish with its sharp bill. It can swim well and then often rests on a convenient perch with its wings spread, allowing its feathers to dry.

SILHOUETTE The narrow, elongated body shape and extendible neck of the Anhinga has led to it becoming known as the Snakebird. Its broad wings, spanning 45 inches (114 cm), are also visible here.

Magnificent Frigatebird

FAMILY Fregatidae
SPECIES *Fregata magnificens*
LENGTH 40 in (102 cm)
HABITAT Open sea
CLUTCH SIZE 1–2

DISTRIBUTION Breeding range includes Florida and the Gulf coast, around to Central America. Also from California southward on the west coast. Resident down to South America.

SOMETIMES DUBBED the pirate of the skies because of the way in which it will harry other birds such as gulls to drop their catches rather than fishing itself, the Magnificent Frigatebird spends much of its time airborne, aided by its 90-inch (229 cm) wingspan. Pairs nest communally, on the ground or in low bushes.

GENDER DIFFERENCES A female is seen here. Males are easily distinguishable by their inflatable orange-red cheek pouches.

CICONIIFORMES   Herons, flamingos, and their allies

Slender in build, long-legged, sometimes secretive and frequently colorful, members of this Order are likely to be encountered in shallow stretches of water. Herons are likely to be lurking among reeds and other aquatic vegetation, others such as spoonbills are much easier to observe, living in what can be large flocks. All these birds feed on small aquatic creatures through to fish and frogs. The Florida Everglades is the area in North America where these wading birds are perhaps most numerous. They are concentrated in warmer areas, where their feeding grounds will not be badly affected by ice in winter.

Green Heron

FAMILY Ardeidae
SPECIES *Butorides virescens*
LENGTH 18 in (46 cm)
HABITAT Wooded waterways
CLUTCH SIZE 3–6

DISTRIBUTION Breeds in the eastern United States into Canada, east of the Great Lakes. Resident in Florida along the Gulf coast. Occurs in the far west.

ADULTS HAVE bluish-gray upperparts with a distinctive greenish suffusion on the back. The wings are dark, but prominently edged with white markings. The sides of the chest have a dull purple hue, with the top of the head being slate-gray while the eyes are orange-yellow. There is a fairly indistinct crest at the back of the crown, which is likely to be held erect if the heron is threatened. At the start of the breeding period, the yellowish legs of the cock bird turn a much brighter orange shade. A pair will nest on their own, constructing a nest of sticks in a well-concealed locality in a tree or bush. Young birds can be recognized by their predominantly brown plumage and will wander off to new territories once they are independent. The adult wingspan is 26 inches (66 cm). Green Herons generally prefer not to wade through water on their relatively short legs when fishing, unlike most other members of the family.

FISHING TECHNIQUE The Green Heron depends on finding a convenient branch from where it can strike at its prey.

Little Blue Heron

FAMILY Ardeidae

SPECIES *Egretta caerulea*

LENGTH 24 in (61 cm)

HABITAT Freshwater/salt
marshland

CLUTCH SIZE 3–7

DISTRIBUTION Coastal areas
from New York south via Florida
and the Gulf coast into Mexico.
Range wider in the southeastern
United States in summer.

THESE HERONS are usually
seen individually outside the
breeding season, but they
will nest communally. Their
legs and feet, including the
long toes, are normally
yellow, but these become
blackish at this time of year.
Even more unusual, however,
is the fact that the young
Little Blue Herons will be
completely white in color
when they leave the nest.
This species' wingspan is
40 inches (102 cm).

DISTINCTIVE COLORING The slate-
blue plumage over the back and
underparts helps to identify this
species. Its head and upper chest
display more purplish coloration.

Snowy Egret

FAMILY Ardeidae

SPECIES *Egretta thula*

LENGTH 24 in (61 cm)

HABITAT Wetland/lakes

CLUTCH SIZE 2–6

DISTRIBUTION Occurs along
both the west and east coasts
of the United States. Summer
range extends to western and
southeastern areas, with some
birds overwintering in Mexico.

THE VERY DELICATE plumes of the Snowy Egret almost
threatened its survival in the 1800s, when these feathers
became highly sought-after as fashion items, to decorate hats in
particular. Thankfully, those days have passed and a healthy
population of these birds now exists throughout their range.

DISPLAY The Snowy
Egret's plumes are less
developed in nonbreeding
birds, such as this individual.
When spread, the wings
measure 41 inches (104 cm).

Tricolored Heron

FAMILY Ardeidae
SPECIES *Egretta tricolor*
LENGTH 26 in (66 cm)
HABITAT Marshland/mangrove
swamps
CLUTCH SIZE 3–7

DISTRIBUTION Eastern coastal area of the United States and throughout Florida. Range extends from New York down into Mexico. In the summer, may wander inland as far as Kansas.

THIS PARTICULAR HERON occurs in fairly open countryside, and can be easily identified by its distinctive coloration. It has a slate-gray head and back, with the plumage having a more purplish hue over the chest area, while the underparts are white. There is a dramatic change in appearance at the start of the breeding season, however, as the yellow facial skin and the base of the bill are both transformed to bright blue. Although they forage for food alone, Tricolored Herons will nest colonially in suitable areas, building in the mangrove swamps, for example, or in a suitable tree. Occasionally, pairs have even been recorded nesting on the ground.

ADULT TRICOLORED HERON Young birds have brown plumage evident on their wings, as well as on the back of the neck. The wingspan measures 36 inches (91 cm).

Great Egret

FAMILY Ardeidae
SPECIES *Ardea alba*
LENGTH 39 in (99 cm)
HABITAT Lakes/marshland
CLUTCH SIZE 3–5

DISTRIBUTION Southeastern United States, extending via the Great Lakes in the summer to southern Canada. Present in California (moving inland during the summer) and Mexico.

THE LARGEST of the egrets found in North America, with a wingspan of 51 inches (130 cm), this species has snow-white plumage, which makes a stark contrast with its black legs. Its strong, tapering bill is yellow in color. The Great Egret is dependent on wetland habitat in order to forage for food, hunting for small aquatic vertebrates in the shallows, which it seizes with its powerful bill. Breeding occurs in large colonies, with the birds nesting in trees or bushes. The young are very similar to their parents when they fledge, although a slightly duller shade of white.

ELEGANT PROFILE These graceful birds move quite slowly and deliberately through shallow water, watching for potential prey.

Great Blue Heron

FAMILY Ardeidae
SPECIES *Ardea herodias*
LENGTH 46 in (117 cm)
HABITAT Wetland
CLUTCH SIZE 3–7

DISTRIBUTION Throughout the United States into Canada during the summer; south of the Great Lakes in the east; in the west, resident up to Alaska.

AS THEIR NAME suggests, most Great Blue Herons are bluish in color, with a black stripe on each side of the head, extending back through the eyes, and on the shoulder area. White areas are restricted to the head and underparts, with white plumes evident over the neck and wings. In Florida, however, there is a totally white form, which used to be regarded as a separate species, while another variant, called Wurdemann's Heron, is characterized by its white head. These herons are solitary outside the breeding period, sometimes flying up to 15 miles (24 km) for food. They breed colonially, on cliffs or in trees or bushes, and occasionally, there may be hundreds nesting together.

BIG IMPACT The Great Blue is the largest heron in North America, having a wingspan of 72 inches (183 cm), and also has the widest distribution.

FIGHTING TALK Two male Great Egrets engage in a territorial dispute. The long, lacy plumes that they develop at the start of the breeding season on their back and tail are clearly evident.

Least Bittern

FAMILY Ardeidae
SPECIES *Ixobrychus exilis*
LENGTH 13 in (33 cm)
HABITAT Reedy wetland
CLUTCH SIZE 4–5

DISTRIBUTION Mainly present in the eastern United States up to southeastern Canada in summer. Resident in southern California, and southern Florida, overwintering in Central America and the Caribbean.

THE LEAST BITTERN is the smallest North American member of the family. Its small size and secretive nature, as well as the marshland habitat, mean that it is hard to observe. If frightened, it tends not to break cover, but freezes, standing immobile with its head raised.

GENDER DIFFERENCES
The black cap identifies this as a male. This area of the body is brown in hens. The wingspan for both sexes is 17 inches (43 cm).

American Bittern

FAMILY Ardeidae
SPECIES *Botaurus lentiginosus*
LENGTH 28 in (71 cm)
HABITAT Marshland
CLUTCH SIZE 2–3

DISTRIBUTION Across northern United States and southern Canada in the summer, overwintering in the southern states, down into Mexico. Resident in areas of the west and east coasts.

AT THE START of the nesting period in the spring, the hen constructs a platform of reeds and other vegetation, while the booming calls of the cock bird echo eerily through the landscape at this stage. It will take nearly a month for the chicks to hatch, and then they will remain in the nest for a further six weeks or so. Their eventual wingspan will be 42 inches (107 cm). If disturbed, the American Bittern will freeze in place with its neck extended upwards.

BLENDING IN WITH THE SURROUNDINGS
The brown and black markings in the plumage of the American Bittern provide very effective camouflage, especially when its head is raised.

Black-crowned Night Heron

FAMILY Ardeidae
SPECIES *Nycticorax nycticorax*
LENGTH 25 in (64 cm)
HABITAT Wet woodland
CLUTCH SIZE 2–6

DISTRIBUTION In summer, central-southern Canada and much of the United States, except northern-central parts; withdraws to coastal areas and into Mexico over the winter.

AS ITS NAME SUGGESTS, the Black-crowned Night Heron is largely nocturnal in its habits, emerging under cover of darkness to hunt for prey such as fish. During the daytime, these herons rest silently under cover in communal roosts. They breed in groups, constructing platform-type nests in trees, often at a considerable height off the ground. Both adults share the task of incubation, which lasts for about 26 days. Young Night Herons develop quite slowly, and may not fledge until they are seven weeks old. They can be easily recognized at this stage, not just by the difference in the coloration of their feathers, but also because their eyes are yellowish-orange, rather than deep red.

FEATHERS Three white plumes extend down over the back of Black-crowned Night Herons, visible here. Their wingspan is 44 inches (112 cm).

Yellow-crowned Night Heron

FAMILY Ardeidae
SPECIES *Nyctanassa violacea*
LENGTH 24 in (61 cm)
HABITAT Wet woodland
CLUTCH SIZE 2–8

DISTRIBUTION Southeastern parts of the United States in the summer, overwintering mainly in Florida, but may be seen from North Carolina as far along the Gulf Coast as western Texas.

YELLOW-CROWNED Night Herons may sometimes be observed hunting during the day. If disturbed, however, they rarely betray their presence by flying off. Instead, these herons freeze where they are, relying on their plumage to conceal their presence. Their wingspan measures 44 inches (111 cm).

MARITIME VISITOR This particular night heron is often seen in coastal areas, where it hunts crabs and fish. It is largely solitary by nature.

Cattle Egret

FAMILY Ardeidae
SPECIES *Bubulcus ibis*
LENGTH 20 in (51 cm)
HABITAT Open areas
CLUTCH SIZE 2–6

DISTRIBUTION Summer range through southeastern United States, up the east coast to Rhode Island. Overwinters in Florida and along the Gulf coast, and also in southern California.

A VERY ADAPTABLE species, the Cattle Egret is not native to North America. Instead, today's population spread here from further south, originally coming from Africa. It breeds in large colonies, in trees or bushes, creating a platform of sticks as a nest. Both parents share the incubation duties, which last just over three weeks. The young egrets then fledge at a month old, eventually reaching the adult wingspan of 36 inches (91 cm).

PLUMAGE The color is mainly white, but birds may also display orange plumes on the crown, back, and chest.

White Ibis

FAMILY Threskiornithidae
SPECIES *Eudocimus albus*
LENGTH 25 in (64 cm)
HABITAT Coasts
CLUTCH SIZE 2–5

DISTRIBUTION From Virginia along the Gulf coast right down into Mexico, and may be seen further inland in the summer. Also occasionally seen in southern California.

THE LONG, DOWN-CURVING BILL of this species helps to set it apart from both herons and egrets. The tips of the White Ibis's flight feathers are black, as is clearly evident when the wings are extended to their full span of 38 inches (97 cm), while both the face and legs are a distinctive bright scarlet.

CONSPICUOUS White Ibises are often seen seeking food in coastal areas, being easy to spot in open terrain.

White-faced Ibis

FAMILY Threskiornithidae
SPECIES *Plegadis chihi*
LENGTH 23 in (58 cm)
HABITAT Freshwater marshland
CLUTCH SIZE 2–7

DISTRIBUTION Central and western parts of the United States over the summer, north to southern Canada. Overwinters in southwestern United States into Mexico.

IN SPITE OF its name, the White-faced Ibis is essentially grayish-brown, although these birds display brighter coloration during the breeding period. Their plumage is then transformed to a reddish-brown shade with green iridescence on the wings and the tail. White feathering on the face develops, too, forming a border around the red facial skin, and their legs become red. Their wingspan is 36 inches (91 cm). They feed on aquatic invertebrates.

FEEDING White-faced Ibis generally forage in freshwater swamps, sometimes venturing into flooded fields after heavy periods of rainfall.

NEAR NEIGHBORS As their name implies, Cattle Egrets (*see* p. 56) live alongside large grazing animals such as these African Buffalo in the Old World where they originate. These birds seize invertebrates disturbed by their movements.

Glossy Ibis

FAMILY Threskiornithidae
SPECIES *Plegadis falcinellus*
LENGTH 23 in (58 cm)
HABITAT Marshland
CLUTCH SIZE 2–7

DISTRIBUTION From southern Maine to North Carolina in the summer, and resident throughout the year from here southwards, through Florida along the Gulf coast into eastern Texas.

THESE IBISES are likely to be observed feeding in small groups, and they also breed communally. They sometimes choose a site on the ground, but generally build their nests in a tree, which affords better protection from predators. The incubation period lasts three weeks.

MATING CHANGE The plumage becomes more glossy and colorful at the start of the breeding period. When spread, the wings measure 36 inches (91 cm).

Wood Stork

FAMILY Ciconiidae
SPECIES *Mycteria americana*
LENGTH 40 in (102 cm)
HABITAT Wetland
CLUTCH SIZE 3–4

DISTRIBUTION Restricted essentially to Florida in North America, extending to southern parts of Georgia and South Carolina in the summer.

FLOCKS OF Wood Storks make an impressive sight when in flight, with their imposing large wings—61 inches (155 cm) in span. They regularly undertake seasonal movements within their range, although the population in Florida is resident throughout the year. The Wood Stork is therefore the only member of the family native to the continent. They hunt for small vertebrates and also larger invertebrates both in water and on land.

FEATHER-FREE The head of the Wood Stork is unfeathered, with its skin here having a rather leathery texture. Its bill is slightly curved.

Roseate Spoonbill

FAMILY Threskiornithidae
SPECIES *Ajaia ajaja*
LENGTH 32 in (81 cm)
HABITAT Wetland
CLUTCH SIZE 2–3

DISTRIBUTION Southern tip of Florida, ranging more widely here in the summer. Also westwards from Louisiana along the Gulf coast down into Mexico, and in the Caribbean.

THE PLUMAGE of Roseate Spoonbills is pinkish, with a darker band of color being evident across each wing. Their wingspan is 50 inches (127 cm). Their most distinctive feature, however, is the enlarged tip to their bill, which looks rather like a spoon in shape. This characteristic helps these birds to feed, allowing them to catch more of the aquatic invertebrates that form the bulk of the Roseate Spoonbill's diet. They also eat small fish. As with many of the water birds from southeastern parts of the United States, Roseate Spoonbills are under threat from habitat change, particularly the drainage of wetland areas, but this does not yet appear to have had an adverse effect on their numbers.

IN FLIGHT When flying, Roseate Spoonbills keep their necks full extended, and land in a similar fashion.

ANSERIFORMES

Waterfowl and screamers

The ducks, geese, and swans comprise by far the largest of the two families that make up this Order, with approximately 159 species recognized worldwide. There are just three species of screamers in contrast, which are confined to parts of South America. The members of the Anatidae are often known collectively as waterfowl, reflecting the fact that they live in the vicinity of water.

Their chicks will start to swim almost immediately after hatching. The description of "fowl" refers to the fact that particularly in the past, many species were an important source of food, alongside domestic fowl.

Trumpeter Swan

FAMILY Anatidae
SPECIES *Cygnus buccinator*
LENGTH 60 in (152 cm)
HABITAT Lakes/rivers
CLUTCH SIZE 2–13

DISTRIBUTION Widely distributed in Alaska and Yukon Territory, overwintering in British Columbia through the northern United States.

JUVENILES Young swans are likely to remain with their parents until they are nearly a year old.

IN COMMON with most swans, the Trumpeter has pure white plumage over its entire body and it is the facial area that allows it to be identified easily. Both the bill and surrounding skin here are black. Young birds differ in appearance, with their plumage being grayish-brown while their bill is pinkish in color.

Tundra Swan

FAMILY Anatidae
SPECIES *Cygnus columbianus*
LENGTH 52 in (132 cm)
HABITAT Lakes/rivers
CLUTCH SIZE 2–7

DISTRIBUTION From western Alaska around the northern coast. Overwinters in the north-western United States, and on the east coast, to North Carolina.

THIS SWAN BREEDS in the far north, heading south in the winter. It is the smallest species of swan occurring in North America, recognizable also by its black bill with a yellow streak on each side of the head, connecting to the eyes. Tundra Swans eat a variety of vegetation, as well as some invertebrates, especially snails.

DEFENSIVE A Tundra Swan defending its nest. Like other swans, it builds a bulky nest of vegetation that helps to insulate the eggs.

Mute Swan

FAMILY Anatidae
SPECIES *Cygnus olor*
LENGTH 60 in (152 cm)
HABITAT Lakes/rivers
CLUTCH SIZE 4–6

DISTRIBUTION Resident in the vicinity of the Great Lakes in the eastern United States, and expanding northward to the east, up to New England.

INTRODUCED FROM EUROPE, the Mute Swan is a large bird with white plumage and a bill that is mainly orange with a black tip. There is also a black knob on the forehead that is especially prominent in the male swan. The male is known as the cob, while the female is called a pen. Swans pair for life. They become very territorial when breeding, with the cob in particular attacking not just other waterfowl, but also dogs and people who venture too close. They can inflict a painful blow with a strike from one of their wings while hissing ferociously. Swans will graze on plant matter both in the water and on land.

YOUNG SWANS Known as cygnets, young swans hatch with their eyes open and have a covering of thick down.

Greater White-fronted Goose

FAMILY Anatidae
SPECIES *Anser albifrons*
LENGTH 28 in (71 cm)
HABITAT Farmland/wetland
CLUTCH SIZE 4–7

DISTRIBUTION Found in Alaska; west of Hudson Bay and on southwestern Greenland. Overwinters in California, but mainly in the southeast from Illinois to Texas, and into Mexico.

THE WHITE BAND at the base of the bill helps to distinguish this species. These geese are brownish overall, with both black markings and pale edging to the plumage on the back and sides of the body. There are regional differences, however, with those breeding in northern-central Canada being larger and darker with less barring than Alaskan or Greenland birds.

SOCIAL BIRDS Greater White-fronted Geese feed and breed in groups. Flocks of thousands may be seen on migration.

Ross's Goose

FAMILY Anatidae
SPECIES *Chen rossii*
LENGTH 23 in (58 cm)
HABITAT Fields/marshland
CLUTCH SIZE 4–7

DISTRIBUTION Breeds on the northern coast of Canada, mainly west of Hudson Bay. Overwinters in California and through the southern states. Also in North Carolina and Virginia.

THESE GEESE undertake an extensive migration back and forth to their breeding grounds each summer. Their coloration is quite distinctive as they are largely white, with their black primary flight feathers becoming evident when the wing is open. Younger birds are grayer.

ADULT ROSS'S GEESE These have the typical look of this species, but there is also a rare, dark-colored variant with a white head and a mottled body.

Brant Goose

FAMILY Anatidae
SPECIES *Branta bernicla*
LENGTH 25 in (64 cm)
HABITAT Bays/marshland
CLUTCH SIZE 1–7

DISTRIBUTION Alaska into the far north, mainly west of Hudson Bay. Winter range includes the Aleutian Islands, plus the west and northeastern coasts of the United States.

THESE GEESE have a circumpolar distribution, occurring in northern Europe and Asia as well as North America. They are sometimes known as Brent Geese. The eastern American subspecies (*Branta bernicla hrota*) has a white abdomen, whereas that of the western race (*B. b. nigricans*) is dark.

MARKINGS Brant Geese display a variable white band on the side of the neck; the head and neck are dark.

Canada Goose

FAMILY Anatidae
SPECIES *Branta canadensis*
LENGTH 45 in (114 cm)
HABITAT Fields/grassland
CLUTCH SIZE 2–12

DISTRIBUTION Summer range extends right up to parts of the continent's northern coastline. Resident down the west coast and generally across an area south of the Great Lakes.

IN SPITE OF THEIR NAME, Canada Geese can be found over virtually the entire North American continent, with their distribution varying according to the season. When migrating, flocks fly in a distinctive V-shaped formation. They are very adaptable by nature, increasingly being seen in areas such as city parks and on golf courses. Flocks can cause considerable damage in fields, by feeding on growing cereal crops, although they normally graze on grass. When nesting, pairs will construct a large nest using vegetation, lining it with down feathers. The female incubates alone, with the goslings hatching after about 25 days.

NESTING Canada Geese are especially protective in the vicinity of their nest, hissing menacingly if disturbed. They breed on the ground near water.

CANADA GOOSE Canada Geese can be identified by the wide area of white plumage on the neck, which runs at an angle beneath the eye. Southern populations of these geese are significantly larger than those from northerly areas.

Fulvous Whistling Duck

FAMILY Anatidae
SPECIES *Dendrocygna bicolor*
LENGTH 20 in (51 cm)
HABITAT Shallow waterways
CLUTCH SIZE 10–20

DISTRIBUTION Occurs in the southeastern United States; resident in the extreme south of Texas and southeastern Florida. Ranges down to Argentina.

WHISTLING DUCKS have a relatively upright stance, not unlike that of a goose, although they are smaller in size. Their calls, sounding like whistles, help to account for the common name of these waterfowl. The Fulvous Whistling Duck can be distinguished by its light brown face, neck, and underparts. The wings are dark brown with relatively broad lighter edging, with both sexes being identical in appearance. These waterfowl frequent open areas of country close to water, such as marshland, and will often choose to nest on the ground.

Occasionally, a pair may decide to nest in a tree cavity, up to 30 ft (9 m) off the ground, which explains why they are also known as tree ducks. More than one pair may even decide to use the same nest.

COLORATION Brown predominates in the plumage, with the bill, legs, and feet being grayish.

Black-bellied Whistling Duck

FAMILY Anatidae

SPECIES *Dendrocygna autumnalis*

LENGTH 21 in (53 cm)

HABITAT Wooded waterways

CLUTCH SIZE 12–16

DISTRIBUTION Isolated resident groups through the southern United States, but mainly found in Texas, ranging further north from here in the summer. Extends south as far as Argentina.

THE RANGE of this whistling duck is extending in southern parts of the United States. It is most likely to be encountered in countryside where there are stands of trees, since it generally prefers to nest in suitable hollows rather than laying its eggs on the ground. The young ducklings will leave the nest when they are newly hatched, though it is likely to be a further two months before they can fly. They will then be similar to their parents, but with paler plumage, and are still easily distinguishable by their gray bills.

CREPUSCULAR These ducks are most likely to be seen when dusk is falling, when they emerge to feed both on plant matter and invertebrates such as snails.

Green-winged Teal

FAMILY Anatidae

SPECIES *Anas crecca*

LENGTH 14½ in (37 cm)

HABITAT Marshland

CLUTCH SIZE 10–12

DISTRIBUTION Widely distributed over much of North America, breeding in the northern half of the continent and overwintering across the entire south, down into Mexico.

THE GREEN AREA on the wings of these teal is present in both sexes, but only the drake has the broad, dark green stripe extending down the neck from behind the eye on each side of the face. Ducks in contrast are predominantly brown in color. Green-winged Teal are very social by nature, sometimes forming large flocks consisting of hundreds of birds during the winter period. Such groups look spectacular when in flight. When feeding, these waterfowl forage in a typical dabbling duck fashion, upending their bodies to feed underwater.

SMALL BUT COLORFUL This species—the drake seen here in breeding plumage—is the smallest of the dabbling ducks in North America.

Northern Pintail

FAMILY Anatidae
SPECIES *Anas acuta*
LENGTH 26 in (66 cm)
HABITAT Lakes/marshland
CLUTCH SIZE 6–12

DISTRIBUTION Summer visitor across the north, south to Colorado; resident in southern Alaska and in western parts of the United States, also overwintering across the south.

THE LONG, narrow pin-like tail feathers serve to identify the drake of this species. Ducks are more nondescript in terms of their appearance, but their relatively large size helps to distinguish them from other species. Both sexes display a brown-green area on each wing in flight.

HABITAT Northern Pintails prefer relatively shallow stretches of water, where they can forage for their food.

American Wigeon

FAMILY Anatidae
SPECIES *Anas americana*
LENGTH 19 in (48 cm)
HABITAT Lakes/marshland
CLUTCH SIZE 6–12

DISTRIBUTION Summer visitor to the far north, largely absent to the south of the Great Lakes. Overwinters on the west coast and across the southern states.

THE WHITE AREA on the crown of the drake has led to these wigeon being nicknamed "baldpate." The bill in both sexes is a distinctive shade of pale bluish-gray, with a prominent black band at its tip. American Wigeon are often seen in fairly urban areas, including parkland. It usually nests in a well-concealed locality in reedbeds, rather than close to water.

OPPORTUNIST Although the wigeon is a dabbling duck, it may steal food from diving ducks, which venture further below the surface.

Cinnamon Teal

FAMILY Anatidae
SPECIES *Anas cyanoptera*
LENGTH 16 in (41 cm)
HABITAT Lakes/marshland
CLUTCH SIZE 10–12

DISTRIBUTION Summer range from southwestern Canada to western Texas into Mexico. Overwinters in southern Texas across the border. Resident across much of California and southwestern Arizona.

THE DISTINCTIVE cinnamon-brown plumage of drakes means that they are easy to identify from a distance. Their eyes are a contrasting shade of bright orange. These dabbling ducks prefer relatively shallow water where they can easily feed, seeking both plants and invertebrates.

SIMILAR SPECIES The Cinnamon Teal is very closely related to the Blue-winged Teal.

Blue-winged Teal

FAMILY Anatidae
SPECIES *Anas discors*
LENGTH 15½ in (39 cm)
HABITAT Lakes/marshland
CLUTCH SIZE 6–15

DISTRIBUTION Widely distributed summer visitor across much of the United States into southern Canada. Generally overwinters in northern South America.

BOTH SEXES DISPLAY the pale blue wing patch that is a feature of this species. Ducks and drakes out of breeding colors are a mottled shade of grayish-brown, with the young being a paler shade of brown with yellow legs. They sometimes occur in very small stretches of water, and may be seen in groups in marshland too.

FEEDING Blue-winged Teal tend not to tip up their bodies like other dabbling ducks when feeding, but simply extend their necks below the surface.

Northern Shoveler

FAMILY Anatidae

SPECIES *Anas clypeata*

LENGTH 19 in (48 cm)

HABITAT Ponds/marshland

CLUTCH SIZE 6–14

DISTRIBUTION Breeds from Alaska right down to northern New Mexico. Resident in the west from British Columbia down to California and Texas, wintering throughout the south.

ONE OF THE DISTINGUISHING features of the Northern Shoveler is its long black bill, described as spatulate because of the way it enlarges at its tip. This helps these waterfowl to obtain food by effectively sieving the water in search of edible items, which include invertebrates as well as plants. The appearance of the drake is transformed outside the breeding season, with the head and breast then becoming grayish in color, with an evident white crescent being present in front of each eye. Females on the other hand are a mottled shade of brown, but again, they can be distinguished from other ducks by their bill shape. In flight, Northern Shovelers display paler blue wing markings, with the underside of the wings being mainly white. A pair will nest close to water, choosing a location that is well-hidden by vegetation.

DISPLAY COLORS A Northern Shoveler drake in breeding plumage. These waterfowl may occasionally venture into coastal areas.

Mottle Duck

FAMILY Anatidae

SPECIES *Anas fulvigula*

LENGTH 22 in (56 cm)

HABITAT Coastal marshland

CLUTCH SIZE 8–11

DISTRIBUTION Summer breeding population centered in northwestern Texas. Resident from the coast of South Carolina down across much of Florida, and along the Gulf states.

THIS PARTICULAR SPECIES favors warmer, southern latitudes. Although often encountered in coastal areas, it can sometimes be seen far inland but populations are generally quite sedentary, remaining in the same area throughout the year. Both sexes have a mottled appearance as their name suggests, with the yellow bill serving to distinguish between them, being of a brighter shade in drakes. The blue-green band present across the flight feathers is only apparent in flight, when the wings are open. Seen from below, the underside of the wing is whitish.

SECLUDED Mottled Ducks tend to be observed on more remote stretches of water, away from human habitation, frequenting marshland over the winter.

Mallard

FAMILY Anatidae

SPECIES *Anas platyrhynchos*

LENGTH 23 in (58 cm)

HABITAT Freshwater/ marshland

CLUTCH SIZE 5–14

DISTRIBUTION Found through Alaska in the summer eastward to Newfoundland. Resident on the western seaboard and across most of the United States.

MALLARDS ARE very conspicuous waterfowl, frequently seen in city parks where there are ponds, as well as on rivers and even in coastal marshes. Drakes have a dark green head and brown chest, and pale flanks, with ducks having a mottled appearance. There are blue patches evident across the wings. Young Mallards resemble adult females, but have dull olive rather than black-marked orange bills. Courting drakes can be very persistent, with a number chasing a single female, and occasionally even exhausting her so that she drowns.

A PAIR OF MALLARDS This species is actually the original ancestor of the majority of today's domesticated breeds of duck.

American Black Duck

FAMILY Anatidae

SPECIES *Anas rubripes*

LENGTH 23 in (58 cm)

HABITAT Ponds/marshland

CLUTCH SIZE 5–17

DISTRIBUTION Breeds right up into eastern Canada and on Newfoundland, resident around the Great Lakes; overwinters through eastern United States.

IN SPITE OF THEIR NAME, American Black Ducks have dark brown rather than pure black plumage. The sexes can be distinguished on the basis of their bill color. This area is yellow in the case of the male, but a much duller yellowish-green, often with blackish markings in the case of the female. They are quite shy birds by nature, and will readily fly off if disturbed. They are most likely to be encountered inland in woodland areas, where there are ponds and streams, while they also favor coastal marshes. Occasionally, they may be seen too on lakes, sometimes in the company of Mallards (*see* p. 73). These species may even hybridize together, and where the American Black Duck is falling in numbers, this crossbreeding is tending to hasten its decline. In areas such as the west of its present distribution, the more adaptable Mallard is being seen increasingly in areas where American Black Ducks used to be common. As a dabbling duck, this species will eat a variety of food, nibbling on underwater plants and also eating invertebrates such as snails. Amphibians too may also be eaten on occasions. When nesting, American Black Ducks will chose a site adjacent to the water, constructing a nest of vegetation. Incubation lasts for about a month. The young ducklings will be able to swim almost immediately, but it will be about nine weeks until they can fly.

IDENTIFICATION The bluish-violet wing markings that are a characteristic of this species will be most evident in flight.

Gadwall

FAMILY Anatidae
SPECIES *Anas strepera*
LENGTH 20 in (50 cm)
HABITAT Small ponds
CLUTCH SIZE 7–15

DISTRIBUTION Summer breeding populations found in southern Alaska and Yukon, but mainly further south, resident in western parts. Overwinters in the southeast, south of the Great Lakes.

FLOCKS OF THESE DUCKS are most likely to be observed on lakes and other open, relatively shallow stretches of water. This allows them to feed easily on vegetation just below the surface. They will also eat aquatic invertebrates. Males have a more colorful breeding plumage.

DRAKE'S PLUMAGE The drake is mainly gray in breeding plumage. Both sexes display a white wing patch.

Wood Duck

FAMILY Anatidae
SPECIES *Aix sponsa*
LENGTH 18½ in (47 cm)
HABITAT Woodland with water
CLUTCH SIZE 8–14

DISTRIBUTION Found in the summer throughout southern Canada and eastern half of the United States, being resident in southern areas here. Resident too along the west coast.

THESE DUCKS ARE UNUSUAL because they roost and breed as high as 50 ft (15 m) off the ground, in a suitable hollow tree. The young ducklings, unable to fly at first, simply tumble down to the ground from the nest site soon after hatching. Their mother watches over them once they take to the water, and the family group will typically remain together for almost two months.

SPECTACULAR The drake, seen here on the right, is one of the most colorful of North America's waterfowl. This species is also known as the Carolina Duck.

Common Eider

FAMILY Anatidae

SPECIES *Somateria mollissima*

LENGTH 24 in (61 cm)

HABITAT Tundra ponds/
coastal bays

CLUTCH SIZE 4–7

DISTRIBUTION Breeds from southern Alaska around the northern coast and Greenland, partly resident here and down the northeastern coast. Also overwinters off Alaska and in Hudson Bay.

COMMON EIDER DUCKS BREED on tundra ponds formed in the summer by the thawing of ice in the upper layers of the ground. They then move to coastal areas to overwinter, feeding on marine invertebrates such as crustaceans and starfish, as well as small fish.

BREEDING PLUMAGE This male Common Eider shows the species' distinctive head profile. The female is brown.

King Eider

FAMILY Anatidae

SPECIES *Somateria spectabilis*

LENGTH 22 in (56 cm)

HABITAT Tundra ponds/
coastal bays

CLUTCH SIZE 4–7

DISTRIBUTION Breeds along the north coast of North America, and up to Greenland. Winters mainly off southern Alaska and down the northeastern coast.

AS THEY INHABIT a cold area of the world, the plumage of eider ducks in general affords them good protection against the cold. Their downy feathering used to be collected to provide the stuffing for eiderdowns. King Eiders are able to dive down to depths of 180 ft (55 m) in search of food, with their wings serving as flippers at this stage.

IDENTIFICATION The gray head and colorful orange shield on the top of the bill of the King Eider distinguish it from its common cousin.

Harlequin Duck

FAMILY Anatidae

SPECIES *Histrionicus histrionicus*

LENGTH 16½ in (42 cm)

HABITAT Streams/coasts

CLUTCH SIZE 5–10

DISTRIBUTION Summer range extends from Alaska to Oregon. Also southern Greenland, north-eastern Canada. Overwinters down to California and Virginia.

THESE DUCKS often spend the winter months swimming in the strong currents in coastal areas at sea, before moving inland to turbulent mountain streams, where they nest adjacent to the water. They are adept at diving for food, and even the young ducklings can swim and dive well, before they gain the ability to fly. Harlequin Ducks will feed on a variety of invertebrates and small fish. It is hard to distinguish the sexes until males start to gain their more colorful breeding plumage at the start of the nesting season.

GENDER DIFFERENCES Drakes have brighter plumage than ducks. The drake in breeding condition keeps the white spot behind the eyes.

Ring-necked Duck

FAMILY Anatidae

SPECIES *Aythya collaris*

LENGTH 17 in (43 cm)

HABITAT Lakes/ponds/ marshland

CLUTCH SIZE 6–14

DISTRIBUTION Summer range from southern Alaska to Nova Scotia, around the Great Lakes and Colorado in the west. Winters down both coasts and across the southern United States.

UNLIKE MANY WATERFOWL, the Ring-necked Duck tends to be quite solitary by nature, and does not occur in large flocks. It tends to frequent stretches of freshwater, but may sometimes be encountered in coastal marshes. A gray wing stripe helps to identify these waterfowl in flight.

BREEDING COLORS This drake clearly displays the whitish stripes evident across the bill.

Lesser Scaup

FAMILY Anatidae
SPECIES *Aythya affinis*
LENGTH 16½ in (42 cm)
HABITAT Ponds/coastal bays
CLUTCH SIZE 9–12

DISTRIBUTION Breeds from Alaska eastward, generally overwintering across the entire United States south of the Great Lakes, down into Central America and the Caribbean, but resident further west.

THIS SPECIES RANGES over a much greater area than its Greater cousin (*see* p. 80), not being confined to coastal areas over the winter. They appear very similar, but aside from being smaller, the Lesser Scaup also has a reduced area of white plumage across each wing.

COLORATION The drake is brownish overall in nonbreeding plumage.

Redhead

FAMILY Anatidae
SPECIES *Aythya americana*
LENGTH 19 in (48 cm)
HABITAT Lakes/marshland
CLUTCH SIZE 7–12

DISTRIBUTION Isolated breeding population in Alaska, and southern Yukon Territory down to west of the Great Lakes. Overwinters in southern United States and Central America.

ALTHOUGH ITS OVERALL COLORATION is not dissimilar to that of the Canvasback (*see* p. 80), the Redhead drake can be identified in breeding plumage by even chestnut-red coloration over the entire head, and its yellow rather than red eyes. The duck in contrast is brown, with the feathering on the crown being of a darker shade. The Redhead's bill is gray with a black tip, providing a further point of distinction between these species.

NESTING Redheads nest in reed beds, constructing a nest here lined with soft down. Unusually, females may lay eggs in other neighboring nests as well.

Tufted Duck

FAMILY Anatidae
SPECIES *Aythya fuligula*
LENGTH 17 in (43 cm)
HABITAT Coasts
CLUTCH SIZE 6–10

DISTRIBUTION Wintertime visitor, ranging from southern Alaska to southern California, and from Newfoundland southward as far as Maryland.

THE LONG BLACK TUFT of feathers evident on the back of the head of the drake is unmistakable, but it will not be until their second year that this characteristic develops fully in young males. The rest of their body, aside from the white flanks, is also a glossy shade of black. The ducks are grayish-brown overall, with the eyes being bright yellow. In flight, both sexes display a white wing bar. They can sometimes be seen out at sea, but also often enter estuaries and forage for food in marshland. Tufted Ducks consume a variety of plant matter, and also eat invertebrates and amphibians, diving beneath the surface to obtain their food. Within North America, they often show strong territorial links, with flocks frequently returning to the same area every year. They may hybridize with related species, such as scaup, with their offspring then displaying shorter crests.

MIGRANT Tufted Ducks may even be seen on ponds in city center parks, but do not breed in North America.

Greater Scaup

FAMILY Anatidae

SPECIES *Aythya marila*

LENGTH 18 in (46 cm)

HABITAT Tundra/coastal bays

CLUTCH SIZE 7–10

DISTRIBUTION Breeds across the north. Overwinters from the Aleutian Islands and southern Alaskan coast to California. Also along the east and Gulf coasts, and areas inland.

THESE WATERFOWL frequent coastal areas, although they breed across the tundra of the far north. Outside the nesting season, the sexes are similar in appearance, but when in breeding condition, they can be distinguished easily. The nest is typically located on the ground, and is hidden in vegetation.

SEASONAL CHANGES This drake is in breeding plumage. During the rest of the year, both sexes are predominantly grayish-brown in color.

Canvasback

FAMILY Anatidae

SPECIES *Aythya valisineria*

LENGTH 21 in (53 cm)

HABITAT Lakes/bays

CLUTCH SIZE 6–9

DISTRIBUTION Westerly breeding grounds from southern Alaska to Nevada, Utah, and Colorado. Winters from British Columbia across the southern states to Central America.

THE PALE COLOR of the drake's back and flanks, resembling the old-fashioned canvas of tents, helps to explain the common name of these waterfowl. The neck and sides of the face are chestnut-red, becoming blackish on the crown, merging into the bill. This area of the body is brown in ducks, with their body being brownish-gray overall. Heavily hunted, partly because of their relatively large size, Canvasbacks prove to be instinctively wary by nature, although on occasions, they may be observed in quite large flocks.

LOCATION Canvasbacks breed in areas of marshland in the summer, and then may be seen in coastal areas at other times of the year.

Oldsquaw

FAMILY Anatidae
SPECIES *Clangula hyemalis*
LENGTH 20 in (51 cm)
HABITAT Coast/tundra pools
CLUTCH SIZE 6–11

DISTRIBUTION Breeds in the far north from the Aleutians to Greenland. Overwinters off Alaska to Washington, down to the Carolinas, and around the Great Lakes.

THE OLDSQUAW is also called the Long-tailed Duck, thanks to the long, narrow white tail feathers of the drake. This feature is most evident when it is in flight, because these feathers may end up being swamped by the swell in water. It is possible to separate the sexes throughout the year, however, partly because the female has a blackish bill, whereas that of the drake has a conspicuous pink-red bar, ending in a dark tip. In the tundra, Oldsquaw congregate on the temporary pools that form here in the brief Arctic summer. Their nest is made from grass, and lined with down feathers, in a well-concealed locality. The hen alone incubates the eggs, with hatching occurring after about three and a half weeks. It will take a further five weeks before the young ducks can begin to fly, in preparation for the journey to their wintering grounds. Here in coastal areas, they may dive down to 200 ft (61 m), seeking prey, which includes crustaceans and other invertebrates.

UNMISTAKABLE SOUND These waterfowl have a very distinctive and loud yodelling call, comprised of three different call notes.

Black Scoter

FAMILY Anatidae
SPECIES *Melanitta nigra*
LENGTH 19 in (48 cm)
HABITAT Tundra/coasts
CLUTCH SIZE 5–8

DISTRIBUTION One population breeds from western Alaska to the Aleutians, overwintering down to southern California. Another in Quebec, wintering on the coast down to Florida.

BLUE MUSSELS are one of the main items in the Black Scoter's diet when they are at sea, although they will also hunt crustaceans and molluscs, diving down to considerable depths for this purpose. On their breeding grounds in the tundra, they will feed on aquatic insects and other invertebrates. Sexing is straightforward, with the plumage of the drake being completely black, where the duck has just a black cap. The rest of her plumage is mottled, with young birds of both sexes resembling the hen. It is likely that young

Black Scoters will not breed until they are about three years old. The nest itself is made on the ground, and hidden as far as possible from potential predators such as Arctic Foxes and Snowy Owls. The young ducklings are still very vulnerable once they have hatched, because they will not yet be able to fly.

ISOLATED This scoter has the most restricted range of the three species occurring in North America, with two widely separated populations.

White-winged Scoter

FAMILY Anatidae
SPECIES *Melanitta fusca*
LENGTH 21 in (53 cm)
HABITAT Rivers/coast
CLUTCH SIZE 6–14

DISTRIBUTION Breeding range mainly from western Alaska eastward to the south of Hudson Bay with a small population in Quebec. Overwinters down the west and east coasts.

IT IS HARD TO SPOT the white wing patches in these scoters when they are not in flight, but the white comma-like patch on each side of the drake's is distinctive. The female lacks black feathering on top of the head, distinguishing her from Black Scoter ducks.

SIZE The White-winged is the largest North American Scoter, occurring both on freshwater and at sea.

Surf Scoter

FAMILY Anatidae
SPECIES *Melanitta perspicillata*
LENGTH 20 in (51 cm)
HABITAT Tundra/coasts
CLUTCH SIZE 5–8

DISTRIBUTION Breeds in the far west, from Alaska to Hudson Bay. Also in Quebec. Overwinters right down the west coast, and to Florida in the east.

WHITE PLUMAGE on the drake's head in the Surf Scoter is present as patches on the forehead, immediately around the bill, and on the nape of the neck. There is a prominent black spot on each side of the horn-colored bill, with reddish markings on the top. Surf Scoters may often be encountered some distance out to sea in the winter. This species nests in the tundra.

SURF SCOTER DRAKE When displaying, several males will compete for the attention of a single female.

Bufflehead

FAMILY Anatidae

SPECIES *Bucephala albeola*

LENGTH 13½ in (34 cm)

HABITAT Woodland waters/ coastal bays

CLUTCH SIZE 6–12

DISTRIBUTION Breeds from Alaska southward and east of Hudson Bay, overwintering over much of the United States down to Central America.

AS THEIR NAME SUGGESTS, Buffleheads have very striking heads, which are relatively large in size, contrasting with their rather short bills. The drake can be easily distinguished by the iridescent green plumage extending from the crown down around the throat, with the area around the neck having a very distinctive purplish hue. The area behind the eyes is white, as is the lower part of the body. Females have gray heads, with an oval-shaped white spot behind each eye. Their backs are dark gray rather than black, providing a further point of distinction from the drake. Buffleheads occur in small flocks in a variety of localities, ranging from ponds where they nest in the summer to coastal areas that are often their favored haunts for the winter. They are tree-nesting ducks, using an old cavity in a trunk for this purpose, sometimes even adopting the abandoned nest of a woodpecker.

BUFFLEHEAD DRAKE This species is the smallest of the diving ducks to be found in North America.

Common Goldeneye

FAMILY Anatidae
SPECIES *Bucephala clangula*
LENGTH 18½ in (47 cm)
HABITAT Lakes/rivers
CLUTCH SIZE 6–15

DISTRIBUTION Breeding range extends through much of Canada, from Alaska to Newfoundland. Overwinters through the majority of the United States, and resident especially around the Great Lakes.

THESE WATERFOWL have been nicknamed "whistler," thanks to the sound of their wings when they are flying. Drakes can be recognized by the large white circular areas on each side of the face, between their golden-colored eyes and their bill. Ducks have a brown head and gray body.

NESTING Common Goldeneyes breed in areas of coniferous forests, nesting in tree holes.

Barrow's Goldeneye

FAMILY Anatidae
SPECIES *Bucephala islandica*
LENGTH 18 in (46 cm)
HABITAT Lakes/rivers
CLUTCH SIZE 9–10

DISTRIBUTION Western population breeds from Alaska to the Northwest Territory, and to British Columbia. Eastern range centered on Newfoundland and Maine.

THESE DIVING DUCKS prefer colder northern waters, not venturing as far south as the Common Goldeneye. Pairs nest in tree cavities. When their young hatch, after about 32 days, they plummet to the ground, which can represent a drop of 50 ft (15 m) or more, and head to water with their mother. It is likely to be two months before they can fly. There are two separate breeding populations in North America: A larger, western one, and a smaller, eastern-based one.

SPECIES IDENTIFICATION
The Barrow's Goldeneye drake (*left*) can be separated from the Common Goldeneye by the fact that is has a crescent-shaped area of white plumage on the face.

Ruddy Duck

FAMILY Anatidae

SPECIES *Oxyura jamaicensis*

LENGTH 15 in (38 cm)

HABITAT Woodland lakes/
rivers

CLUTCH SIZE 5–17

DISTRIBUTION Breeds mainly
in western and central parts up
to Alaska, and near the Great
Lakes. Resident in the
southwest, and winter range
extends through the south.

THESE SMALL DIVING DUCKS often congregate in large flocks.
They can be distinguished easily by their stiff tail feathers, which
may be carried vertically. Even young ducklings will dive in
search of food, rather than dabbling at the surface when they
first take to the water.

GENDER DIFFERENCES
The cock (*left*) is in
breeding plumage. These
ducks may be seen in
bays in winter.

Hooded Merganser

FAMILY Anatidae

SPECIES *Lophodytes
cucullatus*

LENGTH 18 in (46 cm)

HABITAT Woodland ponds/
rivers

CLUTCH SIZE 8–12

DISTRIBUTION Breeds north
to British Columbia, and north
of the Great Lakes; overwinters
on west coast and in southeast.

THE SMALLEST of the
mergansers, the Hooded is
associated with freshwater,
favoring coastal areas in the
winter rather than the more
secluded backwaters where
it associates in small flocks
over the breeding period.
Ducks lay in either hollow
trees or occasionally in
rotting logs. They have
narrow, hooked bills that
help them to catch a variety
of small vertebrates,
including small fish.

DISPLAY The drake's magnificent
breeding plumage includes a black-
bordered white crest, that can be
opened out, as here, rather like a fan.

Common Merganser

FAMILY Anatidae

SPECIES *Mergus merganser*

LENGTH 25 in (64 cm)

HABITAT Woodland lakes/ rivers

CLUTCH SIZE 6–12

DISTRIBUTION Summer breeding range extends right across North America, from Alaska to Newfoundland. Overwinters in the south.

THE LARGE SIZE of these mergansers aids their identification. They also display the narrow bills that are characteristic of this group of ducks. As in other species, the bill is serrated along its upper edge, and this has led to mergansers being referred to as sawbills. This is believed to help them to grab slippery prey such as frogs, which would otherwise be more likely to slip from their grasp. The duck can be recognized by the rusty-red plumage on her head, and white throat and gray body.

MALE PLUMAGE The drake of this species has a white body, contrasting with the dark green head, and the black plumage on the back.

Red-breasted Merganser

FAMILY Anatidae

SPECIES *Mergus serrator*

LENGTH 23 in (58 cm)

HABITAT Woodland waters/ coastal bays

CLUTCH SIZE 8–10

DISTRIBUTION Breeds right across northern North America to Greenland, overwintering along both the east and western coasts; inland in eastern Texas and Oklahoma, and around the Great Lakes.

THE SHAGGY CREST at the back of the head, seen in both sexes, helps to identify these mergansers. In contrast to other species, however, the Red-breasted usually leaves its freshwater haunts in the fall, moving to coastal waters for the duration of the winter.

IDENTIFICATION The drake has a red breast, distinctive red eyes, and a white collar.

FALCONIFORMES

Birds of prey

Although some members of this Order are large in size, others are surprisingly small, reflecting the adaptability of the group as a whole. All members of this Order are predatory birds, but they may not be active hunters. A number of species, notably vultures, scavenge on carcasses, while others will avail themselves of carrion when it is available. All species have a hooked bill, and powerful feet, equipped with curved nails often described as talons. These serve to catch and hold their prey more effectively. As they are at the top of the food chain, birds of prey are generally not very numerous.

Turkey Vulture

FAMILY Cathartidae
SPECIES *Cathartes aura*
LENGTH 27 in (69 cm)
HABITAT Open country
CLUTCH SIZE 1–3

DISTRIBUTION Summer visitor from southern Canada across the United States, resident across the southeastern United States.

IN COMMON WITH other vultures, the Turkey Vulture is essentially bald on its head. This is thought to allow these birds to feed on the carcasses of large animals without fear of their plumage becoming contaminated and matted by blood. The red coloration of the skin here is reminiscent of the appearance of a Wild Turkey (*see* p. 116), explaining this vulture's common name. The keen sense of smell of these birds of prey helps them locate dead animals. They spend much of the day airborne, gliding with their wings outstretched on warm currents of air called thermals, which allow them to stay airborne with minimum effort. When breeding, the hen will lay on the ground, often in a cave on a cliff face, or sometimes even in a deserted building. It will take about 40 days for the eggs to hatch.

LARGE SPREAD The wingspan of these vultures can exceed 67 inches (170 cm) from the tip of one wing to the other.

Black Vulture

FAMILY Cathartidae
SPECIES *Coragyps atratus*
LENGTH 25 in (64 cm)
HABITAT Open country
CLUTCH SIZE 1–3

DISTRIBUTION Resident throughout the southeastern United States, up to southern New England. Ranges right along the Gulf states, well inland, covering most of Texas. Also in southern Arizona.

THE PLUMAGE of these vultures is indeed black, aside from a white area of plumage near the wing tips. The legs and feet are also pale. The bare skin on the head is grayish, as is the powerful bill. This is hooked at its tip, allowing these vultures to rip flesh off the bones of dead animals more easily. Although feeding primarily on carrion, particularly larger herbivores, including domestic farmstock, these vultures may also scavenge on garbage tips, in search of edible food. Black Vultures appear less able to pick up the scent of food than other vultures, but are adept at tracking Turkey Vultures to the site of kills, where they may dispossess their red-headed relatives. Their breeding habits are similar too, with the young vultures finally leaving the nest when they are between 70 and 80 days of age. As adults, their wingspan will be 59 inches (150 cm). These birds of prey are potentially long lived, with a life expectancy measured in decades.

FEEDING HABITS Vultures always feed on the ground at the site of a kill, battling for their share of the spoils.

TURKEY VULTURE (*see* p. 88) A Turkey Vulture alongside a fallen carcass. Although the offical name refers to its resemblance to a Wild Turkey, this species is often known simply as "the buzzard" in some parts of its wide range.

Northern Harrier

FAMILY Accipitridae

SPECIES *Circus cyaneus*

LENGTH 18 in (46 cm)

HABITAT Wetland/open country

CLUTCH SIZE 4–6

DISTRIBUTION Summer visitor across much of Canada southward; resident in central parts of the United States and a winter visitor further south, over the Mexican border.

THE HUNTING HABITAT of this species, with its long wings—on average 44 inches (112 cm) in span—and tail, mean that it is sometimes described as the Marsh Hawk. It is usually seen swooping down low in search of prey, which can range from small birds and rodents to amphibians and small turtles.

GENDER DIFFERENCES The sexes are easily separated: The male (*below*) is mainly gray, while hens are brown.

Cooper's Hawk

FAMILY Accipitridae

SPECIES *Accipter cooperii*

LENGTH 14–20 in (36–51 cm)

HABITAT Open woodland

CLUTCH SIZE 3–5

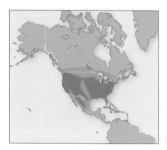

DISTRIBUTION Summer visitor to southern Canada; resident through most of the eastern United States and the west, being a winter visitor in central parts and to southern Florida.

ALTHOUGH SOMETIMES seen perching in the open on telegraph poles, this species generally hunts in woodland, ambushing unwary songbirds in this environment. As with various birds of prey, the hen is decidedly larger in size than the cock bird, and this is the easiest way of distinguishing between the members of a pair. While the hen incubates and cares for the chicks, the cock bird continues hunting, and returns to the nest site regularly with food.

DISTINCTIVE WINGS Cooper's Hawk is a short-winged species, as shown by the distance that the flight feathers extend down the tail feathers. Its wingspan is only 28–34 inches (71–86 cm).

Northern Goshawk

FAMILY Accipitridae

SPECIES *Accipter gentilis*

LENGTH 18–26 in (46–66 cm)

HABITAT Coniferous/mixed woodland

CLUTCH SIZE 2–5

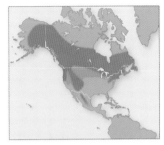

DISTRIBUTION Resident across much of Canada, and down the western United States to the Mexican border.

THIS IS THE LARGEST member of its genus, and rarely seen outside the forests of the far north where it lives and hunts. In flight, its relatively short, distinctive wedged-shaped tail will be apparent. Its wingspan measures 38–46 inches (97–117 cm). Its upperparts are bluish-gray, while there is streaking under the throat, with much finer gray barring on a white background predominating on the underparts, and extending down the legs. Hens in this case can be distinguished both by their larger size and also the coarser nature of the barring. Young birds have brown upperparts and buff rather than white plumage below, broken by thick dark streaking.

Northern Goshawks are very effective hunters, but they tend not to chase their prey, preferring instead to wait until it comes within range. They can then catch it unexpectedly, grabbing it in their strong talons. These birds of prey are able to overpower waterfowl up to the size of a duck, and they will also be able to catch Arctic hares without difficulty. When nesting, a pair will often assemble their bulky nest of twigs up to 60 ft (18 m) off the ground. Northern Goshawks are wintertime visitors across central parts of the United States.

RAISING CHICKS A female Northern Harrier with her chicks, displaying the coarse banding on her feathers. While she looks after the chicks, her partner will be away hunting for the entire family. The young birds will fledge once they are about 45 days old.

Sharp-shinned Hawk

FAMILY Accipitridae

SPECIES *Accipter striatus*

LENGTH 9–14 in (23–36 cm)

HABITAT Thick woodland

CLUTCH SIZE 4–5

DISTRIBUTION Summer range from Alaska to Newfoundland, southward across most of Canada. Resident in western and eastern United States; a wintertime visitor elsewhere.

THESE BIRDS of prey rank as the smallest of all the *Accipter* species, with a wingspan of 20–28 inches (51–71 cm), and they can fly well within their wooded environment. Cock birds have bluish-gray plumage on their upperparts, with barring on the underside of their body. Once again, hens can be identified by their larger size. Pairs construct a bulky nest, which may be located perhaps 60 ft (18 m) off the ground. They feed on a variety of items, including insects caught in flight, as well as rodents and birds.

STRONG GRIP The legs of Sharp-shinned Hawks are very thin, but their feet are usually both strong and effective when restraining prey.

White-tailed Kite

FAMILY Accipitridae

SPECIES *Elanus leucurus*

LENGTH 16 in (41 cm)

HABITAT Open country

CLUTCH SIZE 3–5

DISTRIBUTION Winter range north to the western Oregon-Washington border, and resident through western California. Summer visitor to eastern Texas; resident in the south and in southern Florida.

THESE KITES are quite conspicuous, often choosing to hunt alongside highways. They can be seen hovering above the verges looking for prey on the ground below, particularly mice but also invertebrates and small lizards. In the winter, White-tailed Kites become highly communal, roosting in large groups that may be comprised of hundreds of individuals. Their appearance is quite distinctive, with their head and underparts being white. The back and wings are gray, while the tail feathers are largely white. Their eyes are a vivid red. The sexes are similar in appearance, and young birds resemble their parents, but with buff markings on the back and chest.

VISIBILITY These long-winged kites, with a wingspan of 42 inches (107 cm), can be seen perched out in the open on branches or other vantage points such as telegraph poles.

Mississippi Kite

FAMILY Accipitridae

SPECIES *Ictinia mississippiensis*

LENGTH 14½ in (37 cm)

HABITAT Woodland/swamp

CLUTCH SIZE 1–3

DISTRIBUTION Summer visitor to central and eastern areas of southern United States, north to Iowa. Isolated populations in a number of states.

THIS KITE IS MAINLY a summer visitor to North America, and unusually, can be observed hunting in flocks. Relatively small in size, Mississippi Kites actually sometimes wander much further than their name suggests, turning up in localities as far away as California or in the vicinity of the Great Lakes. In all cases, though, they tend to avoid grassland areas. Along with other kites, this species is very agile in flight. The description of "kite" originates from an old English word, and describes the way in which these birds hover in flight, when hunting prey. Mississippi Kites are primarily insectivorous in their feeding habits.

RECOGNITION Gray coloration predominates in this species. The cock bird (*here*) has a lighter gray head. They have a wingspan of 35 inches (89 cm).

Swallow-tailed Kite

FAMILY Accipitrida

SPECIES *Elanoides forficatus*

LENGTH 23 in (58 cm)

HABITAT Woodland/swamp

CLUTCH SIZE 2–4

DISTRIBUTION Seen in the summer from South Carolina westward via Florida to Louisiana. Also eastern Texas. Overwinters in parts of South America.

THE APPEARANCE of these kites enables them to be identified very easily. The head, underside of the body, and the feathers on the underside of the wings are white in color, with the back and upper part of the wings being essentially black. The wingspan measures 48 inches (122 cm). The Swallow-tailed Kite is a rare species, however, with the total United States breeding population thought not to exceed 1,000 individuals. These birds occasionally wander over a much wider area than usual, having been documented as far north as Nova Scotia. Their aerial agility is such that they can swoop down and catch flying invertebrates. They also prey regularly on small reptiles, and are able to drink by skimming across the surface of a pond with their bill open, just like a swallow.

SILHOUETTE The long, forked tail feathers resembling those of a swallow account for this kite's name.

Zone-tailed Hawk

FAMILY Accipitridae
SPECIES *Buteo albonotatus*
LENGTH 20 in (51 cm)
HABITAT Montane areas
CLUTCH SIZE 2–3

DISTRIBUTION United States summer range comprises Arizona and New Mexico, south from here into Mexico. Also in southwestern Texas, and overwinters right down to South America.

DARK IN COLOR, the Zone-tailed Hawk mimics the Turkey Vulture (*see* p. 88) in its flight pattern, gliding in a similar fashion. It has a wingspan of 51 inches (130 cm). Its bill is pale yellow, corresponding to the color of its legs. The distinctive banding across the tail feathers is less evident in juvenile birds.

DISTINCTIVE The banded tail feathers of this hawk enable it to be identified when it is soaring overhead.

Rough-legged Hawk

FAMILY Accipitridae
SPECIES *Buteo lagopus*
LENGTH 22 in (56 cm)
HABITAT Open country/ marshland
CLUTCH SIZE 2–6

DISTRIBUTION Breeds in the summer through Alaska and across northern Canada. Overwinters further south.

ALTHOUGH THE PLUMAGE of the Rough-legged Hawk is often pale in color, with dark streaks running down the center of the individual feathers, there is also a rare darker-colored variant or "morph." This species occurs further north than other members of the genus during the summer. Pairs nest on cliffs in the Arctic tundra, hunting both lemmings and ptarmigans.

BREEDING A loose pile of twigs serves as a nest for these hawks. Their chicks will hatch after 29 days and fledge six weeks later. The adult wingspan is 56 inches (142 cm).

Red-tailed Hawk

FAMILY Accipitridae

SPECIES *Buteo jamaicensis*

LENGTH 22 in (56 cm)

HABITAT Open country/
woodland

CLUTCH SIZE 1–4

DISTRIBUTION Breeds from central Alaska across Canada to southern Newfoundland, to northern-central United States. Resident through United States.

THE RED-TAILED is one of the most widely distributed and commonly seen North American hawks, ranging over a wide area of the continent, particularly during the summer. They frequent areas of open country where there are stands of trees nearby, which can be utilized for roosting and breeding purposes. These hawks prove very patient hunters, perching in the open. Rodents feature prominently in their diet. In flight, however, their red tail feathers are less evident, because the undersides tend to be whitish. The underparts of the body are whitish too, with darker streaking. Pairs frequently choose to nest at a considerable height, perhaps 70 ft (21 m) or more off the ground. They build a large structure using twigs and other vegetation, either on a cliff or in a mature tree, for their eggs.

PLUMAGE The coloration of the Red-tailed Hawk can vary markedly, with some individuals being a much darker shade of brown than others. Their tail color may vary too. Their wings measure 50 inches (127 cm) across when spread.

Red-shouldered Hawk

FAMILY Accipitridae

SPECIES *Buteo lineatus*

LENGTH 17 in (43 cm)

HABITAT Woodland near
water

CLUTCH SIZE 2–5

DISTRIBUTION Summer range
extends over most of Canada
down to northern-central parts
of the United States. Resident
over the entire continent
further south, into Mexico.

THE RUSTY-RED shoulder patch on the wings of these hawks
is distinctive, alongside wide spotting on the back. They have a
wingspan of 40 inches (102 cm). Their small size enables them
to hunt effectively in a woodland setting. Here they will catch
songbirds as well as rodents, and also prey on amphibians.

DISTINCTIVE FEATURE The
long legs of this species
give it a decidedly vertical
stance on the ground.

Broad-winged Hawk

FAMILY Accipitridae

SPECIES *Buteo platypterus*

LENGTH 16 in (41 cm)

HABITAT Woodland

CLUTCH SIZE 2–3

DISTRIBUTION Breeds in
northwestern Canada down
through southeastern parts of
the United States then flies
south to overwinter down in
northern South America.

THIS IS ANOTHER relatively small
species, found predominately in
woodland areas, with broad wings
spanning 34 inches (86 cm). The tail
feathers too are quite broad and short.
The patterning is relatively plain,
with the back being brownish and
the white underparts streaked with
brownish markings. Broad-winged
Hawks frequently hunt above water,
diving down to capture large
invertebrates such as crayfish, as well
as amphibians. Pairs build their nest
in a tree up to 50 ft (15 m) off the
ground, and both adults are involved
in hatching and rearing the chicks.

HUNTING BEHAVIOR These hawks have
favored perches, especially close to water,
from where they regularly hunt.

Ferruginous Hawk

FAMILY Accipitridae

SPECIES *Buteo regalis*

LENGTH 23 in (58 cm)

HABITAT Arid country/
grassland

CLUTCH SIZE 3–5

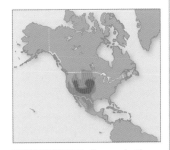

DISTRIBUTION Occurs in the west from southern Canada in the summer to Utah, being resident to the south and west. Overwinters more widely here, down into Mexico.

RUSTY-BROWN COLORATION over the back and wings is offset against pale underparts, in the case of the Ferruginous Hawk. Again, however, there can be considerable variation in the markings, as well as the depth of coloration between individuals. There is a rare dark brown morph, distinguished by its dark reddish-brown plumage. The largest member of the genus, with a wingspan of 53 inches (135 cm), this hawk hunts over open country, with its size enabling it to overpower relatively large quarry such as hares. Pairs may construct their bulky nest in a large, often isolated tree or built among scrub on a hillside. The incubation period lasts for 29 days.

ADULT BIRD Juveniles can be recognized by whitish feathering on their legs, and plainer brown coloration.

Swainson's Hawk

FAMILY Accipitridae

SPECIES *Buteo swainsoni*

LENGTH 21 in (53 cm)

HABITAT Open grassland

CLUTCH SIZE 2–4

DISTRIBUTION Summertime visitor in southwestern Canada southward down through the United States to Mexico. Overwinters in South America.

THESE HAWKS have adapted to changes in the landscape, forming a remarkable relationship with farmers in some areas. They follow harvesting machinery in the fields, swooping down on rodents that are flushed from the vegetation. Swainson's Hawks breed in the United States each year, with pairs often returning to the same site, and repairing their nest in the spring. Incubation, which is shared by both parents, lasts for a month. In flight, these hawks have a slim profile, with a small head. Their wings span 52 inches (132 cm) and are relatively narrow in shape.

VARIETY The coloration of Swainson's Hawk is very variable, with some birds being much darker on their underparts than others.

Osprey

FAMILY Panionidae

SPECIES *Pandion haliaetus*

LENGTH 23 in (58 cm)

HABITAT Coasts/lakes

CLUTCH SIZE 2–4

DISTRIBUTION Summer visitor across much of Canada, also seen in the western United States and the southeast; resident here along the coast and in Florida.

THESE HIGHLY SPECIALIZED fish hawks are very strong and agile, being able to catch and lift their quarry from the surface of the water. Their upperparts are dark brown, with the dark eye stripes serving to highlight the yellow coloration of the eyes.

IDENTIFICATION The Osprey's head and underparts are predominantly white. These hawks prefer to feed off the ground, as here. In this picture, the impressive wings, spanning 63 inches (160 cm), are clearly visible.

Harris's Hawk

FAMILY Accipitridae

SPECIES *Parabuteo unicinctus*

LENGTH 21 in (53 cm)

HABITAT Arid landscapes

CLUTCH SIZE 3–5

DISTRIBUTION Occurs in southern parts of the United States. Resident in south-central Arizona, southern parts of New Mexico into Texas, and also along the Mexican border.

AN IMPOSING HAWK with very distinctive coloring, Harris's Hawk may be seen hunting in family groups after the breeding season. The young hawks need to learn and refine this skill if they are not to face starvation. They can be recognized at this stage by their heavily streaked underparts, which are transformed to a dark shade of chocolate-brown in adults.

GENDER DIFFERENCES As is quite common in the case of birds of prey, both sexes of Harris's Hawk are similar in coloration, but cock birds are smaller. The average wingspan for the species is 46 inches (117 cm).

Golden Eagle

FAMILY Accipitridae
SPECIES *Aquila chrysaetos*
LENGTH 30 in (76 cm)
HABITAT Montane areas
CLUTCH SIZE 1–2

DISTRIBUTION Mainly encountered in the west, from Alaska southward. Resident further south in western parts of the United States and a winter visitor further east.

THE GOLDEN EAGLE is a bird of remote upland areas, flying over large areas of wilderness in the far north of its range. Its coloration is a dark shade of chocolate-brown overall, becoming golden over the nape of the neck. Feathering extends down its legs, and the Golden Eagle's feet are equipped with strong talons that allow it to lift and fly with prey back to its nest, known as an eyrie. They have an impressive wingspan of 80 inches (203 cm). Their strength is such that these eagles can overpower prey up to the size of a small deer, but in contrast to popular myth, they tend not to prey heavily on lambs. When hunting opportunities are restricted, Golden Eagles will even feed on carrion. Their young develop slowly, not fledging until they are at least 10 weeks old.

MAJESTIC A formidable predator, this eagle has a sharp, hooked bill, insuring meat can be ripped away from bone in strips that can be swallowed easily.

OSPREY (*see* p. 100) Ospreys catch and carry relatively large fish in freshwater areas and over the sea, seizing them with their talons just below the water surface. Their feet are also rough, helping them to hold the fish more easily.

Bald Eagle

FAMILY Accipitridae

SPECIES *Haliaeetus leucocephalus*

LENGTH 31 in (79 cm)

HABITAT Coasts/inland waters

CLUTCH SIZE 1–3

DISTRIBUTION Ranges across Canada in the summer; resident along the west and eastern coasts of North America. Resident in the central and western United States, overwintering across the country.

THERE IS NO MISTAKING the identity of the Bald Eagle. Its population had fallen dramatically by the 1970s, because of the build-up of toxic chemicals in its food that adversely affected its breeding. Since legislation banned the most damaging of such chemicals, the numbers of Bald Eagles have grown again, and they can be seen across most of the continent. They will hunt fish themselves, and also rob Ospreys (*see* p. 100) of their catches. Along the shoreland, these eagles will also scavenge on the carcasses of bigger sea mammals washed up here. Larger numbers may congregate in areas where food is readily available. Pairs nest in trees, often as high as 150 ft (46 m) off the ground, with the young eagles remaining here until they are about 10 weeks old.

ICONIC IMAGE A very powerful yellowish bill, a white head plus a brown body and white tail, and a massive wingspan of 80 inches (203 cm), are characteristics of the Bald Eagle.

Crested Caracara

FAMILY Falconidae

SPECIES *Caracara plancus*

LENGTH 23 in (58 cm)

HABITAT Savannah/desert

CLUTCH SIZE 2–4

DISTRIBUTION A small population is resident in southern Arizona. Also represented in eastern Texas, southwestern Louisiana, and central Florida.

EVIDENT ON THE FLAG of Mexico, the Crested Caracara has an unmistakeable appearance, thanks partly to the bare area of reddish skin on the sides of its face that extends from behind the eyes to its nostrils. This skin is paler in young birds, and its presence may be explained by the fact that although Caracaras can hunt, they often scavenge for food alongside vultures. Their wingspan measures 50 inches (127 cm). When nesting, a pair will construct a bulky nest of twigs that will be built off the ground, in a tree or sometimes on top of a large cactus. The incubation period lasts for about 28 days.

ADAPTATIONS The yellow legs of the Crested Caracara are long, reflecting the fact that these birds of prey often feed on the ground. Note the raised crest.

Merlin

FAMILY Falconidae

SPECIES *Falco columbarius*

LENGTH 12 in (30 cm)

HABITAT Wooded areas

CLUTCH SIZE 3–6

DISTRIBUTION Seen in summer across most of Canada; resident in the United States border area, particularly in western parts, and a winter visitor elsewhere.

THESE POWERFUL, small falcons are well-adapted to prey on songbirds, as they can accelerate rapidly toward their target, catching an unwary individual in flight. They also hunt invertebrates. They have a wingspan of 25 inches (64 cm). The Merlin's breeding habits are unusual, because instead of constructing a nest, the hen simply lays her eggs in a tree hole. Unlike most birds nesting in such surroundings, however, the Merlin's eggs are rust-colored rather than white, with darker spots evident over their surface. The young birds fledge when they are a month old.

DIFFERENCES The female Merlin has dark brown upperparts, like young birds of both sexes, but the male has bluish-gray plumage.

Prairie Falcon

FAMILY Falconidae
SPECIES *Falco mexicanus*
LENGTH 17½ in (44 cm)
HABITAT Prairie/arid country
CLUTCH SIZE 3–6

DISTRIBUTION From southern Canada, resident through much of the western United States across the border into Mexico. Winter range extends further west, as far as Kansas.

RATHER THAN DIVING from on high down on to its quarry, the Prairie Falcon uses its agility in open landscape to fly low and fast in pursuit of its quarry, which includes various rodents. Pairs usually adopt the old nests of other birds when breeding.

DISTINGUISHING FEATURES Brown upperparts with sandy barring help to identify this species, with darker streaks running down from the corner of each eye. They have a wingspan of 40 inches (102 cm).

Peregrine Falcon

FAMILY Falconidae
SPECIES *Falco peregrinus*
LENGTH 17 in (43 cm)
HABITAT Cliffs/cities
CLUTCH SIZE 2–4

DISTRIBUTION Found in the west, from southwestern Canada down into Mexico. Mainly resident, but winters further to the east as well, reaching Oklahoma.

A HUNTING PEREGRINE will drop down from the sky on to a bird flying beneath it. This falcon often targets pigeons, but may hunt starlings and other birds of similar size, as well as rodents and even insects. The adult male's plumage is slate-gray with a black cap, and a barred breast, but the female is predominantly brown. Their wingspan measures 41 inches (104 cm).

HIGH NEST Peregrine Falcons traditionally nest on rocky outcrops and ledges, and may utilize highrise buildings in cities for this purpose, too.

Gyrfalcon

FAMILY Falconidae

SPECIES *Falco rusticolus*

LENGTH 22 in (56 cm)

HABITAT Tundra/cliffs

CLUTCH SIZE 3–8

DISTRIBUTION Resident across the far north of the continent, including southern Greenland, and ranges further south across Canada in winter. Summer visitor to northern Greenland.

THIS FALCON is restricted to the far north, with its whitish plumage helping to provide some camouflage in the snowy landscape there. Their underparts are usually much lighter in color than their upperparts. They have the ability to fly quickly, thanks to their powerful wings measuring 47 inches (119 cm) in span, but also with relatively little effort. Gyrfalcons hunt ptarmigans and also rodents, such as lemmings. When nesting, a pair may utilize a ledge on a cliff face for this purpose. The incubation period lasts approximately a month and it will be a further seven weeks before the young falcons fledge.

FEMALE GYRFALCON Individual Gyrfalcons differ quite widely in appearance, with some being much whiter than others. They have long tail feathers, as seen here.

American Kestrel

FAMILY Falconidae

SPECIES *Falco sparverius*

LENGTH 10½ in (27 cm)

HABITAT Open country/cities

CLUTCH SIZE 3–6

DISTRIBUTION Occurs over most of the continent; summer visitor to Canada and northern-central United States, but resident elsewhere in the United States, especially in Texas where it overwinters.

THIS IS THE SMALLEST falcon occurring within North America, and also one of the most common, being found both in rural and city environments, often being seen in the vicinity of parks. Like other falcons, the American Kestrel has keen eyesight, enabling it to spot potential prey on the ground below as it hovers overhead. Sometimes, it may be seen resting on a telephone wire, but it will dive down if a hunting opportunity presents itself. Rodents and invertebrates are the main item in the diet of these kestrels, but they may also take small birds, too.

PAIR OF AMERICAN KESTRELS The more colorful cock bird is evident here on the right, with blue-gray wings. The species' wingspan is 23 inches (58 cm).

GALLIFORMES

Pheasants, partridges, and grouse

These species are generally ground-dwellers, well-adapted to move on foot, although they can fly if danger threatens. Their flight tends to be quite clumsy, however, and they will glide down to another suitable area of cover relatively nearby in most cases. Cock birds can generally be distinguished by their brighter plumage. In some species, polygamy occurs, with a male being surrounded by a group of hens, while in other cases, communal displays permit the hens to choose their own mates. Young birds are able to follow their parents from the point of hatching, although they cannot fly at this stage.

Gray Partridge

FAMILY Phasianidae
SPECIES *Perdix perdix*
LENGTH 12½ in (32 cm)
HABITAT Grassland
CLUTCH SIZE 12–16

DISTRIBUTION Resident from Alberta and Saskatchewan southeastward to northern Illinois, as far south as Nevada and Wyoming.

THESE GAMEBIRDS were introduced from Europe in the 1800s, and are now well-established, particularly in areas of open country and farmland. They spend most of their time on the ground, hiding in grass. If disturbed, a Gray Partridge will only fly a relatively short distance, dropping down into cover again. They feed on seeds and invertebrates.

GENDER DIFFERENCES The prominent chestnut belly patch reveals this to be a cock bird. The orange feathering on the face and throat is also paler in hens.

Chukar

FAMILY Phasianidae

SPECIES *Alectoris chukar*

LENGTH 14 in (36 cm)

HABITAT Arid country

CLUTCH SIZE 10–15

DISTRIBUTION Western range from southern British Columbia south to California, with an isolated population here too, and found in the east from Montana into Colorado.

ANOTHER INTRODUCED species, the Chukar, or Chukar Partridge, has become very adept at avoiding human contact. It is hard to observe in the area where it is now breeds in the wild, in spite of having become established in relatively open countryside. Birds observed in eastern parts of North America are more conspicuous. They will have been released from game farms here.

EASTERN ORIGINS The Chukar occurs naturally in parts of the Middle East and Asia, in arid terrain.

Sharp-tailed Grouse

FAMILY Tetraonidae

SPECIES *Tympanuchus phasianellus*

LENGTH 17 in (43 cm)

HABITAT Open country

CLUTCH SIZE 10–12

DISTRIBUTION Central Alaska and western Yukon Territory. Northern parts of Northwestern Territories to northern Colorado and east to western Quebec.

THE SHARP, pointed tail feathers of the Sharp-tailed Grouse are used in its display, being held erect. The purple air sacs that lie each side of the cock bird's neck are not usually conspicuous, only becoming inflated at this stage in the breeding display. Males congregate each spring, and perform on their traditional display grounds, which are known as leks, in the hope of attracting a mate.

HABITAT Although typically ground birds, these grouse often switch to perch in trees after winter snowfall.

Sage Grouse

FAMILY Tetraonidae

SPECIES *Centrocercus urophasianus*

LENGTH 28 in (71 cm)

HABITAT Sagebrush country

CLUTCH SIZE 7–12

DISTRIBUTION Western-central United States, up to the Canadian border, being largely resident here throughout the year, but may undertake seasonal movements during periods of heavy snow.

AS ITS NAME SUGGESTS, this grouse is essentially confined to the areas of sagebrush, and as this habitat is disappearing, so the numbers of these large grouse are declining too. They feed mainly on sagebrush plants, eating both the leaves and buds. The cock bird has a very striking display, with groups of males congregating each spring on their display grounds, called leks, where they each try to entice the onlooking hens. They inflate the pair of air sacs on each side of their chest, revealing the greenish-yellow skin beneath, while fanning out their pointed tail feathers. After mating, the birds disperse, with hens laying on their own.

COCK SAGE GROUSE DISPLAYING The air sacs are partially inflated here. When deflated as part of the display, they make a sudden popping sound.

Blue Grouse

FAMILY Tetraonidae

SPECIES *Dendragapus obscurus*

LENGTH 20 in (51 cm)

HABITAT Woodland

CLUTCH SIZE 6–10

DISTRIBUTION Occurs from eastern Canada through eastern areas of the United States down close to the Mexican border.

THESE GROUSE live in woodland, but generally frequent open areas, even in the coniferous forest, congregating here. They can be sexed quite easily because only the cock birds display the characteristic bluish-gray plumage. In contrast, hens are significantly duller in coloration, being grayish-brown. They feed on a variety of foods in the summer, such as berries and invertebrates, and less appetizing items such as pine needles during the winter months. Hens lay in a well-concealed nest on the ground.

MARKINGS The hen also displays the bright orange area of bare skin, called a comb, above the eyes.

Spruce Grouse

FAMILY Tetraonidae

SPECIES *Dendragapus canadensis*

LENGTH 16 in (41 cm)

HABITAT Coniferous forest

CLUTCH SIZE 6–12

DISTRIBUTION Resident through much of Alaska and Canada, right across to Newfoundland. Extends to eastern Oregon, also just south of the Great Lakes, and the northeastern United States.

THESE GROUSE LIVE individually in the forests that they inhabit, coming together only briefly for mating, when the male displays by fanning his tail, calling, and strutting to attract a would-be mate. The sexes are easy to distinguish throughout the year, with the cock bird being slate-gray on the back with paler barring on the edges of the feathers, while hens are brown rather than gray here. The female will construct a simple nest in undergrowth, using grass to line a hollow.

Her mottled plumage then helps to conceal her presence when she is incubating the eggs. The young grouse are able to follow her immediately after hatching, but they cannot fly at this stage.

DIET Spruce Grouse feed largely on conifer needles, particularly in the winter when other food is scarce.

Ruffed Grouse

FAMILY Tetraonidae
SPECIES *Bonasa umbellus*
LENGTH 17 in (43 cm)
HABITAT Woodland
CLUTCH SIZE 9–12

DISTRIBUTION Away from the northern coasts of Canada, southward down to California and Utah in the west, and to Georgia and Alabama in the east.

THE NAME OF THESE grouse comes from the ruff of feathers around the neck of the cock bird, which forms a prominent part of their display. They fan their tail feathers at this stage, choosing a prominent spot, such as on top of a log from where to display to hens in the vicinity. The sound of the drumming of the male's wings serves to attract hens to this locality, and he will engage in this behavior for hours. Ruffed Grouse do not spend all of their time on the forest floor. They often perch in the branches, which may afford them greater protection from predators.

DIFFERENCES Ruffed Grouse hens have a smaller ruff and are grayer in color than cocks.

Willow Ptarmigan

FAMILY Tetraonidae
SPECIES *Lagopus lagopus*
LENGTH 15 in (38 cm)
HABITAT Tundra/willow thickets
CLUTCH SIZE 7–12

DISTRIBUTION Resident throughout the far north of North America, extending down in the west to British Columbia. Wintering range may extend further south in central areas.

WILLOW PTARMIGANS typically occur in association with willow thickets, in a part of the world where it is too cold for trees to grow. They feed to a large extent on the willow, eating the catkins in the spring, and pecking off buds and even twigs to sustain them over the bleak winter. At this stage, their plumage is snow-white, reflecting the changing landscape, and they are more likely to be seen in small flocks.

HEN WILLOW PTARMIGAN
Cock birds have chestnut plumage in the summer with white wings and underparts. Both sexes have plumage covering their legs and feet.

SEASONAL APPEARANCE The Willow Ptarmigan alters to match the seasons, relying on its feathering to camouflage its presence. The mottled brown summer plumage merges in very effectively with the earth as shown here.

White-tailed Ptarmigan

FAMILY Tetraonidae
SPECIES *Lagopus leucurus*
LENGTH 12½ in (32 cm)
HABITAT Mountains
CLUTCH SIZE 6–14

DISTRIBUTION Southern Alaska down through British Columbia into Washington and Montana. Also separate populations in northern Utah, as well as Colorado and New Mexico, plus California.

IN THE SUMMER, the white tail feathers of this species aid its identification, but the situation becomes more confused through the winter because, as with many game birds from northern areas, its appearance is transformed. This is the stage when these ptarmigans become completely white in color, helping to camouflage their presence in the snowy landscape. Only their bill remains black, and their feet are feathered as well, protecting against the cold and helping them to walk over the snow. White-tailed Ptarmigans are forced to feed on buds at this stage, but during the summer, they eat a more varied diet of vegetation and invertebrates.

COLOR CHANGE The inset shows one of these ptarmigans in winter plumage, while the main image shows an individual in transition plumage, resulting in a speckled appearance.

Rock Ptarmigan

FAMILY Tetraonidae
SPECIES *Lagopus mutus*
LENGTH 14 in (36 cm)
HABITAT Tundra/rocky areas
CLUTCH SIZE 6–9

DISTRIBUTION Resident throughout the far north, apart from northern Alaska, across to Greenland. May overwinter south in Northwest Territories and south of Hudson Bay.

THESE PTARMIGANS occur at relatively high altitudes within the Arctic region, in rocky areas of countryside. They undergo a seasonal change in appearance at the start of winter, becoming white at this stage, apart from their black tails and a characteristic black stripe above each eye. During the breeding season, however, they can be sexed easily, with the cock bird being dark brown in color with white wings and underparts, while the hen is more mottled. Pairs establish their own territories, which are defended by the cock bird.

INSULATION Feathering extends right down the legs and on to the toes themselves in the case of the Rock Ptarmigan.

Ring-necked Pheasant

FAMILY Phasianidae
SPECIES *Phasinus colchicus*
LENGTH 21–33 in (53–84 cm)
HABITAT Lightly wooded areas
CLUTCH SIZE 7–14

DISTRIBUTION Occurs quite widely across the United States, especially in western and central parts, but local populations may result from recent releases rather than established wild stock.

THIS SPECIES is actually native to Asia, and was introduced to North America in the late 1800s for sporting purposes. These pheasants have since become established across the United States. Cock birds are significantly larger than hens, showing the large red areas of skin on the face, with a white ring of plumage typically evident around the back of the neck. Hens in comparison are significantly duller, being buff in color, with barring on their plumage. There are still some local variations in the appearance of cocks, however, reflecting the fact that several races were originally brought over, and introduced to different areas. Some populations may be darker in color, or lack the white neck collar.

GROUPING A cock pheasant will usually be seen in the company of several hens, foraging in the open.

Wild Turkey

FAMILY Meleagrididae
SPECIES *Meleagris gallopavo*
LENGTH 46 in (117 cm)
HABITAT Oak woodland
CLUTCH SIZE 8–16

DISTRIBUTION Occurs largely within the United States, particularly in the east in suitable habitat, although absent from northern Minnesota, but ranges up to southern Manitoba in Canada.

THIS SPECIES is the ancestor of the domesticated turkey, and is a bird of shady woodland, favoring areas where there are oaks, whose acorns provide a source of food over the winter months. Males are significantly larger in size, and fan their tail feathers as part of their display. There are regional variations, with birds from eastern areas having chestnut tipping to these feathers, whereas those from the west have white tips instead. The head is red and bluish, while the plumage is iridescent in part. Hens have duller feathering and they also lack the long breast tuft of feathers associated with the male turkey, or stag.

FLIGHT Wild Turkeys are able to fly well and will roost in trees at night. Sadly, hunting pressure means this species is now quite scarce.

Northern Bobwhite

FAMILY Odontophoridae
SPECIES *Colinus virginianus*
LENGTH 9¼ in (24 cm)
HABITAT Woodland
CLUTCH SIZE 10–15

DISTRIBUTION Widely distributed through eastern-central parts south of the Great Lakes. Isolated populations in Washington, as well as on the Idaho-Oregon border and in Arizona.

NORTHERN BOBWHITES live on the ground, in flocks numbering as many as 30 birds, which are often described as coveys. These quails feed on seeds and insects. During the spring, pairs nest on their own, choosing a well-concealed locality where the hen will lay her eggs in a small depression on the ground. Both sexes incubate the eggs, and it takes about three weeks for hatching to occur. The young chicks can then follow their parents, although they will not be able to fly at this stage.

GENDER DIFFERENCES The cock bird (*left*) can be identified by its black rather than gray eye stripe, and white areas on the face.

Montezuma Quail

FAMILY Odontophoridae

SPECIES *Cyrtonyx montezumae*

LENGTH 8½ in (22 cm)

HABITAT Open woodland

CLUTCH SIZE 7–14

DISTRIBUTION Southwestern United States, eastern Arizona, and western and central New Mexico with isolated populations in western and central Texas.

THESE PARTICULAR gamebirds are not easy to observe, because they will freeze if disturbed, watching intently and only flying at the very last minute to reveal their presence. Hens have a crest, which gives a characteristically rounded shape to their head, and have mottled brown plumage, compared with the brightly colored cock bird. They live in pairs for much of the year, feeding on a mixture of seeds, acorns, and invertebrates, but the young may remain with their parents through the fall, when groups may join up to form small flocks.

PATTERN The cock Montezuma Quail has a highly distinctive appearance, although the exact pattern of markings vary between individuals.

California Quail

FAMILY Odontophoridae

SPECIES *Callipepla californica*

LENGTH 10 in (25 cm)

HABITAT Open woodland

CLUTCH SIZE 12–15

DISTRIBUTION Extends from southern British Columbia down to California, reaching Baja California, and inland as far as Utah. An isolated resident population also exists in Arizona.

THESE QUAILS may move into urban areas such as city parks during the winter months. They live in groups, being quite common in areas where water is readily available. When breeding, the hen chooses a concealed location, often under a bush, for her nest.

CREST The cock California Quail's forward-pointing crest is a feature shared with Gambel's Quail (*see* p. 118).

Gambel's Quail

FAMILY Odontophoridae
SPECIES *Callipepla gambelii*
LENGTH 11 in (28 cm)
HABITAT Scrub
CLUTCH SIZE 12–20

DISTRIBUTION From south-eastern Nevada and southern Utah into western Colorado. Western range extends to California into Mexico, and east through Arizona and New Mexico to Texas.

THIS SPECIES can be identified by the chestnut coloration of its flanks, streaked with white markings. Both sexes display the unusual forward-pointing black plume that extends right out over the bill from the crown, but this is smaller in the case of hens, allowing the sexes to be distinguished. Immature birds are usually slightly smaller in size, and their coloration is less distinctive. These quail live in large coveys, especially over the winter period when flocks comprised of more than 100 birds may be seen. They eat both plant matter and invertebrates.

HABITAT Gambel's Quail is found in semi-desert areas, taking advantage of thickets in which it can hide and nest. These birds usually stay close to water.

Mountain Quail

FAMILY Odontophoridae
SPECIES *Oreortyx pictus*
LENGTH 11 in (28 cm)
HABITAT Brushland
CLUTCH SIZE 8–15

DISTRIBUTION There is a small population in northern Washington, then from the south of the state across Oregon into California and across the Mexican border.

THE MOUNTAIN QUAIL is found both in the foothills and at higher altitudes within its range, tending to move down to lower levels for the duration of the winter, to avoid the worst of the weather conditions at this stage. They are not particularly easy birds to observe, being shy by nature, and adept at retreating quietly into the brush, rather than flying up and revealing their presence. This species has a fairly vertical, double plume on the head, with these feathers being smaller in the hen. She will incubate the eggs alone, with hatching taking place after a month. The young develop quite rapidly, being able to fly within two weeks of hatching.

CAMOUFLAGE The coloration of these quail helps to conceal their presence. Birds from the west are browner than those occurring inland.

Scaled Quail

FAMILY Odontophoridae
SPECIES *Callipepla squamata*
LENGTH 10 in (25 cm)
HABITAT Arid country
CLUTCH SIZE 9–18

DISTRIBUTION Resident from eastern Colorado and from western Kansas down to western Texas and across the Mexican border. Present as far west as southern Arizona.

THE NAME OF THESE quails stems from the dark edging on the blue-gray plumage of their underparts, which creates a scaled effect. They have a rather fluffy, vertical crest that is white toward the rear, with the crest being smaller overall in the case of hens. The scaled patterning is less apparent in young birds, which join with the adults to create large coveys. A covey may consist of over 100 birds in some areas over the winter months. Breeding success depends very much on climatic factors, because during dry summers, there may not be adequate water available for young hatchlings to survive, along with a shortage of food as well.

NAME The fluffy appearance of their crest is why these gamebirds are often described locally as "cottontops."

GRUIFORMES

Rails, coots, and cranes

The members of this Order found in North America vary significantly in size, from cranes down to rails, but generally they are linked with an aquatic environment. This can vary from saltwater areas through to freshwater, with some species being quite adaptable in this regard. They can be migratory too, as in the case of cranes. Many of these species are often shy birds by nature, and not easy to observe, with the relatively upright and slender body shape of rails especially enabling them to slip through reed beds essentially unnoticed. Nor are the majority of these birds brightly colored.

Sora

FAMILY Rallidae
SPECIES *Porzana carolina*
LENGTH 13¾ in (35 cm)
HABITAT Marshland
CLUTCH SIZE 7–16

DISTRIBUTION Extensive breeding range right up into southeastern Alaska, and across to Newfoundland.

THIS IS ONE of the most common species of rail occurring in North America, being found not only over a wide area but also in a diverse range of habitats through the year. It generally prefers freshwater habitat when breeding, but is likely to move to brackish areas on the coast during the winter period.

MOVEMENTS These rails will fly considerable distances when migrating, flying at night. Otherwise, unless disturbed, they prefer to walk as here, or swim.

King Rail

FAMILY Rallidae
SPECIES *Rallus elegans*
LENGTH 15 in (38 cm)
HABITAT Marshland
CLUTCH SIZE 5–15

DISTRIBUTION In summertime north to Missouri and Illinois, and sporadically elsewhere, including Michigan and Kansas, mainly centered on the coast.

THE LARGE SIZE of the King Rail aids its identification, as it is the largest species of rail found in North America. It also has a particularly long bill combined with a long neck. These birds prefer freshwater areas, rarely being encountered in brackish marshland. They are shy by nature, and are generally not easily spotted.

AUDIBLE The King Rail's presence is likely to be betrayed by its calls, which are most frequently audible at dusk and again at dawn.

Virginia Rail

FAMILY Rallidae
SPECIES *Rallus limicola*
LENGTH 9½ in (24 cm)
HABITAT Wetland
CLUTCH SIZE 5–12

DISTRIBUTION Summertime visitor to southern Canada, north to central Alberta and Saskatchewan, and to Nova Scotia. Widespread through the western United States; overwinters in the southeast.

A PARTICULARLY adaptable species, the Virginia Rail may be found in virtually any type of wetland habitat, either close to the sea or inland. There is a white streak on each side of the head running from above the eye to the bill, with the cheek area being bluish-gray. These rails will eat invertebrates, small fish, and plant matter too.

IDENTIFICATION This species can be identified partly by the red hue of its bill, which is otherwise dark brown on top and toward the tip.

Clapper Rail

FAMILY Rallidae
SPECIES *Rallus longirostris*
LENGTH 14½ in (37 cm)
HABITAT Coastal marshland
CLUTCH SIZE 5–14

DISTRIBUTION Extends north in summer to Massachusetts, Connecticut, and Rhode Island. Present right along the east coast, but scarce in winter north of North Carolina.

AS THE SALTMARSH habitat of the Clapper Rail has been reduced, so its population has declined. It does remains relatively common in suitable areas, however, although it is shy by nature and not easy to observe. Unlike most rails, this species can swim well, and if threatened, an individual may dive under the surface of the water as a way of escaping from danger.

VARIABLE The Clapper Rail varies in size and coloration through its range, with up to 21 different races having been identified.

Purple Gallinule

FAMILY Rallidae

SPECIES *Porphyrula martinica*

LENGTH 13 in (33 cm)

HABITAT Freshwater marshland

CLUTCH SIZE 5–10

THIS IS A PARTICULARLY striking and colorful member of the family, thanks to its purplish head and underparts, as well as its yellow-tipped red bill, with a pale blue forehead shield above. Its appearance is unmistakable. Its long legs, and equally lengthy agile toes, are yellow. These allow the Purple Gallinule to walk effectively over lily pads and similar aquatic vegetation dispersing its body weight so that it does

not sink down into the water. When breeding, the hen lays in a nest of grass and reeds, anchored to aquatic plants. The chicks are covered in down when they hatch, and will start following their mother soon after hatching.

DISTRIBUTION Breeds from South Carolina along the Gulf coast into Texas. Permanently resident in central and southern parts of Florida. May overwinter in Mexico's Yucatan Peninsula.

WALKERS These birds prefer to move by using their feet, although they can swim if necessary, as well as fly.

American Coot

FAMILY Rallidae
SPECIES *Fulica americana*
LENGTH 15½ in (39 cm)
HABITAT Marshland
CLUTCH SIZE 8–20

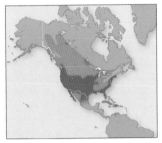

DISTRIBUTION Summer visitor north to Yukon Territory, and eastward to southern Quebec. Resident in western and central parts of the United States; winter migrant in the east.

THE BLACK PLUMAGE of the American coot contrasts with its ivory-colored forehead shield and similarly colored bill. There is a small reddish area at the top of the shield, and a dark band encircling the bill near its tip. The most remarkable feature of these birds is hidden, however, when they are in the water. They have flattened bluish lobed extensions on their toes, which serve as primitive webbing, helping these birds to swim. American Coots have a particularly distinctive style of swimming, nodding their heads forward as they move. They can dive if necessary in search of food, or alternatively, feed at the surface.

URBAN These coots are often resident in city parks where there is a pond nearby. They may forage for invertebrates on the grass in these surroundings.

Common Moorhen

FAMILY Rallidae
SPECIES *Gallinula chloropus*
LENGTH 14 in (36 cm)
HABITAT Freshwater
CLUTCH SIZE 8–12

DISTRIBUTION Breeds mainly in central-eastern parts of the United States, up to Maine. Resident from North Carolina down through Texas and along the Mexican border.

THESE WATER BIRDS are dark in color, but can easily be identified by the red shield on the forehead, which merges into the bill. This in turn becomes yellow at its tip. Common Moorhens are very adaptable, being encountered in a wide range of habitats from ponds and freshwater marshes to rivers. They are quite shy by nature, and may be seen skulking along the edge of the pond, disappearing into reeds here at any hint of a threat. Their long toes assist them in walking across aquatic vegetation.

APPEARANCE Common Moorhens have a white area on the flanks. Although often seen in shallow water, these birds can swim well.

CHARADRIIFORMES

Waders, gulls, and their allies

The Charadriiformes are a diverse group of birds, divided into 19 families, whose representatives are often seen either in coastal areas or in grasslands. Members of this Order include typical shorebirds, observed wandering along the coast line, following tidal movements and congregating on mud flats. They may then move inland to grassland areas during the breeding season. Members of other families, such as the gulls, can be encountered some distance out at sea, and also inland, while others like auks spend most of their lives on the world's oceans.

American Golden Plover

FAMILY Charadriidae
SPECIES *Pluvialis dominica*
LENGTH 10¾ in (27 cm)
HABITAT Tundra/open country
CLUTCH SIZE 4

DISTRIBUTION Breeds in western and central parts of the far north, westward to southern Baffin Island. Overwinters in South America.

THESE LONG-DISTANCE migrants breed in the tundra region in the far north, only being seen elsewhere as passage migrants journeying to and from their wintering grounds in South America. The golden spots of the cock bird are only apparent as part of their summer plumage. In winter, the sexes cannot be told apart, both being predominantly grayish-brown.

MALE BREEDING PLUMAGE Pairs nest on the ground, using a simple scrape lined with lichen as a cushion for the eggs.

Black-bellied Plover

FAMILY Charadriidae
SPECIES *Pluvialis squatarola*
LENGTH 11½ in (29 cm)
HABITAT Tundra/coasts
CLUTCH SIZE 4

DISTRIBUTION Breeds on the northern coast of North America, as far east as the southern Baffin Island. Overwinters along the United States' coastline.

THE BREEDING GROUNDS of this plover lie within the Arctic, with the young birds being reared on the insects that are plentiful here during the brief summer period. The appearance of Black-bellied Plovers varies, with cock birds being mainly black in the summer, with white on the crown and nape, and gray in the winter.

WINTER HABITAT These plovers overwinter mainly in coastal areas, where they can be seen scampering in short bursts over the mud, then pausing to seek worms.

Snowy Plover

FAMILY Charadriidae
SPECIES *Charadrius alexandrinus*
LENGTH 6¼ in (16 cm)
HABITAT Coasts/salt flats
CLUTCH SIZE 3–4

DISTRIBUTION Resident along much of the western United States coast, and parts of the Florida coast, overwintering on the Gulf Coast. Also breeds inland in various localities.

IN SPITE OF ITS NAME, the Snowy Plover is not a bird found in the tundra region—in fact, it does not even occur in Canada. It lives in open areas such as sandy beaches, where it hunts various invertebrates, including small crustaceans. During the breeding period, the cock bird develops a black bar on both sides of the face.

CAMOUFLAGE The Snowy Plover's pale coloration enables it to blend in very effectively against the landscape.

Piping Plover

FAMILY Charadriidae
SPECIES *Charadrius melodus*
LENGTH 7¼ in (18 cm)
HABITAT Beaches/lake sides
CLUTCH SIZE 4

DISTRIBUTION Breeds on the east coast from Nova Scotia to North Carolina; overwinters south along the Gulf coast. Also breeds inland from southern Canada to Nebraska.

THE POPULATION of this plover has plummeted over recent years, so it has now become an endangered species, although the reasons for its decline are not entirely clear. The hen lays her eggs in a depression in the sand, with both members of the pair incubating the clutch. The chicks can run from an early age, and are independent by a month old.

SEASONAL CHANGE Cock birds develop an orange base to the bill, and also a black breast band at the start of the nesting period.

Mountain Plover

FAMILY Charadriidae
SPECIES *Charadrius montanus*
LENGTH 9 in (23 cm)
HABITAT Grassland
CLUTCH SIZE 3

DISTRIBUTION Breeds in Montana and from Wyoming south to New Mexico and Texas. Overwinters in areas of California and along the Mexican border as far as Texas.

THESE PLOVERS are found in areas well away from water, in open countryside, but habitat changes are contributing to a decline in their numbers. They live in small groups, hunting invertebrates and especially grasshoppers. Their nest is a well-disguised scrape on the ground.

HIDDEN The coloration of these rare plovers gives them excellent camouflage, making them hard to spot, even in the areas of open country that they inhabit.

Semipalmated Plover

FAMILY Charadriidae
SPECIES *Charadrius semipalmatus*
LENGTH 7½ in (19 cm)
HABITAT Beaches/lakes
CLUTCH SIZE 4

DISTRIBUTION Summer visitor to the far north, where it is present throughout Alaska, north to Baffin Island, and along Hudson Bay.

SEMIPALMATED PLOVERS breed in the summer in the far north, taking advantage of the temporary pools caused by the meltwater on the tundra where small insects proliferate. For the remainder of the year, they are likely to be seen in coastal areas, on beaches and tidal flats in estuaries, as they overwinter on the east and west United States' coasts. They have a white collar with a black bib, and a white face and underparts. The wings are brownish in color. There is a thin whitish stripe above the eyes, also extending above the bill.

DISTINCTIVE FEATURES The tip of the bill is blackish, with a yellowish-orange area encircling its base. The legs are also yellowish-orange.

Killdeer

FAMILY Charadriidae
SPECIES *Charadrius vociferus*
LENGTH 10½ in (27 cm)
HABITAT Field and shorelines
CLUTCH SIZE 4

DISTRIBUTION Summer visitor to southern Alaska and northwest Canada, and to Newfoundland in the east. Resident up both coasts and across the southern United States.

THESE PLOVERS CAN BE OBSERVED in habitats ranging from grassland to the shores of lakes. Killdeer live in flocks, and feed on a variety of invertebrates, ranging from snails to worms. Their characteristic reddish-orange rump will only be evident when the birds are in flight. They nest on open ground, and both adults take turns to incubate the eggs.

DISTINCTIVE The double chest band of the Killdeer is unique to this species, making identification easy.

Wilson's Plover

FAMILY Charadriidae
SPECIES *Charadrius wilsonia*
LENGTH 7¾ in (20 cm)
HABITAT Coasts/mudflats
CLUTCH SIZE 2–4

DISTRIBUTION Extends to Virginia in summer, and along the Gulf Coast from northern Florida. Resident on Florida's shoreline and in the Caribbean.

THE BLACK CHEST BAND is a feature of cock birds during the breeding period, with this area being sandy brown for the rest of the year, and also in hens. Wilson's Plovers nest on beaches, with their eggs being laid in a scrape in the sand. Their buff coloration gives good camouflage, with their chicks able to scamper around soon after hatching.

IDENTIFICATION An obvious feature of Wilson's Plover is its relatively long and large, thick black bill, which helps to separate it from similar species.

Sandhill Crane

FAMILY Gruidae
SPECIES *Grus canadensis*
LENGTH 42 in (107 cm)
HABITAT Tundra/grassland
CLUTCH SIZE 2

DISTRIBUTION Main summer breeding range extends from Alaska to the eastern coast of Hudson Bay, south and southeast, to northern California and Iowa. Overwinters in southern states.

SANDHILL CRANES vary in size through their range, with those from southern areas being larger than those found in the north. Their appearance is unmistakable, on grounds of their coloration as well as their stature. The top of the head, extending up and around the eyes from the base of the bill is reddish, with the remainder of their plumage being grayish, with a variable brownish hue apparent, particularly over the wings, and a paler, whitish area beneath the throat. In their Arctic breeding grounds, a pair will build a large mound of vegetation as their nest. Once the young cranes hatch, it will be 10 weeks before they can fly.

FEEDING HABITS These cranes are omnivorous, consuming small animals, fish, and plant matter too. They have a large wingspan of between 73 and 90 inches (185–229 cm)

Black Oystercatcher

FAMILY Haematopodidae

SPECIES *Haematopus bachmani*

LENGTH 17½ in (44 cm)

HABITAT Rocky coasts

CLUTCH SIZE 2–3

DISTRIBUTION Resident through the year, from the Aleutian Islands off Alaska's south coast down the west coast of Canada and the United States to southern California.

THESE OYSTERCATCHERS are very distinctive, in terms of their black coloration, with their plumage having a slightly browner hue over the wings. This contrasts with their stout, long red bill and orange eyes, offset against the pale yellow appearance of their legs and feet. They inhabit rocky coastal areas, breeding as individual pairs but coming together to form large flocks of up to 50 birds at the end of this period. Young Black Oystercatchers will be able to feed themselves by five weeks old, and are similar to adults in appearance by this stage, but still distinguishable by the dark tip to their bill.

SPECIALIZED TOOL The stout bill of these birds can be used to tackle a variety of marine invertebrates, and not just oysters. Crabs, limpets, and starfish also feature in their diet.

American Oystercatcher

FAMILY Haematopodidae

SPECIES *Haematopus palliatus*

LENGTH 18½ in (47 cm)

HABITAT Beaches

CLUTCH SIZE 2–4

DISTRIBUTION Summer visitor as far north as Maine, and resident further south, although absent from the tip of Florida, continuing along the Gulf Coast to Mexico.

THIS SPECIES can be easily distinguished from its Black relative by its white underparts, with its legs being pinkish. Pairs nest in a secluded part of the beach, on a scrape in the sand above the high water mark. It takes about 25 days for the eggs to hatch, and as soon as they hatch, the young will start to follow the adults although they are not able to fly at this early age. It will be five weeks before they are independent, being recognizable by their black-tipped bills.

SOCIAL During the winter period, these oystercatchers may congregate together, and they are also seen feeding in the company of other waders.

SANDHILL CRANES (*see* p. 128) These birds extend their head and neck when flying, their long legs and feet roughly horizontal with the body. They fly across the continent, from their northern breeding grounds to southern parts.

Black-necked Stilt

FAMILY Recurvirostridae

SPECIES *Himatopus mexicanus*

LENGTH 14 in (36 cm)

HABITAT Wetland

CLUTCH SIZE 4

DISTRIBUTION Nests in southwestern Canada across the United States border to Montana. Also to the east and south. Resident in southern Florida, California, and southwestern Texas.

THE APPEARANCE of these slender stilts is quite distinctive. Black plumage extends back from the top of the head down over the neck, with the wings often having a slightly browner hue, notably in the case of the hen, with the underparts being white. Young birds of both sexes also resemble hens. The long, straight bill is black, while the long legs are red. The Black-necked Stilt had become a very rare species by the late 1800s, due to hunting, but its numbers have now recovered, and it has recolonized many of its former haunts. It prefers shallow wetlands, where it can use its bill to probe for the aquatic invertebrates that it eats.

NESTING These stilts nest close to water, laying on the ground. The buff coloration of the eggs helps to disguise them here.

American Avocet

FAMILY Recurvirostridae

SPECIES *Recurvirostra americana*

LENGTH 18 in (46 cm)

HABITAT Wetland

CLUTCH SIZE 4

DISTRIBUTION Breeds in southwestern and central Canada through the western United States, from southern California east to northern Texas. On the east coast, overwinters from Virginia southward.

THESE AVOCETS are transformed in the spring by having bright cinnamon plumage on the head and neck, which replaces their gray winter coloration. They use their slender, sensitive upturned bill by waving it from side to side through the water to locate invertebrates in the shallows.

FEATURES There is a prominent white stripe across each wing of this bird, with its long legs being gray.

Lesser Yellowlegs

FAMILY Scolopacidae

SPECIES *Tringa flavipes*

LENGTH 10½ in (27 cm)

HABITAT Tundra/coasts

CLUTCH SIZE 4

DISTRIBUTION Breeds through much of Alaska to the south-eastern side of Hudson Bay. Overwinters in California, and from Virginia throughout Florida down into Central America.

SPECKLED BLACK-AND-WHITE plumage over the back and wings, paler underparts, and yellow legs help to identify these waders. They are largely impossible to distinguish from the Greater Yellowlegs (*see* p. 134), however, except on the basis of their size. Lesser Yellowlegs catch small invertebrates by wading through shallow water, and often occur in small groups. When breeding, a pair may choose a site some distance from water, where they feel relatively secure.

MIGRATION Lesser Yellowlegs make long flights to and from their breeding grounds, being only wintertime visitors to the southern United States.

Greater Yellowlegs

FAMILY Scolopacidae
SPECIES *Tringa melanoleuca*
LENGTH 14 in (36 cm)
HABITAT Shallow wetland
CLUTCH SIZE 3–4

DISTRIBUTION Breeding range extends right across North America, south of Hudson Bay and up to Newfoundland. Overwinters from Washington to Mexico, and along America's east coast.

BASICALLY IDENTICAL in appearance to its smaller relative, apart from its size, the Greater Yellowlegs breeds over a wider area in Canada, although its wintering grounds are more restricted. Here, these birds form mixed flocks with other waders, hunting for invertebrates and small fish.

IDENTIFICATION A slightly upturned bill, long neck, mottled back, and yellow legs all aid identification.

Solitary Sandpiper

FAMILY Scolopacidae
SPECIES *Tringa solitaria*
LENGTH 8½ in (22 cm)
HABITAT Shallow water
CLUTCH SIZE 4

DISTRIBUTION Extends from southern Alaska eastward to Newfoundland, and south to the northern boundary of the Great Lakes. Overwinters mainly in Mexico.

THIS SANDPIPER can be observed in a wide range of habitats, from wet coniferous forest in the far north through to estuaries. Unlike its relatives, the Solitary Sandpiper does not lay on the ground. Instead, it uses an abandoned songbird nest in a tree, with the hen incubating the eggs here on her own. They will take about 23 days to hatch.

ELUSIVE It is not easy to observe Solitary Sandpipers, because they are shy birds, living on their own as their name suggests.

Wandering Tattler

FAMILY Scolopacidae
SPECIES *Heteroscelus incanus*
LENGTH 11 in (28 cm)
HABITAT Streams/coasts
CLUTCH SIZE 4

DISTRIBUTION Breeds mainly in Alaska, as well as the eastern Yukon Territory and northern British Columbia in the summer. Overwinters on the Californian coast, to Baja California.

THE BREEDING GROUNDS of the Wandering Tattler lie in the vicinity of gravel streams in the far north, with these waders then moving a long way south for the winter, being seen in coastal areas at this stage. They are a fairly uniform shade of gray, with a darker gray area between the eyes and the long, pointed bill. Their underparts are pale, but when breeding, this area shows distinctive barring. The relatively short legs are a dull shade of yellow. As with many birds from the far north, Wandering Tattlers display little fear of people and can be approached quite closely as a result.

INDEPENDENT Wandering Tattlers tend not to associate together in flocks even when there may be several birds feeding in the same area.

Spotted Sandpiper

FAMILY Scolopacidae
SPECIES *Actitis macularia*
LENGTH 7½ in (19 cm)
HABITAT Streams/marshland
CLUTCH SIZE 3–4

DISTRIBUTION Breeds from Alaska to Texas, but absent from here to the Carolinas southward. Resident down the west coast. Overwinters in the southern United States.

THE SPOTTED SANDPIPER has an extensive breeding area in North America, being seen in a variety of habitats close to water, in coastal areas as well as inland. It moves with a very distinctive bobbing gait, and flies in quite a stiff way, revealing the white area in each wing. The back is olive-brown, with this coloration extending down the sides of the neck. The eggs are laid in a scrape near water, and it appears that often the cock bird incubates for much of the time on his own.

DISTINCTIVE The Spotted Sandpiper is easily identified during the breeding season, with circular black markings evident on their otherwise white underparts.

Willet

FAMILY Scolopacidae

SPECIES *Catoptrophorus semipalmatus*

LENGTH 15 in (38 cm)

HABITAT Coasts/wetland

CLUTCH SIZE 3–4

DISTRIBUTION Summer visitor to southern-central Canada, extending to Nebraska and California, and on Nova Scotia. Resident along much of the east coast, overwintering on the west coast.

PALE UNDERPARTS, with variable brown markings over the head, back, wings, and tail help to distinguish the Willet. Prominent white and black stripes in the wings are evident in flight. Its bill is grayish, with the legs and feet also being dark gray. There is a white area above the eyes on each side of the head. These sandpipers are surprisingly noisy birds, often being seen in small flocks. They range over a wide area through the year, with breeding taking place in coastal areas and also occurring inland in wetland areas. Willets nest on the ground, in a simple scrape, with both members of the pairs sharing the task of incubation. The young hatch within four weeks, and are able to move almost immediately, being covered in downy feathering at this stage.

ADAPTATIONS The webbed feet of the Willet are evident here. These waders feed on a variety of invertebrates and seeds.

Long-billed Curlew

FAMILY Scolopacidae

SPECIES *Numenius americanus*

LENGTH 23 in (58 cm)

HABITAT Wetland/grassland

CLUTCH SIZE 3–4

DISTRIBUTION Breeds from British Columbia down to California and northern New Mexico and Texas. Overwinters from California east to Texas.

AS THEIR NAME SUGGESTS, these curlews have a very long bill, which curves toward its tip. They have dark brown mottling on their plumage, which tends to be of a lighter tawny shade. In flight, their distinctive cinnamon underwing coverts are clearly apparent. Long-billed Curlews are seen in flocks outside the breeding season, on their wintering grounds, but they breed inland in grassland areas. Here they lay in open country, with their mottled appearance helping to disguise their presence on the nest.

IDENTIFICATION The Long-billed Curlew's profile is unmistakable, thanks to its long bill. Its large size also aids its recognition.

Upland Sandpiper

FAMILY Scolopacidae
SPECIES *Bartramia longicauda*
LENGTH 12 in (30 cm)
HABITAT Grassland
CLUTCH SIZE 4

DISTRIBUTION Breeds in Alaska and northwestern Canada. Also from southern parts of the Northwest Territories around the Great Lakes to the east coast, and south to Oklahoma.

THE HABITS of the Upland Sandpiper are quite different from those of other related species, to the extent that these birds used to be known as Upland Plovers. Not only are they found only in grassland and not coastal areas within North America, but also, they inhabit areas of tall grass. They then become hard to spot, with only their small heads momentarily visible, bobbing in and out of view. Their neck is long, however, enabling them to peer above the grass on occasion, whereas their bill is short. The tail feathers are also distinctive, extending well back beyond the wings, rather than being very short. During the late 1800s, Upland Sandpipers were heavily hunted to the point of extinction, but subsequently, their numbers have recovered. Their breeding behavior is similar to that of other sandpipers, in that they nest on the ground, but again, they choose a well-concealed site in longer grass for this purpose.

SURVEYING Upland Sandpipers commonly use fence posts as vantage points within their breeding territories, as seen here.

WILLET (*see* p. 126) This flock is resting in a characteristic pose in the shallows on a beach. Waders often rest in this way when the tide is coming in, becoming active once it turns, revisiting the newly exposed areas of sand for food.

Marbled Godwit

FAMILY Scolopacidae
SPECIES *Limosa fedoa*
LENGTH 18 in (46 cm)
HABITAT Tidal flats/marshland
CLUTCH SIZE 4

DISTRIBUTION Summer populations found south of Hudson Bay, and in central-southern Canada to Montana and the Dakotas. Overwinters on the west and eastern coasts of the United States.

WHEN IN BREEDING plumage, these godwits have warm tawny-brown plumage above, with black on their upperparts and barring on the underside of the body. They nest inland on the northern prairies. The nest itself is a shallow scrape, close to water and concealed in vegetation. Marbled Godwits overwinter on the United States coasts. During this period, they are less colorful, with buff-brown underparts and mottling above. Adults are impossible to separate from juveniles at this stage.

DISTINCTIVE The dark, slightly upturned tip to the Marbled Godwit's bill contrasts with the flesh-pink base.

Hudsonian Godwit

FAMILY Scolopacidae
SPECIES *Limosa haemastica*
LENGTH 15½ in (39 cm)
HABITAT Beaches/marshland
CLUTCH SIZE 4

DISTRIBUTION Widely distributed breeding populations in the far north extending from Alaska across to Hudson Bay. Overwinters in southern parts of South America.

THE HUDSONIAN Godwit is named after the area where it occurs, Hudson Bay, and it is rarely seen elsewhere, other than to the west. These waders then migrate in flocks down through the central area of the continent after the breeding season. Their coloration is transformed at this stage, when they become grayish above, with white on the lower underparts.

PLUMAGE Their breeding coloration sees a brownish hue to the upperparts, and chestnut coloration below. The Hudsonian is the smallest species of godwit.

Bar-tailed Godwit

FAMILY Scolopacidae

SPECIES *Limosa lapponica*

LENGTH 16 in (41 cm)

HABITAT Tundra/mudflats

CLUTCH SIZE 4

DISTRIBUTION Summer visitor to western Alaska. Migrates back across the Bering Sea to Asia for the winter. Some individuals may wander down the Pacific coast.

THE TAIL FEATHERS are white with barring extending across them. This helps to identify Bar-tailed Godwits throughout the year. In breeding plumage, the back is a mottled shade of brown, with the underparts being chestnut and free from markings. Their appearance is then transformed at the end of the breeding season, when brownish-gray streaking becomes evident over the back, while whitish plumage is apparent below. Hens can be identified by their larger size and paler coloration. Both parents share the task of incubation.

ADAPTATION The long, slightly upturned bill of this godwit is used to probe underwater for food such as worms.

Ruddy Turnstone

FAMILY Scolopacidae

SPECIES *Arenaria interpres*

LENGTH 9½ in (24 cm)

HABITAT Rocky coasts/ beaches

CLUTCH SIZE 4

DISTRIBUTION Breeds in the far north, from northern Alaska across to Greenland. Winters down the west and eastern coasts of the United States.

THIS PARTICULAR turnstone rarely strays far from the shore. Its summer coloration is very distinctive, with adults developing orange-red plumage on the back, and contrasting black feathering on the head and chest, complete with bright orange legs. In the winter, their upperparts become dark brown with black streaking, while the underparts are white. Hens are duller in color than cocks.

BREEDING This species breeds on open ground near the shore. The young birds have scaled rather than streaked patterning on their backs.

Black Turnstone

FAMILY Scolopacidae

SPECIES *Arenaria melanocephala*

LENGTH 9¾ in (25 cm)

HABITAT Rocky coasts/ mudflats

CLUTCH SIZE 4

DISTRIBUTION Breeds on the western coast of Alaska, and overwinters southward from here, right along the Pacific coast of North America to Mexico.

THE DESCRIPTION of "turnstone" for these waders comes from the way in which they feed, turning over pebbles and pushing aside seaweed in the search for anything edible along the shoreline or in the shallows. Most turnstones rarely venture far from the coast and this applies in the case of the Black Turnstone. Black plumage predominates in this species. The summer breeding plumage has a large white spot each side of the head in front of the eye, with a white eyebrow streak too. White spots extend down the neck and the breast, with the belly being white. Patterning is simpler in the winter, with the upperparts and breast being black, while the lower underparts are white. Young birds resemble the adult bird in winter plumage.

SOCIABILITY Pairs are territorial when breeding, but in winter these birds are seen in small flocks.

Surfbird

FAMILY Scolopacidae

SPECIES *Aphriza virgata*

LENGTH 10 in (25 cm)

HABITAT Tundra/rocky beaches

CLUTCH SIZE 4

DISTRIBUTION Summer breeding range centered on Alaska and the northern Yukon Territory. Heads south in winter, along the Pacific coast.

IN THE WINTER when they are found in coastal areas, Surfbirds have gray plumage on the upperparts and breast, with the lower underparts being white. Over the summer, however, they are transformed by developing a rufous patch on each wing, with brownish-black spotting evident over the gray plumage. Pairs nest high in tundra, with the nest being hidden among rocks.

FEEDING The stout bill of the Surfbird is used like a chisel to dislodge molluscs from rocks. It also feeds on other invertebrates.

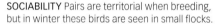

Sanderling

FAMILY Scolopacidae
SPECIES *Calidris alba*
LENGTH 8 in (20 cm)
HABITAT Sandy beaches
CLUTCH SIZE 4

DISTRIBUTION Breeds in the far north of central America, extending to Greenland. Overwinters right down the Pacific coast to Mexico and along the United States' east coast.

IN BREEDING PLUMAGE, this member of the sandpiper clan has blackish, rust, and white mottling on its chest and upperparts, with more evident streaking on the head, while the underparts are white. During the winter, however, its appearance is transformed with the mottling being replaced by gray plumage above, occasionally with a blackish area at the shoulders. Young birds resemble adults in winter plumage, but they are a darker shade of gray, often with white scaling evident on the back as well. The nest is well-concealed on the ground, with both birds taking part in the task of incubation.

FEEDING HABITS Sanderlings are opportunistic when feeding, as they run over the beach and grab invertebrates briefly exposed in the surf using their short bill.

Dunlin

FAMILY Scolopacidae
SPECIES *Calidris alpina*
LENGTH 8½ in (22 cm)
HABITAT Tundra/mudflats
CLUTCH SIZE 4

DISTRIBUTION Along the northern coast of the continent in summer, from Alaska via Hudson Bay, to Greenland. Overwinters down the west and Atlantic coasts.

DUNLINS ARE LIKELY to be seen over the winter months, when their upperparts are brownish-gray, and their plumage is white below. During the summer in the high tundra, they display rufous feathering over the back, offset against a gray-brown head, neck, and upper breast. Dunlin feed in water, moving slowly through the shallows and probing with their long, down-curved bill for small crustaceans and similar invertebrates. Pairs nest on the ground, with incubation taking about three weeks. The young will then be independent after a similar interval.

IDENTIFICATION The Dunlin's black bill is much thicker at its base compared with its tip. It is also slightly downcurved toward its tip.

Baird's Sandpiper

FAMILY Scolopacidae

SPECIES *Calidris bairdii*

LENGTH 7½ in (19 cm)

HABITAT Beaches/damp fields

CLUTCH SIZE 4

DISTRIBUTION Breeds along the northern coast of the continent, from Alaska to Baffin Island. Migrates south in the fall to its overwintering grounds in South America.

THE SEASONAL transformation in plumage is less dramatic in this species compared with some other sandpipers. The grayish-brown plumage seen in winter is altered to a warm shade of brownish-gray, with buff coloring on the chest. Baird's Sandpiper can also be identified by its long wings that extend beyond the tip of the tail. Its legs and feet are gray.

PLUMAGE The summer coloration of these sandpipers helps to provide them with camouflage when they are breeding. Hens lay on the ground.

Red Knot

FAMILY Scolopacidae

SPECIES *Calidris canutus*

LENGTH 10½ in (27 cm)

HABITAT Sandy beaches/ mudflats

CLUTCH SIZE 4

DISTRIBUTION Breeds at various localities in the far north, mainly from Victoria Island north to Greenland, south to Southampton Island. Overwinters from the United States to Argentina.

THE REDDISH UNDERPARTS of this species are only evident during the summer breeding period, offset against grayish-brown, black, and chestnut mottling on the upperparts. In the winter, Red Knots become a pale gray color on the back and wings, with their underparts being white.

CONGREGATING Thousands of Red Knots descend on Delaware Bay in May, to feed on the eggs of the Horseshoe Crab.

White-rumped Sandpiper

FAMILY Scolopacidae
SPECIES *Calidris fuscicollis*
LENGTH 7½ in (19 cm)
HABITAT Mudflats/marshland
CLUTCH SIZE 4

DISTRIBUTION Breeds mainly in northern-central Canada, east to Baffin Island. Overwinters down to southern parts of South America.

THIS FAIRLY NONDESCRIPT sandpiper can be overlooked in mixed flocks of shorebirds. When breeding, adults can be identified by their grayish-brown back, with black streaks on the chest and flanks. Over the winter months, they are dark gray above with white underparts. The sexes are identical in appearance, but their characteristic white rump helps to distinguish them from related species. Young birds resemble adults, but are more of a rufous shade. White-rumped Sandpipers may be seen south of the Arctic breeding grounds over a wider area of North America during the migration periods in the spring and fall, but they do not overwinter on the continent. They nest in a scrape on the ground lined with vegetation, with the buff-green color of their eggs helping to disguise their presence here. The incubation period lasts for approximately three weeks, with this task being shared by both cock and hen. The young sandpipers will then become independent after a similar interval.

FORAGING White-rumped Sandpipers probe for worms and other invertebrates, in shallow freshwater and on tidal mudflats.

Stilt Sandpiper

FAMILY Scolopacidae

SPECIES *Calidris himantopus*

LENGTH 8½ in (22 cm)

HABITAT Shallow pools

CLUTCH SIZE 4

DISTRIBUTION From northeastern Alaska to Victoria Island and around Hudson Bay. Winters in southern Florida, coastal Louisiana and Texas, southern California and Mexico.

THIS SANDPIPER FLIES back and forth over the entire North American continent each year. When in breeding condition, it has chestnut ear patches, with gray-brown upperparts. The underparts have dark brown with white barring. During the winter months, Stilt Sandpipers have a much simpler color scheme, with gray above and white underparts. Their black bill is quite thick along its length, and they feed by probing back and forth for invertebrates of various types. Their legs are green in color.

NO VISIBLE DIFFERENCE It is impossible to tell whether this Stilt Sandpiper on its nest is the cock or hen, as they are identical. Both members of the pair share the task of incubation.

Purple Sandpiper

FAMILY Scolopacidae

SPECIES *Calidris maritima*

LENGTH 9 in (23 cm)

HABITAT Tundra/rocky coasts

CLUTCH SIZE 4

DISTRIBUTION Extends from the northwest of Hudson Bay to Southampton and Baffin Islands, and southern Greenland. In winter, along the eastern Atlantic seaboard to South Carolina.

THE NAME OF THESE SANDPIPERS comes from the color of their winter plumage, which is a purplish-gray shade above, with the underparts being whitish. They are transformed to a brownish-gray, with black streaking over the head, neck, and breast at the start of the breeding season. There is grayish-brown spotting to the plumage on the flanks and belly. In spite of its name, the Purple Sandpiper is most likely to be encountered along rocky rather than sandy shores. They search here largely for molluscs and small crustaceans.

IDENTIFICATION A dumpy body shape with a long, stout bill are characteristic features of the Purple Sandpiper.

Western Sandpiper

FAMILY Scolopacidae

SPECIES *Calidris mauri*

LENGTH 6½ in (17 cm)

HABITAT Coastal flats

CLUTCH SIZE 4

DISTRIBUTION Seen in summer around western Alaska. Overwinters along the United States Pacific coast to Mexico, and from Delaware south down the Gulf coast.

THIS SPECIES IS VERY SIMILAR to the Semipalmated Sandpiper (*see* p. 149). The arrow-like spotting on the belly evident in breeding plumage serves to distinguish the Western Sandpiper, however, and in terms of behavior, it tends to wade more readily when seeking food, rather than foraging at the water's edge. Mottled brown-gray coloring on the head, with more prominent black spotting on the wings are characteristic features. There is an overlay of rusty-red markings on the upperparts behind the eyes and over the wings. During the winter, the coloration on the upperparts becomes much grayer. The hen will lay in a scrape on the ground, with incubation lasting for about three weeks. The young sandpipers will then be independent after a similar period. They have a dark cap, offset against a whitish face.

DISTINCTIVE FEATURES A relatively long, broad bill characterizes the Western Sandpiper. These birds are quite small in size, with a stocky body.

Pectoral Sandpiper

FAMILY Scolopacidae
SPECIES *Calidris melanotos*
LENGTH 8¾ in (22 cm)
HABITAT Marshland/mudflats
CLUTCH SIZE 4

DISTRIBUTION Breeds mainly along the northwestern part of the continent, to the west of Hudson Bay. Winters largely in southern South America.

THESE SANDPIPERS spend more time inland than many related species, even being seen in flooded fields on occasions. Cocks become increasingly vocal at the start of the breeding period, calling loudly as part of their display. Their basic coloration is similar to that of other sandpipers, but there is a very noticeable dividing line between the gray-brown mottling extending down over the breast and the white feathering on the underparts.

DIFFERENCES The male Pectoral Sandpiper is bigger in size than the hen. Groups often forage together in flocks.

Least Sandpiper

FAMILY Scolopacidae
SPECIES *Calidris minutilla*
LENGTH 6 in (15 cm)
HABITAT Rivers/marshland
CLUTCH SIZE 4

DISTRIBUTION Summer range extends over the far north, from Alaska across to Newfoundland. Overwinters down the United States' east and west coast, and across the southern states.

THESE SMALL sandpipers are commonly seen inland in parts of North America when they are migrating. Their appearance in the summer period is rather similar to that of other *Calidris* sandpipers, and these birds may be seen as part of mixed flocks feeding together, making accurate identification harder. Their legs are yellowish, however, unlike those of the Western Sandpiper (*see* p. 147).

SEASONAL CHANGE This Least Sandpiper is in summer plumage. Their upperparts become gray after the breeding period, with their underparts being completely white. Young birds are a more rufous gray in color.

Rock Sandpiper

FAMILY Scolopacidae
SPECIES *Calidris ptilocnemis*
LENGTH 9 in (23 cm)
HABITAT Tundra/rocky shores
CLUTCH SIZE 4

DISTRIBUTION Summer breeding range is on the west coast of Alaska and islands here. Overwinters along the coast from southern Alaska down to northern California.

AS ITS NAME SUGGESTS, this particular sandpiper favors rocky areas of coastline where it overwinters. Similar in size and coloration to the Purple Sandpiper (*see* p. 146), these birds can be distinguished by the presence of a dark gray area of plumage on the lower breast. The bill is again quite long and black in color, curving slightly downward along its length. The legs and feet are yellowish-green. On their breeding grounds, pairs utilize a simple nest, lined with plant matter. The young birds are able to run around as soon as they hatch, covered in downy feathering.

DISTINGUISHING FEATURE When these sandpipers take to the air, it is usually possible to see the white stripe running across each wing.

Semipalmated Sandpiper

FAMILY Scolopacidae
SPECIES *Calidris pusilla*
LENGTH 6¼ in (16 cm)
HABITAT Tundra/mudflats
CLUTCH SIZE 4

DISTRIBUTION Breeds right along the northern coast of the continent, but does not usually overwinter in North America. These sandpipers head instead to Central and South America.

THE NAME OF the Semipalmated Sandpiper stems from the webbing that partially links the front toes of each foot, creating a palm. This allows the bird to walk with relative ease over mud, with little risk of sinking into it. Their summer plumage is less rufous than that of related species, providing a more clearly evident point of distinction.

FAR NORTH The breeding grounds of the Semipalmated Sandpiper lie within the Arctic circle. Both members of the pair look after the chicks.

Short-billed Dowitcher

FAMILY Scolopacidae

SPECIES *Limnodromus griseus*

LENGTH 11 in (28 cm)

HABITAT Tundra/mudflats

CLUTCH SIZE 4

DISTRIBUTION Breeds along the southern Alaskan coast, and also south of Hudson Bay. Winters along the United States' Pacific and Atlantic coasts, down to Central America.

IN SPITE OF ITS NAME, the bill of the Short-billed Dowitcher is not particularly short. These shorebirds favor saltwater localities outside the breeding season. They have brownish-gray upperparts at this stage, with white stripes above the eyes, and white underparts. When in breeding plumage, the area of the neck becomes chestnut-orange, and they have a checkered back, with rufous markings on a brown and white background. Short-billed Dowitchers breed in three separate areas and birds from different areras are distinctly different. Birds from the west have a white belly with darker markings, as do those from the east. Individuals from the central parts of their range, however, have orange underparts. These variations disappear once the birds have molted into winter plumage. When nesting, these

dowitchers breed on dry ground, using a suitable depression for this purpose. Hatching takes three weeks.

COLORATION This particular Short-billed Dowitcher is in winter plumage. The long dark bill ends in a lighter yellowish-green tip.

Long-billed Dowitcher

FAMILY Scolopacidae

SPECIES *Limnodromus scolopaceus*

LENGTH 11½ in (29 cm)

HABITAT Tundra/mudflats

CLUTCH SIZE 4

DISTRIBUTION Summer range restricted to the far northwest, primarily in Alaska. In winter, occurs on both the Atlantic and Pacific United States' coasts, and across the southern states.

CONTRARY TO THEIR NAMES, the bill length in the case of cock birds of this species and that of the Short-billed Dowitcher are almost identical. Where there is an evident variance, however, it is in the case of hens. After leaving their breeding grounds, Long-billed Dowitchers will head to freshwater localities rather than to the coast, unlike their Short-billed relative. They use their long bill to probe for food such as snails and other invertebrates in environments that may vary from shallow pools to marshland. The eggs of the Long-billed Dowitcher tend to blend in against the area of surrounding grass where they are laid, being green with dark spots. The eggs will be incubated by both parents and should hatch after about three weeks.

PLUMAGE When in breeding condition, the Long-billed Dowitcher cock bird has chestnut-orange on the neck, and orange underparts. The back is overlaid with rufous plumage.

Wilson's Snipe

FAMILY Scolopacidae

SPECIES *Gallinago delicata*

LENGTH 10½ in (27 cm)

HABITAT Marshland/wet fields

CLUTCH SIZE 4

DISTRIBUTION Ranges up to Alaska and to Newfoundland in the summer. Resident in western United States especially, and also overwinters widely across the southern United States.

THESE BIRDS ARE hard to observe, because of their secretive natures, and their mottled coloration helps them to blend into the background in their marshy habitat. When flushed from cover, they fly in a very distinctive zig-zag pattern. Wilson's Snipe uses its long bill to catch invertebrates of various types, probing in mud for worms. The hen lays on the ground, lining the scrape with grasses as a cushion for her eggs. The incubation period lasts for approximately 20 days, and the young will be independent after a similar interval.

WARY BEHAVIOR It is rare to spot a Wilson's Snipe out in the open. These birds are very alert to any hint of danger.

Red-necked Phalarope

FAMILY Scolopacidae
SPECIES *Phalaropus lobatus*
LENGTH 7¾ in (20 cm)
HABITAT Tundra/coasts
CLUTCH SIZE 2–4

DISTRIBUTION Occurs across the northern part of the continent, from Alaska to Labrador in the summer. Winters at sea in southern latitudes.

THE PLUMAGE OF THESE PHALAROPES alters significantly through the year. During the winter, their coloration is relatively subdued, having gray upperparts with white below. The back is streaked with lighter markings, and there is black feathering behind the eyes and on the crown. Just prior to the breeding season, however, they molt, but in a reversal of the more usual situation within the avian kingdom, the hen's breeding plumage is more colorful that that of her partner. She can be recognized by the rusty-red area on the neck, with the throat area being white. There are buff stripes apparent over the back. She will guard the nest site from interlopers, leaving it to the cock bird to incubate the eggs. The chicks should hatch three weeks later.

HABITS Although they can wade in the shallows, as seen here, Red-necked Phalaropes may also be observed swimming offshore.

Wilson's Phalarope

FAMILY Scolopacidae
SPECIES *Phalaropus tricolor*
LENGTH 9¼ in (24 cm)
HABITAT Marshland/lakes
CLUTCH SIZE 3–4

DISTRIBUTION Breeds mainly in the west, from British Columbia south to New Mexico, and across to Quebec. Overwinters down to South America.

DURING THE WINTER, Wilson's Phalarope has gray plumage on the head, back, and wings, with white on the underparts, but is then transformed in the spring. Black and chestnut stripes are evident on the neck, with rusty areas to the sides of the chest, with cock birds being of a paler shade than hens. The bill in this case is very thin, allowing these phalaropes to pick up small aquatic creatures, as well as seeds. They nest in reedbeds, with the cock incubating the eggs.

DISTRIBUTION Wilson's Phalarope is a migratory species, but unlike other members of its family, it is never seen on the coast, being restricted to freshwater areas.

American Woodcock

FAMILY Scolopacidae
SPECIES *Scolopax minor*
LENGTH 11 in (28 cm)
HABITAT Damp woodland/fields
CLUTCH SIZE 4

DISTRIBUTION Summer visitor from southeastern Canada down to Missouri, and then resident southward. Overwinters from eastern Texas along the Gulf coast to Florida.

THE RELATIVELY LARGE EYES of the American Woodcock are an indicator of its nocturnal lifestyle. Males even undertake their elaborate courtship dance at night. Hiding in woodland areas during the day, these birds will emerge into nearby fields under cover of darkness to hunt for worms that they can grab with their long bill. Their mottled plumage helps to conceal their presence, and their short legs mean they can drop to the ground to escape detection. They prefer to hide rather than fly from potential danger.

WELL HIDDEN This shy, cryptic species is very hard to spot, with its plumage providing excellent camouflage, even at close quarters.

Long-tailed Jaeger

FAMILY Stercorariidae

SPECIES *Stercorarius longicaudus*

LENGTH 22 in (56 cm)

HABITAT Tundra/open sea

CLUTCH SIZE 2

DISTRIBUTION Breeds mainly west of Hudson Bay to Alaska; and from Baffin Island to Greenland. Overwinters at sea off South America.

THE JET BLACK CAP, coupled with the long tail streamers, help to identify this particular jaeger. It nests on the tundra, and then migrates not over land, but heads back to the sea. Long-tailed Jaegers are a predatory species, feeding not just on lemmings but also raiding the nests of other birds breeding in this part of the world.

PLUMAGE This is an adult bird, as reflected by its tail streamers, which are not seen in the grayer juveniles. The species has a wingspan of 40 inches (102 cm)

Parasitic Jaeger

FAMILY Stercorariidae

SPECIES *Stercorarius parasiticus*

LENGTH 19 in (48 cm)

HABITAT Tundra/open sea

CLUTCH SIZE 2

DISTRIBUTION Summer visitor to the far north, from Alaska to northern Quebec and Labrador. Overwinters along the southern coasts of the United States.

ITS GRAY CAP helps to identify this species, with its tail being relatively short. Its wingspan is around 42 inches (107 cm). As with other seabirds, there is also a darker form, with the white plumage being replaced by brown. The sexes are identical in appearance. The unusual name "jaeger" means "hunter" in German, and describes the predatory nature of these birds. They steal eggs and nestlings from other species breeding on the tundra, as well as preying on lemmings. At sea, however, they harry other seabirds into dropping their catches.

FEEDING HABITS This species is known as the Parasitic Jaeger because of the way in which it steals food. Its upper bill is hooked at the tip.

Herring Gull

FAMILY Laridae
SPECIES *Larus argentatus*
LENGTH 25 in (64 cm)
HABITAT Coasts/lakes
CLUTCH SIZE 2–3

DISTRIBUTION Breeds across a broad area of northern North America. Resident in northeastern parts. Winters through the southeast and in the west.

ADULTS OF THIS SPECIES can be identified by their bill color, which is yellowish with a prominent red spot on the lower mandible, near its tip. The head, neck, and underparts are white, and the wings gray. The flight feathers are black, with white spots at their tips. In winter plumage, the neck is streaked with brown, and the red on the bill becomes less distinctive. Herring Gulls will feed on fish, but they are effectively scavengers, eating anything edible. This has seen them move further inland, away from the coast, often into cities where they may nest on the roofs of tall buildings. Pairs have very protective parental instincts, dive-bombing people who venture too close to the nest or chicks after they have fledged.

COLORATION This is a young Herring Gull, as shown by its mottled brown plumage and dark bill. As an adult, its wingspan will reach 57 inches (145 cm)

Laughing Gull

FAMILY Laridae
SPECIES *Larus atricilla*
LENGTH 16½ in (42 cm)
HABITAT Sea/marshland
CLUTCH SIZE 3–4

DISTRIBUTION Resident from North Carolina along the Gulf Coast, and inland Florida in winter. In summer may range up to Nova Scotia.

THE SOUND OF the calls of this gull helps to explain its common name—they resemble the sound of someone laughing. It is primarily found along the coast, but moves further inland, typically to areas of salt marsh, when nesting. These birds breed here in colonies. The young gulls should hatch after a period of about three weeks, but it will take three years for them to acquire adult coloring and a wingspan of 40 inches (102 cm). During the winter, Laughing Gulls have largely white heads, with some darker speckling evident here.

IDENTIFICATION A Laughing Gull in summer plumage, as reflected by the black plumage on the head. The sexes are identical in appearance.

HERRING GULL A young herring gull scavenges a dead crab. It is molting into adult plumage, with the emerging gray plumage evident on the wings, indicating that it is just over two years old. These gulls can live for 15 years or longer.

California Gull

FAMILY Laridae
SPECIES *Larus californicus*
LENGTH 21 in (53 cm)
HABITAT Coasts/lakes
CLUTCH SIZE 2–3

DISTRIBUTION Summer visitor to central Canada to the northwestern United States; resident in a few localities. From southern British Columbia to California in winter.

THESE GULLS LIVE and breed inland during the summer months, returning to the coast in the fall. They have a relatively limited area of distribution around the prairie lakes, nesting here on the islands where they are relatively safe from predators. Pairs breed on the ground, creating a mound of vegetation as their nest. Both birds share the task of incubation, which lasts just over 21 days. When they fledge, the young gulls have brown feathering on the back, with pink legs and a dark bill. It will take a series of molts over four years for them to acquire full adult plumage. The adult wingspan is 54 inches (137 cm). On the prairies, California Gulls eat a range of invertebrates—this species is credited with eating a plague of locusts, preventing the early Mormon settlers from starving when their crops were under threat from these insects. They will also catch rodents.

APPEARANCE This adult California Gull is in summer plumage. During the winter, brown stripes will be evident on the neck.

Mew Gull

FAMILY Laridae
SPECIES *Larus canus*
LENGTH 16 in (41 cm)
HABITAT Coasts/lakes
CLUTCH SIZE 2–3

DISTRIBUTION From Alaska to the Northwest Territories and northern Manitoba, and south on the west coast. Winter visitor here from Washington to California.

A NARROW YELLOW BILL and yellow legs help to distinguish the Mew Gull. The plumage over the back and wings is grayish, with the underparts being white. Over the winter period, the white area on the head and neck has a brownish suffusion. Mew Gulls nest in colonies, sometimes alongside other species of gull in their northern breeding range. They then overwinter along the coast. This species feeds on invertebrates such as worms and molluscs, rather than scavenging. Young birds can be recognized by their brown, mottled appearance, and it takes three years for them to acquire full adult plumage. Their eventual wingspan will be 43 inches (109 cm). Juveniles lack the white spots at the tips of the flight feathers, and have brown spotting on their underparts.

DISTINCTIVE SOUND The call of the Mew Gull has been likened to the miaowing sound made by a cat! They also have a more guttural call note.

Ring-billed Gull

FAMILY Laridae
SPECIES *Larus delawarensis*
LENGTH 17½ in (44 cm)
HABITAT Coasts/inland waters
CLUTCH SIZE 3

DISTRIBUTION Central Canada east to Newfoundland in summer. Resident in the north-western United States and the Great Lakes. Overwinters across much of the south.

THE MOST DISTINCTIVE feature of this gull is the dark tip around its bill, which is otherwise yellow in color. The legs too are yellow, and its basic coloration corresponds to that of other species. There is a narrow red area of bare skin encircling the eyes. Although young birds fledge with blackish bills, the distinctive dark tip will be apparent here by their first winter. They will grow to have a wingspan of 48 inches (122 cm). Ring-billed Gulls are a relatively common and adaptable species, eating a variety of invertebrates and also scavenging on occasions.

WIDESPREAD The Ring-billed may be the most common North American gull, with its population comprising nearly four million birds.

Glaucous Gull

FAMILY Laridae

SPECIES *Larus hyperboreus*

LENGTH 27 in (69 cm)

HABITAT Coasts/open sea

CLUTCH SIZE 2–3

DISTRIBUTION Breeds in western Alaska, and resident from here down to Washington. Winter range extends southward via California into Mexico.

THESE GULLS are unusual in breeding exclusively in the far north, often on the Arctic tundra if not along the coast. Their large size, with a wingspan of 60 inches (152 cm), and very pale coloration help to distinguish them from other species. They have glaucous-gray plumage over the back and wings, with the rest of the body being white. Pale brown streaking on the head is apparent in the winter, with the sexes being identical in appearance. It will take four years for young birds to gain their adult plumage.

AGGRESSIVE The Glaucous Gull is a predatory species, which will seize eggs and nestlings of other birds, and harries sea ducks to drop fish.

Great Black-backed Gull

FAMILY Laridae

SPECIES *Larus marinus*

LENGTH 30 in (76 cm)

HABITAT Coasts/lakes

CLUTCH SIZE 2–3

DISTRIBUTION The Labrador coast to Newfoundland in summer. Resident to North Carolina, inland to the Great Lakes, wintering south to Florida.

THESE LARGE AND AGGRESSIVE gulls have expanded their range from the coast, moving inland and they have now started to colonize the area adjacent to the Great Lakes. Although they eat fish and are well-recognized as nest-raiders, these gulls will also visit garbage dumps regularly in search of food. The extensive black plumage over its back and wings, combined with its large size and wingspan of 65 inches (165 cm), helps to identify the Great Black-backed Gull. The bill is yellow, with a red spot.

BEHAVIOR Great Black-backed Gulls are social, usually breeding in colonies, and noisy by nature.

Franklin's Gull

FAMILY Laridae
SPECIES *Larus pipixcan*
LENGTH 14½ in (37 cm)
HABITAT Marshland
CLUTCH SIZE 3

DISTRIBUTION From Alberta in Canada, south to Utah, northern Colorado, and western Nevada. Westward to southwestern Ontario and South Dakota. Overwinters on South America's Pacific coast.

THIS SUMMER VISITOR to North America frequents inland areas of the continent, breeding in colonies on marshland in the prairies. They construct their nests using reeds and grasses, with the incubation period, shared by both members of the pair, lasting for approximately three weeks. Franklin's Gull is a red-billed, black-headed species with prominent crescents of white feathering above and below each eye, but in winter the black hood is restricted to the back of the head, with white plumage extending back from the bill. Its wingspan is 36 inches (91 cm).

HABITAT The nest of these gulls is constructed on the ground, often concealed in among reeds. Invertebrates of various types feature prominently in their diet.

Bonaparte's Gull

FAMILY Laridae
SPECIES *Larus philadelphia*
LENGTH 13½ in (34 cm)
HABITAT Coasts/forest
CLUTCH SIZE 2–3

DISTRIBUTION In summer from Alaska to Hudson Bay, not breeding within the United States. Winters on the west and east United States' coasts, and across the southeast.

THESE SMALL GULLS, having a wingspan of only 33 inches (84 cm), breed amid the coniferous forests of the far north, near lakes and marshy areas where they can find food. Pairs construct their nests in the branches up to 20 ft (6 m) above the ground. Over the winter, on the coast, they will prey on fish and marine invertebrates. Sometimes, these gulls are harassed by jaegers, which will steal their catch from them as they return to shore. Their flight is very graceful, being rather like that of terns.

SEASONAL CHANGE Bonaparte's Gulls only have black plumage on the head in summer. It becomes white, apart from dark markings behind the eye in the area of the ear coverts, during the fall.

Black-legged Kittiwake

FAMILY Laridae

SPECIES *Rissa tridactyla*

LENGTH 17 in (43 cm)

HABITAT Coasts/sea

CLUTCH SIZE 2

DISTRIBUTION Summer visitor to the northwestern and northeastern coasts. Resident around Newfoundland. Occurs off the west coast and to South Carolina in winter.

THESE OCEAN-DWELLING GULLS are not normally encountered inland, as they spend most of their lives at sea. Very adept in flight, with a wingspan of 36 inches (91 cm), Black-legged Kittiwakes can swim well, aided by their webbed feet. They do not feed exclusively at the surface, however, but can dive effectively as well, pursuing fish here. On occasions, they may even be seen following fishing boats, feeding on the waste thrown overboard. The bill is yellow, and the legs and feet are black, which aids their identification. When breeding, pairs nest in large colonies on very narrow and often quite exposed cliff faces, constructing a nest of seaweed for their eggs. It is thought that by choosing a very narrow shelf, they protect themselves against potential predators. Young birds have a black collar around the back of the neck, with a black area behind each eye, with the bill too being black. It takes three years for them to acquire full adult plumage.

COMMON COMBINATION Like many gulls, Black-legged Kittiwakes have a white head and body, offset against gray wings.

Least Tern

FAMILY Sternidae

SPECIES *Sterna antillarum*

LENGTH 9 in (23 cm)

HABITAT Beaches/sandbars

CLUTCH SIZE 2–3

DISTRIBUTION The United States' Atlantic seaboard and Gulf Coast. Also southern California and inland parts of the United States. Overwinters from Mexico to South America.

THIS SUMMERTIME visitor ranks as the smallest of the terns likely to be seen in North America, having a wingspan of only 20 inches (51 cm). When in breeding condition, adults develop a black cap on the head, extending down the nape, with a white triangular area on the forehead. The sexes are identical in appearance. Pairs nest in loose colonies, breeding on the ground.

MARINE DIET A male Least Tern displays to a hen with a fish in his bill. In addition to small fish, they also eat crustaceans.

Caspian Tern

FAMILY Sternidae

SPECIES *Sterna caspia*

LENGTH 21 in (53 cm)

HABITAT Coasts/inland waters

CLUTCH SIZE 2–4

DISTRIBUTION Very scattered breeding range from southern Alaska down to California and east to North Carolina. Resident along the Gulf coast.

AT THE OTHER EXTREME from the Least Tern, the Caspian is the largest tern occurring on the continent, with a wingspan measurement of 50 inches (127 cm). This species can be recognized in breeding condition by its black cap and pale gray body coloration, which is darker over the wings. In winter plumage, these terns have white streaking on the head. They have a distinctive pattern of feeding, usually diving down from high above the surface of the water in search of fish.

NESTING The eggs are laid on the ground in a simple scrape, hatching after three weeks.

Elegant Tern

FAMILY Laridae
SPECIES *Sterna elegans*
LENGTH 17 in (43 cm)
HABITAT Coasts
CLUTCH SIZE 1–2

DISTRIBUTION Southern California and Mexico in summer, but may wander further north. Winters along the Pacific coast of South America.

THESE TERNS HAVE a particularly slender body shape, and a drooping black crest that is apparent on the back of the head. This coloration extends forward around the eyes. The bill is orange-red, and the legs are a distinctive shade of black. Nesting takes place on islands, and there can sometimes be hundreds of birds in these breeding colonies. Young birds are easily distinguished by their yellow bill color.

PLUMAGE From January until June, Elegant Terns have a black cap on the head. The front area here then becomes white with blackish spotting in summer. They have a wingspan of 34 inches (86 cm).

Forster's Tern

FAMILY Laridae
SPECIES *Sterna forsteri*
LENGTH 14 in (36 cm)
HABITAT Beaches/marshland
CLUTCH SIZE 3–4

DISTRIBUTION Sporadic summer range from Alberta to the northern United States. Occurs along the United States' Pacific and Atlantic coasts and on the Gulf coast.

FORSTER'S TERNS often nest in inland areas in the vicinity of marshes during the summer months, although in some areas, they also breed on the coast. They not only feed on fish, but also invertebrates. The black cap which is again a feature of these terns is quite extensive, running back from the bill below the eyes and down the neck. Their wingspan measures 31 inches (79 cm).

COLORATION The bill color of Foster's Tern is yellowish-orange with a fairly prominent dark tip, while the legs are a deeper shade of orange.

Common Tern

FAMILY Laridae

SPECIES *Sterna hirundo*

LENGTH 14½ in (37 cm)

HABITAT Beaches/inland waters

CLUTCH SIZE 2–3

DISTRIBUTION Breeds from the southern Northwest Territories and eastern Alberta to Newfoundland, and down the eastern United States' coast. Overwinters from Texas southward.

THE RANGE OF the Common Tern is more extensive than that of any North American species, although it is only likely to be seen here during the summer months. Pairs will nest on the ground at this stage, seeking sandy areas close to water for this purpose, including islands. Both adult birds take turns to incubate the eggs, which should hatch after a period of about 24 days. It will then be a further month before the young birds start to fly themselves. At this stage, they have brownish rather than gray markings on the back and it will be three years before they finally attain adult plumage and a wingspan of 30 inches (76 cm). Adults have a bright red bill, with a dark tip. They dive into the water to obtain food, and feed largely on small fish.

FLIGHT The long tail streamers associated with this species can be seen here, extending beyond the forked tail feathers, back from beyond the flight feathers. Common Terns depart for the winter between August and September each year, and start to return in April.

Royal Tern

FAMILY Laridae

SPECIES *Sterna maxima*

LENGTH 20 in (51 cm)

HABITAT Beaches/coastal marshland

CLUTCH SIZE 1–2

DISTRIBUTION North to New England in summer; resident from North Carolina to Mexico. Also in southern California and in central Florida in winter.

HUGE NUMBERS OF THESE TERNS congregate at the start of the breeding season and nest communally on small sandy islands and sandbars adjacent to the sea. The Royal Tern is a relatively large species, with a wingspan of 41 inches (104 cm), displaying a black cap with a small crest at the back of the head. Its forehead then becomes white with some spotting as the breeding season progresses. The large bill is a pale orange shade, with the legs being blackish. The sexes cannot be distinguished visually.

MARINE HABITAT A Royal Tern in winter plumage standing in the shallows. These birds feed further out at sea, diving from the sky.

Gull-billed Tern

FAMILY Laridae
SPECIES *Sterna nilotica*
LENGTH 14 in (36 cm)
HABITAT Marshland/beaches
CLUTCH SIZE 3–5

DISTRIBUTION Summertime in southern California, and Atlantic coast from New Jersey down to eastern Florida. Also from Louisiana to western Florida. Overwinters in Central

UNLIKE MANY TERNS, the Gull-billed has a black beak. In breeding plumage, there is an extensive black area present on the crown of the head, which extends back down the neck. Adult birds have a wingspan of 34 inches (86 cm). These terns catch flying insects on the wing, and also feed on fish and amphibians, but they do not dive into the water to catch their prey.

BEHAVIOR These Gull-billed Terns are facing away from the direction of the prevailing wind, sheltering on the sand as far as possible.

Sandwich Tern

FAMILY Laridae
SPECIES *Sterna sandvicensis*
LENGTH 15 in (38 cm)
HABITAT Beaches/islands
CLUTCH SIZE 1–2

DISTRIBUTION Eastern seaboard from Maryland south to Georgia and western Florida to Louisiana in summer. Resident around Florida and the Gulf coast of Texas, overwintering further south.

A BLACK CAP with a ragged crest at the back of the head, and black legs help to identify this species. Its bill is black, with a yellow tip, and its wingspan is 31 inches (79 cm). The Sandwich Tern is a plunge diver, as far as obtaining food is concerned, feeding on shoals of fish and squid. It breeds in large colonies.

PLUMAGE This Sandwich Tern is in summer plumage. The black forehead grows less conspicuous, appearing speckled over the winter months.

Arctic Tern

FAMILY Laridae
SPECIES *Sterna paradisaea*
LENGTH 15½ in (39 cm)
HABITAT Tundra/beaches
CLUTCH SIZE 2–4

DISTRIBUTION Summer visitor across Alaska to the western coast of Hudson Bay, then around the coast to Newfoundland and Nova Scotia. Overwinters in the Antarctic region.

THESE TERNS FLY almost from one end of the earth to the other, being summer visitors to the far north. They are the ultimate long-distance migrants, although having flown south to the Antarctic, young Arctic Terns may not immediately undertake the return journey north during the following spring, remaining here instead until the following year. Distinguishing Arctic Terns is not especially easy, however, as they are quite similar both to the Common and Forster's Terns, although they have a slightly longer wingspan of 34 inches (86 cm). The bill coloration can

help, as this is only red in the case of the Arctic Tern, lacking the black tip seen in Common Terns. They have a black cap in breeding plumage, with pale gray coloration on the body and a whitish area around the cheeks. These terns are very defensive of their nest sites, not hesitating to mob any would-be intruders, with the aim of driving them away. Their eggs take about 21 days to hatch, with the chicks flying once they are about three weeks old. They will then attain full adult plumage in their third year.

ON THE DEFENSIVE Even other terns that approach too closely to a nesting pair will be driven away.

Brown Noddy

FAMILY Laridae
SPECIES *Anous stolidus*
LENGTH 15½ in (39 cm)
HABITAT Coasts/sea
CLUTCH SIZE 1–2

DISTRIBUTION Summer range in North America restricted to the Dry Tortugas in Florida, with these birds overwintering out across the tropical area of the Atlantic Ocean.

NODDIES ARE a group of tropical terns, with this species ranging further north into temperate latitudes. The Brown Noddy is grayish-brown in color with a dark bill and legs. The top of the head is paler, however, and white rings of plumage encircle the eyes. The sexes are similar. They have long wings with a span of 32 inches (81 cm) and a wedge-shaped tail. These terns spend most of their time skimming over the sea, catching food at the surface, but they come ashore to breed.

NESTING BEHAVIOR Brown Noddies frequently lay on the ground, especially on small islands, but equally, a pair may build a nest in the branches of a shrub or tree, often using seaweed.

Black Tern

FAMILY Laridae
SPECIES *Childonias niger*
LENGTH 9¾ in (25 cm)
HABITAT Lakes/marshland
CLUTCH SIZE 2–3

DISTRIBUTION Breeds from Alberta down across southern Canada to the northern United States, reaching south as far as California, eastward to Colorado. Overwinters in tropical Pacific waters.

THESE TERNS are mainly black in color, with gray wings with a span of 24 inches (61 cm) and a relatively short, forked tail. They also have white undertail coverts. During the winter, the appearance of Black Terns is transformed, so they then appear mainly white, with an area of black plumage on the head and at the shoulders. They are unlikely to be seen in North America at this stage, although occasional individuals have been recorded as overwintering off the Californian coast. Black Terns breed inland, in small colonies using mats of floating vegetation to support their eggs. They feed not by diving, but by hovering and scooping up prey directly from the water's surface. Small fish and invertebrates such as crustaceans feature in their diet.

SURVEYING These birds will catch insects in flight, hawking them in a similar way to swallows.

GENDER DIFFERENCES The bill of the male Black Skimmer is larger and longer than that of the hen.

Black Skimmer

FAMILY Laridae
SPECIES *Rynchops niger*
LENGTH 18 in (46 cm)
HABITAT Beaches/sea
CLUTCH SIZE 4–5

DISTRIBUTION Summer range includes inland parts of California and from Massachusetts to Virginia. Resident from here along the coast to Central America, and on the Californian coast.

ONE OF THE MOST striking features of the Black Skimmer is the length of its upper and lower bills, with the latter being much longer. This is related to the way in which these birds feed, flying over the water, with the lower bill angled just below the surface. Once contact is made with a small fish, the bird clamps its upper bill down, enabling it to seize its prey. The bill itself is red at its base, and black along its length. Black Skimmers are seen almost entirely out over the sea, although they may move to inland waters if the sea becomes very rough. The head and nape are black during the summer, with the back and wings being dark while the underparts are white. In the winter, the lower neck becomes whitish. Sexing is straightforward on the basis of size, as cock birds are significantly larger than hens. The average wingspan is 44 inches (112 cm). Breeding takes place on sandy areas of the coast.

Razorbill

FAMILY Alcidae
SPECIES *Alca torda*
LENGTH 17 in (43 cm)
HABITAT Cliffs/open sea
CLUTCH SIZE 1

DISTRIBUTION Breeds around Greenland, Baffin Island, and northeastern Canada. Resident in an area from Newfoundland to Nova Scotia, and also overwinters further south, off the Atlantic coast.

THE FLATTENED, broad shape of the bill helps to identify this species. It is also short, being encircled by a white band. The head, back, wings, and throat are black, apart from white edging across the rear of the wings. The underparts are white too, with white feathering extending over the throat when Razorbills are in winter plumage. They are able to walk effectively on land, having a similar gait to that of a penguin. Furthermore, these seabirds are able to fly well, often skimming close to the waves, and they will dive too, down to depths of 60 ft (18 m), in search of squid, fish, and crustaceans. Razorbills often venture close inshore, even sometimes being seen in estuaries, and this leaves them vulnerable to oil spills. Pairs nest in colonies, often on cliffs, and prove to be quite noisy in such surroundings.

PLUMAGE CHANGES A white stripe runs from the eyes to the top of the bill when Razorbills are in breeding condition.

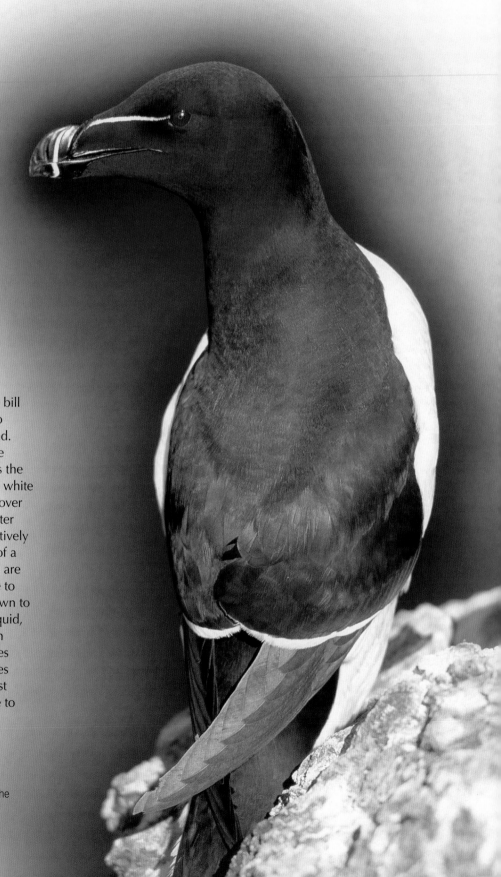

Pigeon Guillemot

FAMILY Alcidae
SPECIES *Cepphus columba*
LENGTH 13½ in (34 cm)
HABITAT Rocky shores/sea
CLUTCH SIZE 1–2

DISTRIBUTION Breeds from the northwestern coast of Alaska down to southern California. Also resident from southern Alaska down to British Columbia and northern Washington, and off California.

THESE GUILLEMOTS have a pointed black bill, with red legs and feet, which are webbed between the toes. Their appearance varies markedly through the year, as in breeding plumage, both sexes are predominantly black in color, aside from having white patches on their wings. In the winter, however, they are transformed to appear mainly white, with black coloration restricted to the wings, with black and white barring on the back and rump. Young birds resemble adults out of breeding color, but usually display barring on the head and neck as well. These seabirds take a varied diet, based on fish and marine invertebrates such as crustaceans, catching food beneath the waves. The incubation period for these guillemots lasts about 24 days, with both parents sharing this task.

SILHOUETTE The profile of the Pigeon Guillemot helps to explain its common name, with its body shape being similar to that of a pigeon.

Black Guillemot

FAMILY Alcidae
SPECIES *Cepphus grylle*
LENGTH 13 in (33 cm)
HABITAT Rocky shores/open sea
CLUTCH SIZE 1–2

DISTRIBUTION Resident off the northern coast of Alaska, and from Greenland to north-eastern Canada, overwintering in adjacent areas. Regularly sighted down to Long Island.

THIS SPECIES is very similar to the Pigeon Guillemot in appearance, but in breeding plumage they can be distinguished as there is no black plumage intruding into the white patches on the Black Guillemot's wings. Their area of distribution is also quite separate, apart from a small area of overlap on Alaska's west coast. In winter plumage, the difference in wing coloration is apparent, although again, Black Guillemots become predominantly white. Their wings are quite broad and rounded in shape, not only enabling these birds to fly effectively, but also to swim well underwater, combining with their webbed feet to act as flippers.

CHARACTERISTIC POSE It is not uncommon to see Black Guillemots resting on rocks and calling loudly. They utter a series of whistles and high-pitched sounds resembling screams.

Rhinoceros Auklet

FAMILY Alcidae

SPECIES *Cerorhinca monocerata*

LENGTH 15 in (38 cm)

HABITAT Sea

CLUTCH SIZE 1

DISTRIBUTION Southern visitor from the Aleutians down to British Columbia. Ranges as far south as Baja California in winter, being resident in some localities further north.

THE APPEARANCE of the Rhinoceros Auklet is transformed at the end of the nesting period, when birds of both sexes lose the horn-like growth on the bill. This helps to confirm that these particular auklets are most closely related to puffins rather than auks. The white down-curving streaks of plumage on each side of the lower bill become less apparent over the winter period, as do the stripes extending back above the eyes. Further evidence of the affiliations of the Rhinoceros Auklet is apparent from its breeding habits since pairs choose to nest in underground burrows, just like puffins. They also lay just a single egg. Both parents share the task of incubation. It will take about 35 days for the egg to hatch, and it is likely to be a further 42 days before the youngster will leave the nest.

DISTINCTIVE FEATURE The small, vertical horn at the base of the upper bill explains the name of these seabirds.

Dovekie

FAMILY Alcidae

SPECIES *Alle alle*

LENGTH 8¼ in (21 cm)

HABITAT Rocky coasts/open sea

CLUTCH SIZE 1

DISTRIBUTION Resident in western Alaska and Greenland, with its summer range extending further north. Overwinters in the Atlantic as far south as North Carolina.

ALSO KNOWN AS the Little Auk, this species has a distinctive small, stubby bill. Its head, breast, back, and wings are black in color, with the underparts being white. In winter plumage, however, the breast is white, and white plumage extends up behind the eyes. The sexes are identical in appearance. When swimming, their compact body shape is very apparent, and they will dive regularly. Their main breeding grounds are not on the North American mainland, but in Greenland and parts of Europe and Russia within the Arctic Circle.

SEA-BASED Dovekies are most common off the coast of northern Canada, but they tend not to come close inshore. However, groups, known as "wrecks," may sometimes be driven inland by fierce gales.

Common Murre

FAMILY Alcidae

SPECIES *Uria aalge*

LENGTH 17½ in (44 cm)

HABITAT Open sea

CLUTCH SIZE 1

DISTRIBUTION Summer visitor to northwestern Alaska and northeastern Canada. Resident to California and Nova Scotia. Overwinters offshore in the Pacific and Atlantic Oceans.

MURRES ARE now the largest living alcid, following the extinction of the Great Auk in the mid-1800s, and is also known as the Common Guillemot. The Common Murre's appearance resembles that of most seabirds, being predominantly black and white in color. In the summer, pairs nest on narrow cliff ledges where they are relatively safe from predators such as gulls that are inclined to steal eggs and young chicks. The egg of the Common Murre is pear-shaped to prevent it from rolling off the edge of the ledge.

COLORATION When in breeding plumage, the Common Murre has a white stripe running from each side of the bill across the cheeks to the eyes. The sexes are indistinguishable in appearance.

Thick-billed Murre

FAMILY Alcidae

SPECIES *Uria lomvia*

LENGTH 18 in (46 cm)

HABITAT Open sea

CLUTCH SIZE 1

DISTRIBUTION Breeds in northwestern Alaska, overwintering off the southern coast. Also around Baffin Bay in the east; resident in northeastern Canada around Newfoundland, ranging further south in winter.

IT CAN BE DIFFICULT to distinguish this species from the Common Murre, although it is slightly larger in size. The bill is shorter and thicker, as its name implies, but perhaps the most evident distinguishing feature is the white edging running along the bill. This pale streak is apparent throughout the year. Thick-billed Murres nest in large colonies on traditional breeding grounds, with both members of the pair sharing the task of incubation, which lasts for about 30 days. After a month, the chick will ultimately plunge off the cliff face directly into the sea below, accompanied by its parents. At this stage, young Thick-billed Murres can be identified by the whitish plumage on the throat, which resembles that of adults in winter plumage.

CAMOUFLAGED The solitary egg blends in well against the rocky cliffs where these murres nest.

Atlantic Puffin

FAMILY Alcidae
SPECIES *Fratercula arctica*
LENGTH 12½ in (32 cm)
HABITAT Open sea
CLUTCH SIZE 1

DISTRIBUTION Western Greenland down to the coast of Newfoundland, mainly resident from here to Nova Scotia. Overwinters in the Atlantic and further south, to North Carolina.

THIS IS THE ONLY species of puffin occurring on the Atlantic seaboard of North America. Its brightly colored and large, distinctive bill means that it can be identified easily. These puffins nest in colonies in underground burrows, although they may occasionally nest under rocks. The hen incubates alone, with the male bringing her food. The incubation period lasts for about 30 days, with the young fledging after about seven weeks. The bill is grayish at this stage, and its distinctive coloration develops slowly, over the course of about five years.

MARINE BIRDS Atlantic Puffins live mainly at sea, only coming ashore for breeding purposes each spring, and prefer to nest on islands.

Horned Puffin

FAMILY Alcidae
SPECIES *Fratercula corniculata*
LENGTH 15 in (38 cm)
HABITAT Open sea
CLUTCH SIZE 1

DISTRIBUTION Breeds along the western and southern coasts of Alaska, and through the Aleutians. Overwinters in the Gulf of Alaska westward and southward, in the ocean.

LARGER IN SIZE than its Atlantic counterpart, the Horned Puffin also has a bigger bill. The so-called "horn" is created by the wattle that extends vertically upward from each eye. These disappear at the end of the breeding season and the face becomes significantly darker, being grayish. The bill plates that result in the brightly colored bills of breeding birds of both sexes are also shed at this stage, so the bill assumes a greenish-brown appearance with a dull red tip over the winter. Young birds have a relatively slender grayish-black bill on fledging.

NESTING These puffins nest in colonies, frequently on cliff faces where the hens lay in among the rocks, or sometimes further inland, often under boulders.

Tufted Puffin

FAMILY Alcidae

SPECIES *Fratercula cirrhata*

LENGTH 15 in (38 cm)

HABITAT Open sea

CLUTCH SIZE 1

DISTRIBUTION Summer visitor off the northwestern coast of Alaska right down along the coast to central California. Overwinters in this region, but occurring away from land.

IN ADDITION TO the brightly colored orange bill, with its notched appearance and colorful base, these puffins also develop remarkable tufts of blond plumes extending back on each side of the head from above the eyes down the sides of the neck. The legs and large, webbed feet are also orange; the feet have dark claws. There are prominent white areas on each side of the head at this stage, with the remainder of the plumage being black. In the winter, the white feathering and the plumes are lost, with these puffins then appearing predominately black. The bill is also much duller, losing the prominent pale olive-green area on the upper mandible, so it appears constricted at its base here. Tufted Puffins spend most of their lives at sea, only coming ashore in the summer to breed. Their nesting burrows can be up to 7 ft (2 m) in length.

DISTINCTIVE APPEARANCE The bright coloration of the puffin's bill when in breeding condition means that this group of birds are sometimes misleadingly described as sea parrots. They feed not just on fish, but will also catch crustaceans as well as various molluscs.

ATLANTIC PUFFIN (*see* p.174) The sand eels this Atlantic Puffin has caught form a significant part of a puffin's diet, and indiscriminate commercial fishing can impact adversely on the food supply of puffins and other seabirds.

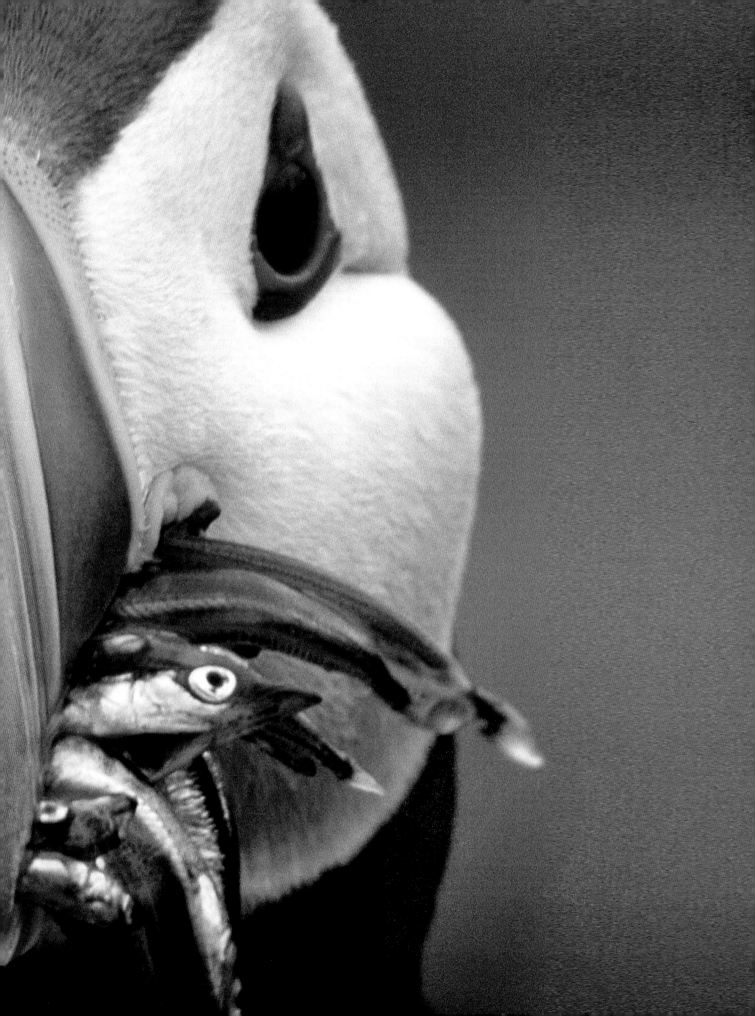

COLUMBIFORMES

Pigeons and doves

These birds are generally common, in localities from city centers to rural areas. One of the reasons for their success is their breeding habits. They are opportunistic, nesting whenever conditions are favorable rather than having a set breeding season. They can also rear their young easily. Both members of a pair produce a special protein-rich secretion called crop milk, which they will regurgitate for their offspring. Should a nest fail, however, then a pair will usually start to breed again very quickly afterward. There is no strict division between pigeons and doves—pigeons simply tend to be larger in size.

Band-tailed Pigeon

FAMILY Columbidae
SPECIES *Columba fasciata*
LENGTH 14½ in (37 cm)
HABITAT Forest
CLUTCH SIZE 1

DISTRIBUTION Summer visitor to British Columbia and southwestern parts of the United States. Resident down the west coast.

THE BAND-TAILED ranks as the largest of the pigeons occurring in North America, and is also distinguishable by the band across its tail. Pairs breed in woodland areas, building a loose nest of twigs often as high as 40 ft (12 m) off the ground. Young Band-tailed Pigeons lack the white collar around the neck.

DISTINCTIVE MARKINGS There is a narrow white collar around the neck, with a wider area of iridescent green plumage below. The yellow bill has a black tip.

Eurasian Collared Dove

FAMILY Columbidae
SPECIES *Streptopelia decaocto*
LENGTH 12½ in (32 cm)
HABITAT Suburbs/urban areas
CLUTCH SIZE 2

DISTRIBUTION Expanding its range rapidly. Extends across southern United States, to North Dakota and South Carolina.

THESE DOVES are not native to North America. Their ancestors were released in the Bahamas during the 1970s and spread to Florida, with their United States range having since expanded considerably. They have adapted well to urban living, particularly in the suburbs where they are regular visitors to backyard bird tables, nesting on buildings or in trees.

COLORATION Eurasian Collared Doves have generally grayish-buff plumage, with a black half collar around the neck.

Rock Dove (or Feral Pigeon)

FAMILY Columbidae

SPECIES *Columba livia*

LENGTH 12½ in (32 cm)

HABITAT Parks/urban areas

CLUTCH SIZE 2

DISTRIBUTION Found throughout the entire continent, as far north as southern Canada, from British Columbia across to Newfoundland. Isolated populations further north.

THIS IS ANOTHER species that was introduced to the United States from Europe, evolving back from domesticated stock to a free-living existence, which is why these pigeons are now described as feral, hence their alternative name. Nevertheless, they are often seen in close proximity to buildings both in cities and further out in the suburbs. Rock Doves are very effective scavengers, eating virtually anything discarded such as old sandwiches. They often congregate in parks and similar public places, seeking scraps of food from visitors here. They will also descend on bird tables, eating a variety of seeds. They will breed virtually in any month of the year, particularly in southern parts of their range. The cock will pursue his intended mate, engaging in a bowing display. The nest may be built in a tree or shrub, but equally, it may be on an outside ledge or even inside an abandoned building. Both members of the pair take turns incubating their white eggs for a period lasting for two weeks or so.

PLUMAGE In this pair of blue Rock Doves, the larger cock bird (*left*) displays great iridescence.

Inca Dove

FAMILY Columbidae

SPECIES *Columbina inca*

LENGTH 8¼ in (21 cm)

HABITAT Parks/suburbs

CLUTCH SIZE 2

DISTRIBUTION Resident from California, southern Nevada, and Utah across the southern states to eastern Louisiana. Summer range extends further north in parts of New Mexico.

SCALLOPED-EDGING to the plumage serves to identify this relatively small dove. It associates closely with people, frequently being seen feeding in backyard areas and may nest on the ledges of buildings. Incubation and fledging take about 12 and 14 days respectively, and although the young are similar to their parents in terms of coloration, they lack the darker edging to the individual feathers, making them easy to identify. Several broods—perhaps as many as five—may be reared in rapid succession by a pair of Inca Doves under favorable conditions.

ORIGINS The name of the Inca Dove reveals that its origins lie further south across the Mexican border, in the lands that used to be occupied by the Inca people.

Common Ground Dove

FAMILY Columbidae

SPECIES *Columbina passerina*

LENGTH 6½ in (17 cm)

HABITAT Brushland/woodland

CLUTCH SIZE 2

DISTRIBUTION Occurs across the southern states. Resident in southern California, Arizona, and New Mexico. Also southern Texas, and from Mississippi via Florida to South Carolina.

THESE SMALL DOVES are often seen in pairs, searching the ground for seeds, which make up the bulk of their diet. In flight, it is possible to spot the rusty-red coloration of their flight feathers. Pairs usually nest quite low down, often in bushes.

IDENTIFICATION A yellow base to the bill helps to identify these small doves, along with random dark markings on the wings.

White-winged Dove

FAMILY Columbidae
SPECIES *Zenaida asiatica*
LENGTH 11½ in (29 cm)
HABITAT Arid areas
CLUTCH SIZE 2

DISTRIBUTION Summer range from southern California and Oklahoma, north to Colorado. Resident further south, and along the Gulf coast, overwintering here too. Resident in southern Florida.

THE RANGE OF THE White-winged Dove varies through the year. They can be recognized by their grayish-brown coloration, and the prominent white areas of plumage running down the outer side of each wing. There is also a bright blue area of bare skin encircling each eye, and the tail id relatively short. Pairs construct a typical flimsy platform of twigs and other vegetation for a nest, often in a tree, but they may alternatively choose a large cactus for this purpose, which gives them added protection against predators. Their eggs will take approximately two weeks to hatch, with the chicks fledging after a similar period.

FEEDING White-winged Doves have a varied diet, feeding not just on seeds of various types, but also on the berries and fruits of cactus.

Mourning Dove

FAMILY Columbidae
SPECIES *Zenaida macroura*
LENGTH 12 in (30 cm)
HABITAT Brushland/suburbs
CLUTCH SIZE 2

DISTRIBUTION Summer range across southern Canada and down into the northern-central United States. Resident in parts of Newfoundland down the east coast, and across much of the United States.

THE MOURNFUL CALLS of this dove account for its common name. Mourning Doves can be sexed by sight, since cock birds are brighter in color than hens, with a pinkish suffusion to the brown feathering on the breast. The lack of blue skin around the eyes, and a longer narrow tail helps to distinguish the Mourning Dove from its White-winged relative in areas where they overlap. Pairs will nest in a bush or tree, and they are likely to rear several broods in succession.

BEHAVIOR Mourning Doves often search for food on the ground and visit bird tables. The spotted patterning on the wings can differ from one individual to another.

CUCULIFORMES

Roadrunners, anis, and cuckoos

One of the best-known characteristics of cuckoos relates to their breeding behavior, as they have a reputation for being brood-parasites, with hens laying their eggs in the nests of other birds. Although many species reproduce in this way, however, some members of this family actually rear their own young. In virtually all cases, although the sexes are similar in appearance, hens can be identified by their slightly larger size. A few species, such as the Greater Roadrunner, are terrestrial in their habits, but still display the fairly slim body shape and long tail associated with their arboreal relatives.

Greater Roadrunner

FAMILY Cuculidae
SPECIES *Geococcyx californianus*
LENGTH 23 in (58 cm)
HABITAT Arid scrub/woodland
CLUTCH SIZE 3–6

DISTRIBUTION Resident across much of southwestern United States, extending north to Nevada and surrounding states.

THE POWERFUL LEGS of the Greater Roadrunner allow these birds to run at speeds equivalent to 15 mph (24 kph) if in danger, preferring to run back to cover rather than flying. They are essentially predatory in their feeding habits, hunting down reptiles, invertebrates, rodents, and even small birds, although they will also eat fruit and berries.

HUNTING ADAPTATION Alert by nature, this species has keen eyesight which allows it to spot quarry—often small reptiles.

Groove-billed Ani

FAMILY Cuculidae
SPECIES *Crotophaga sulcirostris*
LENGTH 13½ in (34 cm)
HABITAT Woodland/scrubland
CLUTCH SIZE 3–6

DISTRIBUTION Summer visitor to southern Texas. Overwinters eastward along the Texas coast, occasionally even recorded from Florida.

THE INDENTATIONS on the bill explain the Groove-billed Ani's name. Unlike most cuckoos, these birds are highly social, with several pairs often nesting communally together. They may hunt invertebrates and small vertebrates in the trees, as well as chasing prey on the ground. Anis are not strong fliers, often gliding between perches.

APPEARANCE Black in color, with some hints of green or purple iridescence in the plumage, the Groove-billed Ani has a prominent bill and a long tail.

Oriental Cuckoo

FAMILY Cuculidae

SPECIES *Cuculus saturatus*

LENGTH 12½ in (32 cm)

HABITAT Woodland near water

CLUTCH SIZE 1 per nest

DISTRIBUTION Seen in summer on the Aleutian Islands, the Pribilofs, and St. Lawrence, and on the Alaskan mainland. Overwinters in Asia, with its range extending to Australia.

AS ITS NAME SUGGESTS, this species originates from Asia, being only a summer visitor. Two different color morphs exist, differing widely in appearance. In the case of the gray morph, the plumage is gray over the head, becoming darker over the back and wings, and lighter on the chest, with the lower underparts being barred. The hepatic morph is heavily barred, and reddish-brown in color above, with the lower underparts tending to display brown barring on a whitish background. Oriental Cuckoos feed on invertebrates and fruit. They are parasitic in their breeding habits, with hens laying individual eggs in the nests of other birds which then rear the cuckoo chicks.

GENDER DIFFERENCES Cock birds of this species are usually gray, but gray hens are sometimes recorded.

Yellow-billed Cuckoo

FAMILY Cuculidae

SPECIES *Coccyzus americanus*

LENGTH 12 in (30 cm)

HABITAT Woodland near water

CLUTCH SIZE 2–4

DISTRIBUTION Summer visitor mainly to eastern parts of the United States, from the Great Lakes to Florida and east to Arizona. Overwinters in South America, to Argentina.

GRAYISH-BROWN UPPERPARTS help to identify the Yellow-billed Cuckoo, with the underparts being a dull white. The slightly curved beak is mainly yellow, but with black markings on the upper bill. This species is easily overlooked in woodland areas, with its coloration helping it to disguise its presence. Pairs build a platform of twigs, leaves, and similar material in a tree, with the hen laying her greenish-blue eggs here. Incubation lasts for approximately 14 days, being shared by both members of the pair. The young cuckoos will be able to leave the nest after a similar interval, having been reared largely on invertebrates, with caterpillars being a favorite food. Berries will also be eaten when they are in season. Young Yellow-billed Cuckoos differ from adults by having a completely dark bill.

PLUMAGE The rufous coloration in each wing is visible here, but is more evident when the cuckoo is flying.

Black-billed Cuckoo

FAMILY Cuculidae

SPECIES *Coccyzus erythropthalmus*

LENGTH 12 in (30 cm)

HABITAT Woodland near water

CLUTCH SIZE 2–5

DISTRIBUTION Breeds from Nova Scotia to Tennessee. Also westward across to Alberta and Kansas. Overwinters in northern parts of South America.

THE BLACK-BILLED CUCKOO overlaps in some parts of its range with its Yellow-billed cousin, but it can be distinguished by the color of its upperparts, which are a purer shade of brown. The bill is also black. Young Black-billed Cuckoos have a buff-colored throat and undertail coverts when they first leave the nest, with the white tips to the individual tail feathers being less distinctive. The skin around the eyes is paler in color too. Although these cuckoos are not uncommon in some areas, their population has declined in various parts of their range. It can actually be quite difficult to spot these birds in their woodland habitat, as they are shy by nature. Pairs rear their own young, with their breeding biology corresponding to that of the Yellow-billed Cuckoo.

IDENTIFICATION The bright red area of bare skin encircling the eyes helps to distinguish this species.

STRIGIFORMES

Owls

Owls have large, rounded faces, with their eyes being directed forward to aid their hunting abilities. Their bill is narrow yet powerful, and they have strong feet equipped with sharp claws that help them to grab their prey. Small rodents are a major item in the diet of many species. Owls are essentially nocturnal hunters, as this is the time when rodents emerge from their daytime hiding places. After eating a meal, an owl regurgitates the skin, bones, and other indigestible remains of its prey. These form a so-called "owl's pellet," confirming the presence of these birds in an area.

Northern Pygmy Owl

FAMILY Strigidae
SPECIES *Glaucidium gnoma*
LENGTH 6¾ in (17 cm)
HABITAT Dense woodland
CLUTCH SIZE 2–6

DISTRIBUTION Largely resident from Washington south to California. Also east to Colorado and New Mexico, with the species' range continuing into Central America.

LIVING IN DENSE woodland, these small owls are often active during the day. Nevertheless, their small size and tendency to perch high up in trees means that they can be hard to observe. However, the commotion resulting from other forest birds mobbing one of these owls may betray itspresence in an area.

PLUMAGE Coloration varies through this owl's range. Browner individuals like this bird originate from the Pacific coastal region and northern areas.

Elf Owl

FAMILY Strigidae
SPECIES *Micrathene whitneyi*
LENGTH 5¾ in (14 cm)
HABITAT Arid areas
CLUTCH SIZE 3–4

DISTRIBUTION Summertime visitor to the southwest United States, being sighted in California, southern Arizona, New Mexico, and southwestern Texas. Resident in Baja California; overwinters in Mexico.

THIS IS THE smallest species of owl occurring in North America. Its size and nocturnal habits mean that it is very hard to observe. Furthermore, studies suggest that it appears to be quite scarce through its range, and it is now almost extinct in California.

DIET The Elf Owl feeds on large invertebrates such as beetles and grasshoppers. It may also tackle dangerous prey such as scorpions.

Boreal Owl

FAMILY Strigidae
SPECIES *Aegolius funereus*
LENGTH 10 in (25 cm)
HABITAT Dense forest
CLUTCH SIZE 3–7

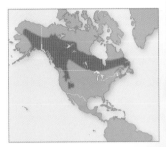

DISTRIBUTION Resident from Alaska eastward, south of Hudson Bay, extending to Newfoundland. Range is largely Canadian, but occurs in the west south to Colorado and New Mexico.

A SPECIES OF THE far north, the Boreal Owl occurs in remote areas of forest. It is often quite conspicuous in such localities when sighted, however, having little instinctive fear of people. Its basic coloration is a milk chocolate-brown, with white streaking on the underparts, combined with spotting on the head, back, and wings. The eyes are a rich shade of yellow, and its bill is horn in color, and narrow in shape. These owls hunt small rodents and will also prey on large invertebrates. They remain resident in their territory throughout the year, with a pair breeding in a suitable hollow within a tree trunk, often high off the ground. The hen incubates the eggs on her own, with hatching taking about a month.

BUILD Boreal Owls have a relatively large head and a stocky body. Their white wing markings are highly individual.

Burrowing Owl

FAMILY Strigidae
SPECIES *Speotyto cunicularia*
LENGTH 9½ in (24 cm)
HABITAT Open country
CLUTCH SIZE 5–7

DISTRIBUTION Southern-central Canada through the western United States in the summer. Resident in Florida, and from California along the Mexican border.

THESE OWLS are unusual because they nest underground in suitable burrows, being found in areas where tree cover is scarce. This means that they can range into suburban areas, inhabiting golf courses for example. They do not tunnel underground themselves, but take over burrows excavated by rodents such as ground squirrels, or may even adopt those dug by gopher tortoises in Florida.

DIET Burrowing Owls catch rodents and invertebrates on the ground. They may be seen on fence posts, scanning the surrounding area for prey.

Eastern Screech Owl

FAMILY Strigidae

SPECIES *Megascops asio*

LENGTH 8½ in (22 cm)

HABITAT Woodland/parks

CLUTCH SIZE 4–6

DISTRIBUTION Resident throughout the eastern part of the United States, just extending across the Canadian border to the northwest and as far as Montana in the west.

HABITAT When nesting, the Eastern Screech Owl will seek out a hollow in a tree, either a natural hole or one created by woodpeckers.

THE COLORATION OF the Eastern Screech Owl is quite variable, ranging from gray to a reddish-brown, with vertical black streaking on the underparts. The eyes are yellow, and there are distinctive ear tufts of plumage on the head. Individuals of widely differing coloration may arise in the same brood, being seen in the same area, although generally those from the Great Plains are grayer overall than those found in the southeastern parts of their range. Nocturnal hunters, these owls may sometimes dive to catch fish.

Flammulated Owl

FAMILY Strigidae
SPECIES *Otus flammeolus*
LENGTH 6¾ in (17 cm)
HABITAT Oak and pine wood
CLUTCH SIZE 3–4

DISTRIBUTION Summer visitor from southern British Columbia through western Texas and into Mexico. Scattered populations in southern California; overwinters in Central America.

THE SMALL SIZE of the Flammulated Owl, combined with its coloration, means that it is not an easy species to detect, particularly in view of its nocturnal habits. Its eyes are dark, with its plumage being grayish-brown, lighter on the underparts. White speckling and rusty markings help to conceal its presence. It has short ear tufts, which are also not very conspicuous. In some areas, a number of pairs may effectively share a territory, nesting in close proximity to each other in suitable tree holes.

HUNTING Flammulated Owls will catch a wide range of prey under cover of darkness.

Western Screech Owl

FAMILY Strigidae
SPECIES *Megascops kennicottii*
LENGTH 8½ in (22 cm)
HABITAT Woodland/parks
CLUTCH SIZE 4–6

DISTRIBUTION Extends from the extreme south of Alaska along the British Columbian coast, and more widely across the western United States to western Texas and into Central America.

THE WESTERN SCREECH OWL is very closely related to its Eastern cousin, although now they are regarded as being separate species. A point of distinction is that the Western Screech Owl is encountered in desert areas. Its plumage tends to be gray, again displaying vertical streaking and dark cross-hatching on the underparts. Northwestern populations tend to have a more brownish tone to their plumage overall. The bill is a dark yellowish-green color, with a white tip. They feed largely on rodents and even invertebrates.

WELL HIDDEN It can be quite easy to overlook the presence of a Western Screech Owl, because its plumage provides very effective day-time camouflage.

Whiskered Screech Owl

FAMILY Strigidae
SPECIES *Otus trichopsis*
LENGTH 7¼ in (18 cm)
HABITAT Mountain forest
CLUTCH SIZE 3–4

DISTRIBUTION Range restricted to a very small part of southeastern Arizona, adjacent to the border with New Mexico. Extends from here across the Mexican border.

THESE RELATIVELY small owls have streaked and barred grayish plumage, with whitish eyebrows above their bright yellowish-orange eyes. This enables them to blend in very effectively again the dark woodland areas which they inhabit. They are found in coniferous and deciduous forests, typically at an altitude of 4,000–6,000 ft (1,220–1,830 m). They emerge under cover of darkness to hunt prey, which consists largely of invertebrates, including spiders, although they are opportunistic in their feeding habits, and will also hunt small rodents and lizards. Their name derives from the bristle-like plumage around the base of the bill, reminiscent of whiskers. Pairs nest in tree hollows.

DISTINCTIVE The calls of the Whiskered Screech Owl are quite eerie, echoing through the forest. The short ear tufts are not apparent, lying flat in the case of this individual.

Short-eared Owl

FAMILY Strigidae
SPECIES *Asio flammeus*
LENGTH 15 in (38 cm)
HABITAT Open country
CLUTCH SIZE 5–9

DISTRIBUTION Alaska and most of northern Canada in summer. Resident in northwestern parts of the United States—ranging more widely in winter—but not in the southeast.

THE FACE OF THIS OWL appears rounded, due partly to its very short ear tufts. The Short-eared is a relatively common and also easily seen species, compared with some other members of the family, since it is active during the day. During the winter, these owls may form small flocks. They may even hunt collectively, flying back and forth across an area, looking for rodents, which make up the bulk of their diet. Pairs nest on the ground, choosing a well-concealed area for this purpose. The eggs hatch after about three weeks, with the young fledging approximately six weeks later.

PLUMAGE Mottled brown above, with streaking on the underparts, are identifying characteristics of this species, although the exact patterning differs between individuals.

Barn Owl

FAMILY Strigidae
SPECIES *Tyto alba*
LENGTH 16 in (41 cm)
HABITAT Farmland/cliffs
CLUTCH SIZE 5–11

DISTRIBUTION Resident in western, southern, and eastern areas of the United States, extending further north in the summer, and west to Canada.

IDENTIFIYING FEATURE
The down-curved, sharp but narrow bill of the Barn Owl is clearly apparent here.

ELEGANT AND EASILY IDENTIFIABLE thanks to its distinctive coloration, the Barn Owl may be seen out hunting from dusk onward. The back is tan with grayish markings, with the face and underparts being whitish, with some dark speckling on the underparts. It is possible to sex these owls on the basis of their coloration, since males are lighter in terms of their overall coloration, compared with females. Although the species used to roost on cliffs, it has adapted to the spread of agriculture by adopting barns for this purpose, breeding as well as roosting in this type of environment. The hen incubates the eggs on her own, with hatching taking about 35 days. The young birds should grow rapidly and will leave the nest for the first time once they reach eight weeks of age. Rodents, in the guise of rats and mice, are their favored prey.

BARN OWL A keen sense of sight is vital to these birds, helping them to locate potential prey as they swoop over the ground. The position of their eyes right at the front of the face allows them to target their quarry very accurately.

Long-eared Owl

FAMILY Strigidae
SPECIES *Asio otus*
LENGTH 15 in (38 cm)
HABITAT Dense woodland
CLUTCH SIZE 3–8

DISTRIBUTION Breeds across southern Canada apart from the west. Resident in the northwestern United States, extending in a narrow band across the continent. Winter visitor to the south.

IN SPITE OF THIS OWL'S NAME, the areas of plumage on the top of the head are not related to the ear openings, but simply tufts of long feathers. Unusually, these owls may sometimes be encountered in small groups, although they are quiet by nature and not easy to observe, even when hunting their rodent prey. The presence of a Long-eared Owl in an area of woodland may, however, be revealed by smaller birds, which swarm angrily around, trying to drive it away.

FEATHERS In flight, the ear tufts of the Long-eared Owl are held flattened against the head. The depth of coloration of this owl's plumage varies, with some being a richer tawny shade than others.

Great Horned Owl

FAMILY Strigidae
SPECIES *Bubo virginianus*
LENGTH 22 in (56 cm)
HABITAT Forest, open desert, urban areas
CLUTCH SIZE 2–4

DISTRIBUTION This owl has a massive range, being resident over the entire North American continent except the extreme north, extending down to Mexico.

THE MOST WIDELY DISTRIBUTED of the North American owls, the Great Horned Owl is at home in a wide variety of habitats, even nesting successfully in urban spaces such as parks. Its extensive distribution partly reflects the fact that it is highly adaptable in its feeding habits. A wide variety of mammals, including squirrels, may fall prey to these predators, as well as other birds up to the size of geese. They are not always easy to spot, however, because they are essentially nocturnal in their habits, resting quietly during the day.

HORNS The feather tufts on the head of this Great Horned Owl are flattened, rather than being held erect.

Northern Hawk Owl

FAMILY Strigidae
SPECIES *Surnia ulula*
LENGTH 16 in (41 cm)
HABITAT Coniferous forest
CLUTCH SIZE 3–7

DISTRIBUTION Essentially resident over northern parts of North America, from Alaska, south of Hudson Bay, eastward to Newfoundland.

INSULATION The feet of the Northern Hawk Owl are well-feathered, helping to protect against the wintertime cold.

THE DESCRIPTION OF "hawk owl" refers to the relatively long flight feathers of these birds. Like other species found within the Arctic Circle, where there can be almost constant darkness or daylight depending on the season, the Northern Hawk Owl may be observed hunting both during the day and at night. Lemmings and other rodents feature prominently in its diet, but it may also catch small birds too, especially in the winter when the ground is carpeted with snow, making rodents harder to find. Pairs breed in the spring, sometimes adopting the nest of another bird such as a woodpecker for this purpose. The incubation period lasts for just over three weeks, with the young owls fledging by the time they are five weeks of age. Their plumage is much duller at this stage. Although mostly resident to the far north, the Northern Hawk Owl may be seen in the United States.

Great Gray Owl

FAMILY Strigidae
SPECIES *Strix nebulosa*
LENGTH 27 in (69 cm)
HABITAT Dense forest
CLUTCH SIZE 2–5

DISTRIBUTION Resident in eastern Alaska and northwestern Canada, south of Hudson Bay, just across the United States' border here. Extends to Wyoming in the west.

AS ITS NAME SUGGESTS, the Great Gray Owl is the largest species of owl occurring in North America. Even the facial disks, which are the flattened areas on each side of the face, are grayish in color, with some darker, concentric markings evident here too. There is a white area on the chin on each side of the face, with a central black area. The narrow bill is a pale shade of greenish-yellow, with the eyes being pale yellow. The plumage on the body is grayish with streaks and barring. Especially in the far north of its range, the Great Gray Owl may be seen hunting during the day, seeking rodents and mice which constitute most of its diet; further south, it is strictly nocturnal, only emerging from its daytime roost under cover of darkness. These owls often take over the nests of birds of prey, although they also nest on cliffs.

DISTINCTIVE SHAPE The flattened, circular face of the Great Gray Owl is clearly apparent in this photograph.

Barred Owl

FAMILY Strigidae
SPECIES *Strix varia*
LENGTH 21 in (53 cm)
HABITAT Dense woodland/ swamp
CLUTCH SIZE 3–4

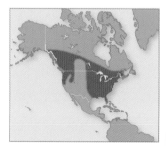

DISTRIBUTION Ranges from British Columbia eastward to Nova Scotia, down to northern California and southeastern parts of the United States.

BARRING ACROSS the upper chest is very evident in the case of this species, which is brownish-gray in terms of its overall coloration. In contrast, the underparts are streaked. It has a stocky appearance overall, with a short tail. The varied calls of the Barred Owl may reveal its presence in a forest, often being uttered during hours of daylight. Aside from their typical hooting calls, more unusual and distinctive are the cackling notes which these owls often make. Barred Owls feed mainly on mice.

IDENTIFICATION A rounded head, dark eyes, and a relatively pale bill are characteristic features of the Barred Owl. The gray facial disks are highlighted with black borders.

Northern Saw-whet Owl

FAMILY Strigidae

SPECIES *Aegolius acadicus*

LENGTH 8 in (20 cm)

HABITAT Dense forest

CLUTCH SIZE 4–7

DISTRIBUTION Resident in southern British Columbia, and in summer, eastward across the rest of Canada. Resident mainly in the western and eastern United States, but seen elsewhere too.

THESE SMALL OWLS have brown upperparts with white streaking particularly on the forehead and crown. Their underparts are much whiter, broken by reddish-brown streaks. They have a compact body shape, emphasized by their short tail and long wings. Their eyes are yellow, and their bill black. This secretive species inhabits areas of dense woodland, and hides away during the daytime. Northern Saw-whet Owls are so-called because of the sounds of their calls. They feed on small rodents and invertebrates. When breeding, a pair will occupy a nest hole that may have originally been created by a woodpecker, or a natural cavity in a tree. The white eggs are incubated by the hen, and hatch after about four weeks.

HABITAT Coniferous forests are home to these owls, although they may also be found in mixed woodland areas.

Snowy Owl

FAMILY Strigidae

SPECIES *Nyctea scandiaca*

LENGTH 23 in (58 cm)

HABITAT Tundra/open country

CLUTCH SIZE 5–9

DISTRIBUTION Ranges extensively across the far north, being resident here on the mainland. Overwinters widely across much of Canada, apart from the east, crossing into the northern United States.

THE SEXES CAN BE distinguished in this species because mature cock birds are almost pure white. In contrast, adult female and young Snowy Owls of both sexes will display quite heavy black barring on their bodies. Living within the Arctic Circle means that during the summer months, when it is permanently light, these owls will often choose to hunt during the day, eating carrion too. In the absence of trees, pairs nest on the ground. The hen incubates the eggs on her own, with hatching taking just over four weeks.

ADAPTATION Feathering continues down to cover the toes, enabling Snowy Owls to walk over snow in the winter and helping to protect them from frostbite.

SNOWY OWL AND LEMMING Lemmings form the central part of the Snowy Owl's diet, but the population of these rodents fluctuates on a seven-year cycle, increasing and then collapsing. Few chicks are reared in the lean years.

CAPRIMULGIFORMES

Nightjars and nighthawks

As their common name suggests, these birds are shy, and they are secretive in their habits, often nocturnal by nature. They typically emerge under cover of darkness to catch cicadas, moths, and other invertebrates that fly at night. They spend much of the daytime resting on the ground, where their plumage helps to conceal their presence. A remarkable attribute of some species is the way in which they can survive adverse weather conditions, particularly severe cold spells, by becoming torpid. Their metabolism falls but, like hibernating reptiles, they become active again when conditions improve.

Lesser Nighthawk

FAMILY Caprimulgidae
SPECIES *Chordeiles acutipennis*
LENGTH 8½ in (22 cm)
HABITAT Arid scrubland
CLUTCH SIZE 2

DISTRIBUTION Southwestern United States in the summer. Overwinters and resident from northwestern Mexico down to South America.

THIS SPECIES is a summertime visitor to the United States, being the only member of the family to breed here. Lesser Nighthawks arrive from the start of March onward, although they are not easy to observe. Instead, their presence is more likely to be revealed by the trilling calls of cock birds, which are uttered around dusk.

DIFFERENCE The white stripe on the cock bird's throat, as seen in this case, helps to distinguish the sexes. The plumage here is buff in hens and immature birds.

Chuck-will's-Widow

FAMILY Caprimulgidae
SPECIES *Caprimulgus carolinensis*
LENGTH 12 in (30 cm)
HABITAT Dense woodland
CLUTCH SIZE 2

DISTRIBUTION Widespread across southern states in summer; winters in Florida, the Caribbean, and Central America.

THIS IS LARGEST of the nightjars occurring in the United States, with cock birds being bigger than their mates. The wide gape of these birds enables them to catch large flying insects, including moths. They start to leave for their wintering grounds from mid-August, and will have largely disappeared by late October.

NOCTURNAL During the day, these nightjars rest on or near the ground, with their cryptic plumage providing excellent camouflage.

Whip-poor-will

FAMILY Caprimulgidae

SPECIES *Caprimulgus vociferus*

LENGTH 9¾ in (25 cm)

HABITAT Woodland

CLUTCH SIZE 2

DISTRIBUTION Centered on the northeast, extending to Canada, with a smaller population in the southwest United States, extending across the Mexican border. Some birds overwinter in Florida.

THIS NIGHTHAWK is so-called because of the sound of its song, which is most likely to be heard at dusk. The hen lays her whitish spotted eggs directly on the ground, with the nest site itself usually being concealed among vegetation. The chicks hatch after about three weeks.

SPREADING The range of the westerly population of the Whip-poor-will has expanded over recent years.

Common Poorwill

FAMILY Caprimulgidae

SPECIES *Phalaenoptilus nuttallii*

LENGTH 8 in (20 cm)

HABITAT Rocky scrub

CLUTCH SIZE 2

DISTRIBUTION Found over a wide area of western and central parts of the United States in the summer, and may be expanding its range further northeast.

THIS IS THE SMALLEST of the nightjars occurring in North America, and favors open countryside. The majority of the population will retreat southward into Mexico for the winter. Some individuals remain in the United States, however, and they have the ability to become dormant in cold weather, sheltering in travel rocks, where they can also remain largely hidden from predators.

CAMOUFLAGE The hunched posture of the Common Poorwill helps it to remain hidden on the ground. It will often hide away under rocks.

Pauraque

FAMILY Caprimulgidae

SPECIES *Nyctidromus albicollis*

LENGTH 12 in (30 cm)

HABITAT Brushland

CLUTCH SIZE 2

DISTRIBUTION Centered on Mexico, but extends across the United States' border into southern Texas, being recorded as far as north as Maverick, Bastrop, Grimes, and Calhoun counties.

THIS NIGHTJAR is most likely to be observed along roadsides at night, with its eyes glowing red when illuminated by headlights. It is drawn to hunt insects attracted by the lights here, catching them close to the ground in flight. During the day, Pauraques hide away in vegetation, and they also nest on the ground in a simple scrape lined with leaves.

DISTINCTIVE The long, slender body shape of the Pauraque helps to identify this species.

Common Nighthawk

FAMILY Caprimulgidae

SPECIES *Chordeiles minor*

LENGTH 9½ in (24 cm)

HABITAT Woodland/suburbs

CLUTCH SIZE 2

DISTRIBUTION Summertime visitor from northern parts of Canada, southward across the entire United States, apart from the southwest. Overwinters in South America, down to Argentina and Uruguay.

BLACKISH-BROWN mottling helps to conceal the presence of this nighthawk, breaking up its profile. Its has a very slender body, accentuated by its long, narrow wings and its forked tail. The hen lacks the white tail band seen in cocks, and has a buff-colored throat, as do young birds. There are some regional variations in coloration too, with those seen in northern parts of North America tending to be relatively gray, while those from the east are browner. Common Nighthawks usually nest on the ground.

BEHAVIOR Common Nighthawks hunt insects in flight, becoming active at dusk and hiding away travel vegetation during the daytime.

APODIFORMES

Swifts and hummingbirds

The hummingbirds represent the largest grouping within this Order, comprising some 340 species. They are found only in the Americas, being most numerous in northern South America. Despite their small size, most hummingbirds seen in the United States in summer will fly a considerable distance to their wintering grounds further south. They are also surprisingly aggressive. Much of their life is spent in flight, as is the case with swifts, the other group in this Order. Swifts feed on the wing, and undertake long migratory flights, although they are larger and their coloration is more subdued.

Chimney Swift

FAMILY Apodidae
SPECIES *Chaetura pelagica*
LENGTH 5 in (13 cm)
HABITAT Woodland/towns
CLUTCH SIZE 4–5

DISTRIBUTION Seen over much of eastern North America during the summer, ranging as far north as Canada. Overwinters in Peru and adjacent parts of South America.

CHIMNEY SWIFTS start to return to North America from mid-March onward, reaching the most northerly parts of their range by the middle of May. In the past, they built their nests, which consist of vegetation held together with their saliva, inside trees. However, they will also breed inside barns and, in more urban areas, they have adapted to use chimneys for this purpose, which explains their common name. They leave their breeding grounds by mid-November. Although brownish-black in color, the plumage of some individuals becomes even darker thanks to the soot within chimneys. These swifts do not roost on branches, but rest by clinging to vertical surfaces.

APPEARANCE These swifts are often described as resembling cigars with wings, thanks to their narrow, cylindrical body shape. They are very agile in flight.

Vaux's Swift

FAMILY Apodidae

SPECIES *Chaetura vauxi*

LENGTH 4¾ in (12 cm)

HABITAT Woodland

CLUTCH SIZE 4–5

DISTRIBUTION Mainly a summertime visitor to western North America, typically not seen to the east of the Rockies. Overwinters largely from central Mexico down to northern South America.

AN AERIAL ACROBAT, Vaux's Swift can climb and turn sharply when pursuing the swarms of flying insects that it hunts in the sky. Although pairs breed mainly in hollow trees, it is adapting to nesting in buildings, in the same manner as the related Chimney Swift.

SOCIABLE Vaux's Swift spends most of its time on the wing, forming huge flocks after the breeding season.

White-throated Swift

FAMILY Apodidae

SPECIES *Aeronautes saxatalis*

LENGTH 6½ in (17 cm)

HABITAT Mountain/cliffs

CLUTCH SIZE 3–6

DISTRIBUTION Breeding range extends over central western parts of North America. May overwinter as far north as California, extending southward into Mexico.

ALTHOUGH TRADITIONALLY favoring canyons and cliffs, White-throated Swifts are not uncommonly seen flying above freeways and increasingly in urban areas. They will cover large distances hunting various flies and other winged insects, catching them in flight. These swifts are one of the fastest and most agile of all North America's birds, able to reach a speed equivalent to 145 mph (234 kph).

RECOGNITION It is not always easy to pick out the distinctive white plumage of these swifts in flight, especially when the light is poor.

Blue-throated Hummingbird

FAMILY Trochilidae
SPECIES *Lampornis clemenciae*
LENGTH 5 in (13 cm)
HABITAT Wooded canyons
CLUTCH SIZE 2

DISTRIBUTION Two separate United States populations: Into Mexico from the southwest mountains; and the Chisos Mountains in western Texas.

THIS IS THE largest hummingbird occurring in North America, typically being observed in shady areas where there is water nearby. Here the hen will construct her small cup-shaped nest, in a well-hidden locality. She then incubates the eggs on her own; the young will remain here for the first three weeks of their lives.

GENDER DIFFERENCES Only the male Blue-throated Hummingbird displays the brilliant blue throat coloration. In hens the feathering here is a dusky gray shade.

Violet-crowned Hummingbird

FAMILY Trochilidae
SPECIES *Amazilia violiceps*
LENGTH 4½ in (11 cm)
HABITAT Wooded canyons
CLUTCH SIZE 2

DISTRIBUTION Extends from semiarid areas in the southwestern United States across the border into western Mexico.

THIS HUMMINGBIRD sometimes nests in the United States, but generally breeds in Mexico. During the winter, there is a small resident population that remains in southeastern Arizona. Occasionally, it is seen much further north, having been recorded as a vagrant in northern California. The plumage of both sexes is identical, which is unusual for hummingbirds.

IDENTIFICATION With a crown of violet-blue, whitish underparts, and a long red bill with a dark tip, this species is unmistakable.

Magnificent Hummingbird

FAMILY Trochilidae
SPECIES *Eugenes fulgens*
LENGTH 5¼ in (13 cm)
HABITAT Montane areas
CLUTCH SIZE 2

DISTRIBUTION Found in the mountains of southern Arizona, New Mexico, and Texas, in the United States, and ranges as far south as northeastern Nicaragua in Central America.

THIS IS A RELATIVELY large species of hummingbird, characterized also by its long yet relatively narrow bill. In spite of its size, its calls are quite loud, with the notes sometimes running together to create a chattering sound. As with its relations, the Magnificent Hummingbird uses its long bill to probe flowers for their nectar. This sugary solution provides them with a source of energy, while at the same time, they transfer pollen from flower to flower as they feed, which means that the blooms may be fertilized by these small birds. Tiny flies and similar insects are also hunted by hummingbirds, particularly when there are young in the nest, as they offer a valuable source of protein to aid the growth of the nestlings.

PLUMAGE The brilliant green iridescence of the plumage evident on the throat is a characteristic of the male.

Buff-bellied Hummingbird

FAMILY Trochilidae
SPECIES *Amazilia yucatanensis*
LENGTH 4¼ in (11 cm)
HABITAT Woodland edges
CLUTCH SIZE 2

DISTRIBUTION The North American race ranges from the lower Rio Grande Valley in southern Texas across the border to northeastern Mexico.

DISTINCTIVE Buff coloration on the underparts helps to identify these particular hummingbirds, along with the rufous-red coloration of their tail feathers.

THIS SPECIES BREEDS quite commonly in Texas, from April onward through the summer months, and then over the winter period they wander more widely, occasionally along the Gulf coast to Florida. As in the case of other hummingbirds, the Buff-bellied female is responsible for building the nest and rearing her brood by herself, with no help from the cock bird. The nest itself is made from plant fibers and lichens, being located on the bough of a tree well off the ground. The incubation period lasts for approximately 14 days, with the young birds growing rapidly and leaving the nest after a similar interval. At this stage, they all resemble adult females, but males can be distinguished by their black bills, which will ultimately gain their characteristic red coloration by the time they are a year old.

Black-chinned Hummingbird

FAMILY Trochilidae

SPECIES *Archilochus alexandri*

LENGTH 3¾ in (10 cm)

HABITAT Wooded lowland

CLUTCH SIZE 2

DISTRIBUTION Found as far north as southwestern British Columbia in the summer, down through the western parts of the United States into Mexico.

THESE HUMMINGBIRDS begin to arrive in their northern breeding grounds by May, and then start to move south again between August and September. They generally overwinter in Mexico, although individuals may occasionally be seen in south-eastern parts of the United States at this stage, too.

DIFFERENCES Only the cock displays the characteristic black plumage on the throat. This area is white in adult hens and the young of both sexes.

Ruby-throated Hummingbird

FAMILY Trochilidae

SPECIES *Archilochus colubris*

LENGTH 3¾ in (10 cm)

HABITAT Gardens

CLUTCH SIZE 2

DISTRIBUTION Occurs widely in eastern North America, and overwinters in Central America from Mexico south to Panama. Rarely seen in Florida in winter.

IN SPITE OF their small size, Ruby-throated Hummingbirds undertake a remarkable journey, migrating back and forth across the Gulf of Mexico every year. In North America, where they spend the summer, they are frequent garden visitors, often attracted by tubular nectar feeders. The red tips of such drinkers appeal to them in the same way as the color of their favorite flowers. Like most hummingbirds, however, they are quarrelsome by nature, chasing each other away from the source of food. Males are again also more colorful in appearance than hens.

MATURITY The ruby throat coloration is characteristic of mature males. Young cocks are whitish here until their first winter molt.

Lucifer Hummingbird

FAMILY Trochilidae

SPECIES *Calothorax lucifer*

LENGTH 3½ in (9 cm)

HABITAT Arid country

CLUTCH SIZE 2

DISTRIBUTION Mainly Mexico, but also some southern parts of the United States: Southeast Arizona, southwest New Mexico, and western Texas.

CONSPICUOUS Lucifer's Hummingbird is a summertime visitor to the United States, most likely to be observed in desert canyons.

THIS SPECIES can be identified partly by the shape of its bill, which is curved along its length rather than being straight. The description of "hummingbird" comes from the noise produced as these small birds fly. As they hover in front of a flower to extract its nectar, their wing beats are so fast that they are invisible to the naked eye. The sound of the movements of their wings in flight creates the humming noise, which is only audible at close quarters. Their aerial agility also allows hummingbirds to catch small invertebrates; these form an important part of their diet.

Broad-tailed Hummingbird

FAMILY Trochilidae

SPECIES *Selasphorus platycercus*

LENGTH 4 in (10 cm)

HABITAT Mountain meadow

CLUTCH SIZE 2

DISTRIBUTION Occurs widely in western and central North America during the summer. May be observed as far north as British Columbia.

AS ITS NAME SUGGESTS, the tail feathers of the Broad-tailed Hummingbird do not taper significantly along their length. When displaying to their would-be mates, males have a remarkable display flight, which sees them effectively dive down through the air, falling in this way for up to 30 ft (9 m). The hen builds the nest on her own, and raises the chicks by herself. After the breeding season, they start migrating southward again from August onward, and some individuals may be seen farther east at this stage.

GENDER DIFFERENCES Only the cock bird has the rose-red area on the throat. It is white with darker streaking in hens and immature birds.

Allen's Hummingbird

FAMILY Trochilidae
SPECIES *Selasphorus sasin*
LENGTH 3½ in (9 cm)
HABITAT Suburban woodland
CLUTCH SIZE 2

DISTRIBUTION Breeding range extends from southwestern Oregon to southern California, including the Channel Islands; overwinters in Mexico.

THESE HUMMINGBIRDS rank among the earliest migrants to reach North America from their wintering grounds to the south, arriving from January onward, but equally, they are among the first to depart, leaving again in June after the breeding season. Strangely, however, the population of Allen's Hummingbirds that is present on the islands off the coast of California remains resident there throughout the year. These used to comprise a separate group, and the birds forming the island population were fractionally larger in size with correspondingly longer bills. Recently, however, some of these island birds have crossed to the southern Californian mainland, where they can be seen throughout the year, sometimes breeding with their smaller migratory relatives.

IDENTIFICATION A female Allen's Hummingbird displays the characteristic speckling on the throat and buff coloration on the sides of the body.

Rufous Hummingbird

FAMILY Trochilidae
SPECIES *Selasphorus rufus*
LENGTH 3¾ in (10 cm)
HABITAT Woodland
CLUTCH SIZE 2

DISTRIBUTION Breeds in northwestern North America, overwintering in Mexico, although occasionally recorded in southeastern parts of the United States in winter.

IN THE CASE of this species, and other members of the genus, the typical buzzing sound associated with hummingbirds is created when they are flying rather than hovering. Rufous Hummingbirds are seen in their North America range from the end of February through until September.

COLORATION In keeping with its name, the male of this species is mainly rufous-brown in color.

Calliope Hummingbird

FAMILY Trochilidae
SPECIES *Stellula calliope*
LENGTH 3 in (8 cm)
HABITAT Mountain meadow
CLUTCH SIZE 2

DISTRIBUTION Breeds in inland western North America, and may sometimes be observed through the Great Plains and Texas in the fall; overwinters in Mexico.

THE SMALLEST breeding bird in North America, the Calliope Hummingbird is often to be seen in areas where there are woodland streams close to the upland meadows that provide flowers for these nectar feeders. They can be sexed easily: Although the males do not have a solid area of iridescent plumage forming the gorget, their throat area is clearly streaked with reflective purple.

IDENTIFICATION Hens have bronzy-green spots superimposed on white throat plumage. Young cocks are similar until they molt for the first time.

SPECTACULAR The display flight of the male Rufous Hummingbird is very distinctive. It will plunge in a J-shaped dive, rather than undertaking a U-shaped dive, as is seen in the case of the related Allen's Hummingbird.

Anna's Hummingbird

FAMILY Trochilidae
SPECIES *Calypte anna*
LENGTH 4 in (10 cm)
HABITAT Coastal areas/scrub
CLUTCH SIZE 2

DISTRIBUTION Breeds in western parts of North America from southwestern British Columbia south as far as northwestern Baja California, and into northern Mexico.

ANNA'S HUMMINGBIRD is present within the North American part of its range throughout the year, and the species may also be seen in northern Mexico at this stage. Cock birds have iridescent plumage covering the entire head, which is known as a helmet in this case.

DISTINCTIVE FLIGHT Anna's Hummingbird tends to hold its tail feathers closed, as shown here, when hovering in flight.

Costa's Hummingbird

FAMILY Trochilidae
SPECIES *Calypte costae*
LENGTH 3½ in (9 cm)
HABITAT Arid country
CLUTCH SIZE 2

DISTRIBUTION The breeding range is centered around the arid southwestern part of the United States, extending down to southwestern Baja California and northwestern Mexico.

IN SOME LIGHTS, the male of this species appears to have blackish plumage on the head. But in reality, the crown and gorget are violet-purple in color. Occurring essentially in desert areas, these hummingbirds seek out the nectar from plants such as red beardtongue, which is a particular favorite. Hen birds have dark upperparts of a brownish color, and are pale below.

SILHOUETTE Costa's Hummingbird has a stocky appearance, thanks to its thick neck, with its compact shape emphasized by its short tail.

Green Violet-ear

FAMILY Trochilidae
SPECIES *Colbri thassinus*
LENGTH 4¾ in (12 cm)
HABITAT Highland forest
CLUTCH SIZE 2

DISTRIBUTION The main range is from Mexico through South America to Argentina, but it may be seen occasionally in the southern United States.

THE GREEN VIOLET-EAR is a very widely distributed species, with its range extending across South America where hummingbirds as a family are most numerous. It is the nominate race of this species, known ornithologically as *Colibri thassinus thalassinus*, that may be seen in the United States, although it is more usually resident in the pine-oak forests of the Mexican highlands. These hummingbirds are most likely to be observed between May and August, with the majority of sightings being made in Texas. Their appearance is unmistakable, to the extent that they are unlikely to be mistaken for any other hummingbird normally seen in North America. Hens can be identified by having a less iridescent plumage than cock birds, being duller in appearance, with the violet coloration on the chest and behind the eyes also being reduced in size.

DISTINGUISHING FEATURE The violet-blue coloration on the chest is distinctive of this race of Green Violet-ear, along with its larger size.

GREEN VIOLET-EAR Hummingbirds in general bathe frequently, sometimes splashing in shallow pools of water or shower on branches when it is raining. This helps to keep their plumage in good condition.

Broad-billed Hummingbird

FAMILY Trochilidae
SPECIES *Cyanthus latirostris*
LENGTH 4 in (10 cm)
HABITAT Scrubland/gardens
CLUTCH SIZE 2

DISTRIBUTION The race of this species (*Cyanthus latirostris magicus*) seen in the United States extends south across the Mexican border to Nayarit, in the northwest of the country.

THE MAIN AREA where the Broad-billed Hummingbird occurs is in Mexico, but it is quite commonly seen in southern Arizona over the summer months, during which time it will often breed. A characteristic that sets it apart from other hummingbirds is that it tends to perch for longer periods.

COLORATION The bill of these hummingbirds is reddish-orange at its base, with those of hens being duller in color.

White-eared Hummingbird

FAMILY Trochilidae
SPECIES *Hylocharis leucotis*
LENGTH 4 in (10 cm)
HABITAT Montane areas
CLUTCH SIZE 2

DISTRIBUTION Although it may be seen over the summer in the mountains of southern Arizona, appearing as far east as Texas, the species' range is centered on Central America.

THIS SPECIES is generally encountered at quite high altitudes in North America; it typically visits between April and October. The hens will collect moss from the pine and oak woodland that is favored by the species, using this as the basis to create their cup-shaped nests. Conifer needles, lichens, and even spiders' webs may also be used in their construction.

DISTINCTIVE Dark plumage on the head, with a bright white stripe on each side of the face extending down the neck characterizes both sexes.

TROGONIFORMES

Trogons

Members of this family are found mainly in Central and South America, with the Elegant Trogon being the only representative that is encountered regularly in North America. Other members of the Order do, however, occur in parts of Africa and Asia, in tropical areas. Males of the family in particular have highly colorful plumage but this coloration is not always immediately evident in the dappled light of the forests in which they occur. They are sluggish birds by nature, and their lack of movement also means they can be difficult to spot in these surroundings. Their body is quite compact, and the tail feathers are long and broad.

Elegant Trogon

FAMILY Trogonidae
SPECIES *Trogon elegans*
LENGTH 12½ in (32 cm)
HABITAT Woodland
CLUTCH SIZE 3–4

DISTRIBUTION Most common in the United States in summer in southeastern Arizona and sometimes southern Texas; its main range is Central America.

THIS IS A RARE SPECIES in Arizona, and its population may decline during droughts. Numbers normally increase in the spring with an influx of breeding birds from across the Mexican border occurring in April. Breeding takes place in cavities in hollow trees, but these birds are susceptible to disturbance at this stage, and repeated, intrusive observations by birdwatchers have led to some nests being abandoned over recent years. Elegant Trogons become very scarce in the state over the winter months, but some do remain resident. They feed mainly on fruit, supplemented with some insect fare. Their calls consist of a series of croaks.

GENDER DIFFERENCES The cock, shown here, has much brighter and more iridescent green plumage compared to the hen and immature birds, which are a duller, olive-green.

CORACIIFORMES

Kingfishers

The majority of the ten Families forming this Order do not actually occur in North America, although some, such as the Todies (Todidae) and Motmots (Momotidae), are present elsewhere in the New World. In contrast, Hornbills (Bucerotidae) are confined to the Old World. Kingfishers as a group are represented, however, with a small number of species present, but their family is quite widely distributed over the continent. These birds tend to be found close to water. Although small fish are their main quarry, some kingfishers also catch insects, such as dragonflies, that occur in a similar type of environment.

Belted Kingfisher

FAMILY Alcedinidae
SPECIES *Ceryle alcyon*
LENGTH 13 in (33 cm)
HABITAT Near water
CLUTCH SIZE 5–8

DISTRIBUTION Resident in much of Canada, coastal British Columbia, and the western United States; also below South Dakota. It is a winter visitor in the extreme south.

THIS IS THE MOST widely distributed kingfisher in North America, typically inhabiting areas of woodland near water, ranging from streams to lakes. Solitary and territorial by nature, Belted Kingfishers only come together during the breeding season in the spring. Males can be easily distinguished from females by their lack of a rust-red band across the lower belly, so that this part of the body is entirely white. When seeking food, kingfishers have favored vantage points overlooking a stretch of water. Here they will remain, essentially immobile, until a fish or amphibian swims within reach. The kingfisher then dives down into the water, seizing its quarry in its powerful bill.

SOUND ALERT The calls of these kingfishers are loud and quite harsh, usually uttered during flight.

Ringed Kingfisher

FAMILY Alcedinidae
SPECIES *Ceryle torquata*
LENGTH 16 in (41 cm)
HABITAT Rivers/lakes
CLUTCH SIZE 4–5

DISTRIBUTION Occurs on the Pacific and Atlantic coasts of Mexico. Wanders across the United States border mainly in the vicinity of the Lower Rio Grande Valley, Texas.

THIS LARGE SPECIES of kingfisher has grayish-blue upperparts, and a similar area of plumage on the chest, separated by a white collar that extends around the neck. In the case of hens, there is also a further white patch on the lower chest, with a reddish area below. Cock birds can be easily distinguished as they are entirely reddish-brown on their underparts, aside from their white undertail feathers. Ringed Kingfishers are found near relatively large stretches of water, and hunt patiently, waiting for perhaps two hours or so without moving for fish and frogs to swim within range. They carry their prey back to a perch, banging it against the wood, and then swallowing it whole, head first. This

is a much safer method than eating a fish the other way around, when scales and sharp fins could catch in the throat and cause a blockage. Ringed Kingfishers also use their strong bills to excavate a breeding tunnel in a suitable bank, typically above a river. This can be up to 36 inches (91 cm) in length, being enlarged into a nesting chamber at the far end, where the hen will lay her eggs straight onto the ground.

GENDER DIFFERENCE Only the female Ringed Kingfisher displays a blue patch on the underparts. This species has a restricted range in North America.

MALE BELTED KINGFISHER WITH A FISH (*see* p. 218) Note the rough feathering of the crest. Kingfishers can see underwater, and can swim well while submerged, helping them to grab their quarry before returning to the surface.

Green Kingfisher

FAMILY Alcedinidae

SPECIES *Chloroceryle americana*

LENGTH 8¾ in (22 cm)

HABITAT Near streams

CLUTCH SIZE 4–6

DISTRIBUTION This is primarily a Central American species, but it is resident in both the extreme south of Arizona and also over a wider area of southern Texas.

THE CENTRAL AREA of distribution for this kingfisher lies further south, in Central America, but in areas of North America where it does occur, it can be seen throughout the year. However, Green Kingfishers are shy birds by nature and this, coupled with their relatively small size, means that they are not easy to observe. They also blend in well with the terrain where they occur, in areas of forest close to water. In common with other members of the family, they have a long, powerful bill that tapers to a sharp point. The head is a dark metallic green, as are the back and wings, and they have an insignificant crest at the back of the crown. There is a broad white stripe encircling the neck. Sexing is easy as the cock bird has a broad red breast band, while the hen displays green spotting over the breast along with much paler reddish-brown feathering in this area. Pairs nest in a bank, having created a tunnel that is about 36 inches (91 cm) in length. They do not use any nesting material: The hen simply lays her eggs on the bare earth. The eggs hatch after about three weeks, and the young leave the nest when they are approximately a month old.

BEHAVIOR The unmistakably colored Green Kingfisher frequently hunts from a relatively low vantage point above the water.

PICIFORMES

Honeyguides, toucans, and woodpeckers

Three families, comprising the Toucans (Ramphastidae), Honeyguides (Indicatoridae), and Woodpeckers (Picidae), make up this Order, but only the latter group occurs in North America. Woodpeckers are remarkably adaptable birds, because although they rely heavily on trees, both for food and nesting, a number are found in arid areas, where they have switched to using giant cacti for these purposes instead. Their claws and tails are sharp, enabling them to anchor on and move easily up a trunk. Furthermore, their bills can be used as drills and chisels, helping them to reach invertebrates lurking around the tree or cactus.

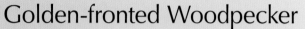

Golden-fronted Woodpecker

FAMILY Picidae

SPECIES *Melanerpes aurifrons*

LENGTH 9¾ in (25 cm)

HABITAT Dry brushland

CLUTCH SIZE 4–6

GOOD GRIP Like other members of the group, the Golden-fronted Woodpecker uses its stiff, pointed tail feathers and strong legs to support itself when climbing.

DISTRIBUTION Its range is centered on Texas, but it is also present in southwestern parts of Oklahoma. Occasionally recorded in New Mexico.

THIS IS A VERY colorful woodpecker. It has golden-yellow plumage above the bill and the underparts are buff, contrasting with the vivid black-and-white-striped markings on the back. The nape of the neck is golden-orange, and cock birds can be distinguished by the crimson-red area on the top of the head. Golden-fronted Woodpeckers eat not just insects, but also consume plant matter such as acorns. A pair will nest in a hollow in a dead tree, usually at some height from the ground. The incubation period lasts for about two weeks, with the young leaving the nest when they are a month old. At this stage, both sexes resemble the adult hen.

Red-bellied Woodpecker

FAMILY Picidae
SPECIES *Melanerpes carolinus*
LENGTH 9¼ in (24 cm)
HABITAT Mixed woodland
CLUTCH SIZE 4–6

DISTRIBUTION Resident over most of the southern United States, south of the Great Lakes, from the Dakotas via Oklahoma to central Texas.

THIS IS A VERY adaptable species, occurring over an extensive area and being found in a wide range of habitats from the swamps of Florida to backyards and city parks. It is also quite flexible in its feeding habits; in addition to eating invertebrates and seeds, in Florida, these woodpeckers may pierce oranges with their bills, and suck out the juice. The Red-bellied Woodpecker is similar to the Golden-fronted Woodpecker, but can be recognized by the deeper red plumage on the nape of the neck. This extends over the entire top of the head in the case of the cock bird. There is also reddish suffusion to the plumage of the underparts, as its name suggests.

VARIETY OF NESTS This woodpecker nests not just in tree holes, but may also utilize utility poles, boring into the wood with its bill.

Red-headed Woodpecker

FAMILY Picidae
SPECIES *Melanerpes erythrocephalus*
LENGTH 9¼ in (24 cm)
HABITAT Woodland
CLUTCH SIZE 4–6

DISTRIBUTION Occurs mainly in the east; west into Montana and New Mexico in summer. Western range is northeastern Texas; overwinters in the south.

THE NUMBERS of this woodpecker appear to be declining in some parts of its range, partly because the dead trees that it favors for nesting purposes are being felled as part of commercial forest management practices. This means that competition for the remaining available nest sites is intensified, with these birds losing out, sometimes to introduced species such as the European starling (*see* p. 307).

TWO BROODS In areas where they can breed unmolested, Red-headed Woodpeckers may raise a couple of broods of chicks in succession.

Acorn Woodpecker

FAMILY Picidae

SPECIES *Melanerpes formicivorus*

LENGTH 9 in (24 cm)

HABITAT Oak woodland

CLUTCH SIZE 4–5

DISTRIBUTION Western United States, from Oregon to California. Scattered locations in Colorado and Utah; present in Arizona and New Mexico, south to western Texas.

AS ITS NAME SUGGESTS, acorns play an important part in the diet of this woodpecker. It starts to collect them in the fall, and stores them in holes drilled in trees and posts through its territory. This enables these birds to build up a food store to last through the winter when there may be snow on the ground. Another unusual feature of the Acorn Woodpecker is that it lives in small flocks, possibly family groups, which share these feeding holes and refill them each year. When a pair is breeding, other members of the group may also bring food to help with the rearing of the young.

GENDER Sexing these woodpeckers is fairly straightforward. The forehead is white in the case of the cock, shown here, while the hens have a black band on their forehead.

Lewis's Woodpecker

FAMILY Picidae

SPECIES *Melanerpes lewis*

LENGTH 10¾ in (27 cm)

HABITAT Open woodland

CLUTCH SIZE 5–8

DISTRIBUTION Resident from Washington to California; visits British Columbia, South Dakota, and Nebraska in summer. Southwestern birds move closer to Mexico in winter.

THE FEEDING HABITS of Lewis's Woodpecker are somewhat unusual, in that it catches insects in flight, rather than boring into the bark to find them like most woodpeckers. When nesting, their chicks will hatch after a period of about 12 days, and then remain in the nest for a month or so. Young birds can be distinguished from their parents at this stage by their lack of a gray collar, and they have only a hint of red on their underparts, appearing duller in terms of their overall coloration.

HIGH NESTS This woodpecker favors tall trees, where it will breed in hollows often 60 ft (18 m) or more off the ground.

Gila Woodpecker

FAMILY Picidae

SPECIES *Melanerpes uropygialis*

LENGTH 9½ in (24 cm)

HABITAT Arid country

CLUTCH SIZE 3–6

DISTRIBUTION Southeastern California to Baja California and southern Arizona into Mexico. Recorded in Nevada.

DRY COUNTRYSIDE is home to the Gila Woodpecker, and rather than nesting and feeding in trees, it has adapted to thrive among the giant cactuses that grow within its range. It may bore into these with its bill, creating a secure nest site, often over 20 ft (6 m) off the ground. The sharp spines on the trunk of the cactus offer further protection from predators. Both cock and hen share the task of incubation, which lasts for approximately two weeks. The young woodpeckers will be ready to leave the nest when they are about a month old, and the adult birds may soon be nesting again. The Gila Woodpecker's relationship with the giant saguaro cactus is mutually beneficial as the bird helps to protect the cactus from attack by plagues of insects, hunting and

PRICKLY HOME The Gila Woodpecker regularly nests in giant cactus, but will use trees where available.

eating such pests and so helping to insure its long-term future. This is quite a conspicuous bird, with its loud calls attracting attention, and in some parts of its range, it is not an uncommon bird table visitor. There is very evident black and white barring across the back and wings, with the head and underparts being buff-gray in color. The white underside of their wings is apparent when they are in flight, and only cock birds display the crimson-red cap on the crown.

White-headed Woodpecker

FAMILY Picidae
SPECIES *Picoides albolarvatus*
LENGTH 9¾ in (25 cm)
HABITAT Coniferous forest
CLUTCH SIZE 3–5

DISTRIBUTION Southern British Columbia in Canada, to the southwestern United States, including mountains in southwestern California.

THE WHITE PLUMAGE on the head and throat of these woodpeckers enables them to be identified easily, with the rest of their plumage being entirely black, apart from a small white patch on each wing. The area at the back of the head is red in the case of cock birds. Unusually for woodpeckers, this species is a quiet bird, rarely betraying its presence in an area by hammering at the bark of trees with its bill. This means that the White-headed Woodpecker can be difficult to spot, particularly in the poorly lit, dense coniferous forest where it makes its home.

RELATIVELY COMMON The White-headed Woodpecker is not uncommon within its range, preferring to nest high up in pine trees, often 50 ft (15 m) or more above the ground.

Black-backed Woodpecker

FAMILY Picidae
SPECIES *Picoides arcticus*
LENGTH 9½ in (24 cm)
HABITAT Coniferous forest
CLUTCH SIZE 4–5

DISTRIBUTION Extending right across North America, from Newfoundland to southern Alaska, south to California in the west and New York state.

THE BACK OF THIS woodpecker is black, as its name suggests. Its head is also black, aside from a small white line behind each eye, and a broader white streak running across the cheeks from the bill. The flight feathers are speckled with white markings, and the flanks are barred. It is easy to distinguish the sexes in this case, as only the cock bird has the yellow cap on its head.

DEAD TREES These birds like to nest in a dead or dying tree, excavating a suitable nesting chamber. They move very easily up tree trunks using their specially adapted feet.

Red-cockaded Woodpecker

FAMILY Picidae

SPECIES *Picoides borealis*

LENGTH 8½ in (22 cm)

HABITAT Coniferous forest

CLUTCH SIZE 2–5

DISTRIBUTION Southeastern United States, from Virginia to Louisiana; not southern Florida. Scattered in Arkansas, eastern Texas, and southern Oklahoma.

AS THE MATURE TREES favored by the Red-cockaded Woodpecker are declining, so its numbers are falling as well, to the extent that it is now considered an endangered species. These woodpeckers prefer to nest in trees afflicted by heartwood disease, which is caused by a fungus, as this makes it easier to bore into them. But such trees are frequently felled at an early stage, because they are unhealthy. This then deprives the woodpeckers of nesting opportunities. An unusual feature of this woodpecker's breeding habits is that several pairs will nest communally, sharing a suitable tree. The hen incubates during the day, while the cock bird sits at night.

HEADDRESS The male woodpecker has a small red cocade behind each eye, although this is not easy to spot.

Downy Woodpecker

FAMILY Picidae

SPECIES *Picoides pubescens*

LENGTH 6¾ in (17 cm)

HABITAT Woodland

CLUTCH SIZE 4–7

DISTRIBUTION Occurs over much of North America, from central Alaska to Newfoundland, south to California, and reaching Florida and eastern Texas.

THE DOWNY WOODPECKER is the smallest member of this family occurring in North America, and is a very adaptable species, being found in a wide variety of habitats, including city parks and suburban areas. These woodpeckers may also be regular visitors to backyard bird tables, usually being attracted by nuts and suet balls. Their bills are short in comparison with other species. It is relatively easy to identify the sexes, as males have a red patch on the nape, which is absent in hens, and tend to be slightly larger as well. In the case of birds from the Pacific northwest, the black plumage on the back and underparts is replaced by grayish-brown feathering.

SHARED PARENTING Downy Woodpeckers breed in hollows in dead trees, and both parents share the task of incubation, which lasts about 14 days. The young fledge when they are just over three weeks of age. It is then not uncommon for the nesting pair to rear a second brood.

Ladder-backed Woodpecker

FAMILY Picidae

SPECIES *Picoides scalaris*

LENGTH 7¼ in (18 cm)

HABITAT Arid country

CLUTCH SIZE 4–5

DISTRIBUTION Southwestern United States: Central California, southern Nevada, Utah, and Colorado to northeastern Baja California,

THE NATURAL TERRAIN of the Ladder-backed Woodpecker is semi-desert, and it nests in this habitat by making holes into large, drought-resistant plants, such as yuccas, that are found in such areas. The woodpecker plays a valuable role in maintaining the health of such plants by feeding on agave beetle larvae, for example. On occasions, they may also use manmade structures, such as utility poles. It is a relatively small species, with a very distinctive pattern of fine black and white barring on its back. The facial feathering is buff with black markings, becoming more grayish on the underparts, with spotting evident on the flanks. It is easy to distinguish the sexes from some distance away, since while the crown of the cock bird is red, that of the female is black.

WELL-NAMED The common name of this woodpecker derives from the fact that the barring across the back is relatively horizontal, reminiscent of the steps of a ladder.

Three-toed Woodpecker

FAMILY Picidae

SPECIES *Picoides tridactylus*

LENGTH 8¾ in (22 cm)

HABITAT Coniferous forest

CLUTCH SIZE 4–5

DISTRIBUTION Occurs widely in North America, from Alaska to Newfoundland and south from Montana to Nevada and into northwestern New Mexico.

THE MAJORITY OF woodpeckers have four toes on each foot, two of which point upward, and two of which point down when the woodpecker is grasping the bark. An adaptation seen in some woodpeckers, including this one, is a change in the number of toes, enabling them to move up a tree more easily. This species has only three toes on each foot, all of which point forward, helping the bird to maintain its grip more easily. The sexes can be separated easily by sight, since only cock birds have a yellow cap.

UNDER THE BARK The Three-toed Woodpecker does not drill into the bark to obtain grubs and other insects. Instead, it chisels the bark off.

Hairy Woodpecker

FAMILY Picidae

SPECIES *Picoides villosus*

LENGTH 9¼ in (24 cm)

HABITAT Forest

CLUTCH SIZE 4–7

DISTRIBUTION Occurs widely from Alaska to southern New Mexico, and to Newfoundland. Also Florida to eastern-central Texas. Found in Central America.

THE HAIRY WOODPECKER has a white back and its wings are predominantly black but display individual white spotting at the edges. The underparts are also white. On the head there is a broad black stripe running through each eye on males and females, but only the cock birds display a red area on the nape of the neck.

This is quite a noisy species, using its bill not just to bore into the bark in search of insect life, but also banging to create a drumming sound. This banging is used by many woodpeckers as a way of marking their territories, although at ground level, it is not always easy to pinpoint the direction of the sound.

HIGH LIFE This adaptable species usually prefers areas of mature woodland, nesting high up in the dead limb of a tree.

DISTINCTIVE FEATHERS A Three-toed Woodpecker (*see* p. 228) on a branch clearly reveals the distinctive white barring that extends across the flight feathers of most members of this family of birds.

Red-naped Sapsucker

FAMILY Picidae
SPECIES *Sphyrapicus nuchalis*
LENGTH 8½ in (22 cm)
HABITAT Deciduous woodland
CLUTCH SIZE 4–6

DISTRIBUTION Mainly around the Rocky Mountains and the Great Basin, from southwestern Canada to the southwestern United States. Winters in Baja California and northern Mexico.

SAPSUCKERS ARE SO-CALLED because they will use their bills to burrow into trees to reach the sap. These woodpeckers also feed on insects and fruit. Clear red marking at the back of the head helps to distinguish this sapsucker from its close relatives. At one point, the Red-naped Sapsucker was believed to be simply a race of the Yellow-bellied Sapsucker, as was the Red-breasted Sapsucker, but these are each now regarded as valid species. Young Red-naped Sapsuckers lack the contrasting markings of their parents, and their plumage is predominantly brown when they fledge, after nearly a month in the nest. They will then achieve their adult coloration during their first winter.

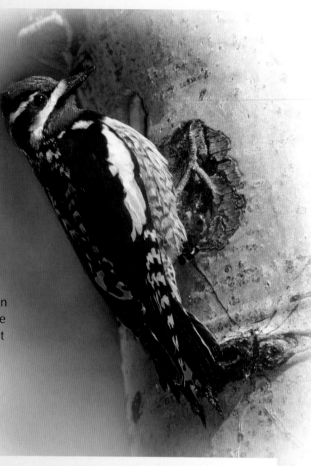

RED CHIN The Red-naped Sapsucker has a red chin; this area is white in the hen.

Red-breasted Sapsucker

FAMILY Picidae
SPECIES *Sphyrapicus ruber*
LENGTH 8½ in (22 cm)
HABITAT Mixed woodland
CLUTCH SIZE 4–6

DISTRIBUTION Coastal areas of southern Alaska and Oregon to the Sierra Nevada of southern California and western Nevada. Populations tend to move south in winter.

THE RED PLUMAGE in this species extends from around the throat down on to the chest. There is some variation in coloration between those birds from the northerly areas of North America, which display yellow spots on the lower underparts, and birds from further south, which are whiter in appearance. The Red-breasted Sapsucker also interbreeds with other sapsuckers.

NEST HOLES Sapsuckers nest in holes in dead trees, often at a considerable height off the ground. The incubation period is two weeks.

Williamson's Sapsucker

FAMILY Picidae

SPECIES *Sphyrapicus thyroideus*

LENGTH 8½ in (22 cm)

HABITAT Coniferous forest

CLUTCH SIZE 3–7

DISTRIBUTION From British Columbia south to northern Baja California, Arizona, and New Mexico. Overwinters in southern California and southern states into Mexico.

THIS IS THE LARGEST species of sapsucker and it has a very distinctive pale lemon-yellow coloration on the underside; the female is barred. When nesting, a pair will use a nest hole in a dead branch, and may return to the tree to breed again in the following year, creating a new nest site.

A COCK BIRD This male Williamson's Sapsucker clearly shows the pale lemon plumage on its belly.

Yellow-bellied Sapsucker

FAMILY Picidae

SPECIES *Sphyrapicus varius*

LENGTH 8½ in (22 cm)

HABITAT Deciduous forest

CLUTCH SIZE 4–6

DISTRIBUTION In summer it occurs widely from Alaska to Newfoundland and Nova Scotia. It overwinters in the southeastern United States and into Central America.

THIS SPECIES has yellow colored underparts and a prominent black breast band. Sapsuckers in general have relatively long wings, a characteristic that is emphasized by the long white band running down the edge of the wing. Sapsuckers drill into trees with their bills. This causes the sap to ooze out through the hole, and the sapsucker will drink this regularly as part of its diet.

RED MALE This is the male Yellow-bellied Sapsucker. Hens have white throats and their red plumage is restricted to the crown.

Pileated Woodpecker

FAMILY Picidae
SPECIES *Dryocopus pileatus*
LENGTH 16½ in (42 cm)
HABITAT Mature woodland
CLUTCH SIZE 3–5

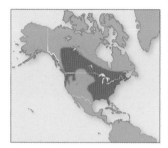

DISTRIBUTION Found in southern British Columbia to Nova Scotia, and central California, ranging from Illinois to Virginia, Florida, and Texas.

IT IS LIKELY that this is now the largest species of woodpecker occurring in North America, as in spite of a possible recent sighting, the Ivory-billed Woodpecker (*Campephilus principalis*) is believed to be extinct here. The Pileated Woodpecker is predominantly black, with a white stripe on each side of the face, extending down the neck. The plumage under the wings is also white, while the top of the head in both sexes is a brilliant red. This area of plumage is larger in the case of the cock, however, who also displays a red mustache. These woodpeckers favor mature trees, and may be seen in forested areas or more open parkland.

PERMANENT RESIDENTS This species remains resident in an area throughout the year. In the breeding season, they make nests in dead limbs of trees, up to 70 ft (21 m) off the ground.

Gilded Flicker

FAMILY Picidae
SPECIES *Colaptes chrysoides*
LENGTH 11½ in (29 cm)
HABITAT Arid country
CLUTCH SIZE 5–10

DISTRIBUTION Southwestern United States, from southeast California to Arizona and possibly New Mexico. Also occurs in Baja California.

THIS LARGE WOODPECKER has a grayish face with a cinnamon brown crown; cock birds are distinguished by their red mustache. They occur in dry country, often choosing to nest in a saguro cactus, its sharp spines providing some protection from predators. The eggs take about two weeks to hatch, and the chicks leave the nest after a further three weeks or so. Ants feature prominently in the diet of these woodpeckers, which hunt for their food on the ground. Aside from invertebrates, they will also eat some berries.

TREELESS HABITAT This woodpecker rarely hunts for invertebrates in or on the bark of trees as these are uncommon in its habitat.

Northern Flicker

FAMILY Picidae
SPECIES *Colaptes auratus*
LENGTH 12½ in (32 cm)
HABITAT Open woodland
CLUTCH SIZE 5–10

DISTRIBUTION Very widely distributed throughout North America: From Alaska and Newfoundland in the north south to the Mexican border.

THE NORTHERN FLICKER is far more widely distributed than the Gilded Flicker. The two species are similar in appearance, to the extent that they used to be considered to be members of the same species. In the Northern Flicker two distinctive color variations are now recognized: Red-shafted and yellow-shafted. Those birds from the north and west of the species' range are yellow-shafted. This is because of the yellow underwing and undertail feathering. Other more evident characteristics are the gray plumage on the crown, combined with the tan facial plumage and a red crescent marking on the neck. In the case of the red-shafted variant, the yellow areas are red, the crown is brown, not gray, and there is no red on the nape, but the mustache is red, contrasting with a gray face.

RED-SHAFTED NORTHERN FLICKER This variant occurs in eastern areas, and may interbreed where it meets with yellow-shafted individuals.

PASSERIFORMES

Perching birds

The largest of the avian orders, the Passeriformes covers a wide range of different genera, found around the world. Some families, such as the Tyrant Flycatchers (Tyrannidae), which is the largest member of the group, are found exclusively in the New World, whereas others, such as the buntings, grouped in the Family Emberizidae, occur in both the Old and New Worlds. Passeriformes are often reasonably small birds, many of which tend to display shades of brown and gray in their plumage, rather than being vividly colored. Many are quite social by nature, and live in flocks.

Alder Flycatcher

FAMILY Tyrannidae
SPECIES *Empidonax alnorum*
LENGTH 5¾ in (14 cm)
HABITAT Boggy woodland
CLUTCH SIZE 3–4

DISTRIBUTION Breeds in an area that extends from Alaska right across northeastern Canada and in the vicinity of the Great Lakes. Overwinters in South America.

THIS FLYCATCHER used to be grouped as a single species with the Willow Flycatcher (*see* p. 239), being referred to under the older name of Traill's Flycatcher. It is really only their vocalizations that enable them to be separated, rather than any distinctive plumage differences. It favors areas where alder is growing, as its name now suggests.

TRAVELERS These birds migrate long distances, overwintering as far south as Bolivia. They tend to fly across Central America, around and not over the Gulf of Mexico.

Yellow-bellied Flycatcher

FAMILY Tyrannidae
SPECIES *Empidonax flaviventris*
LENGTH 5½ in (14 cm)
HABITAT Boggy woodland
CLUTCH SIZE 3–5

DISTRIBUTION Breeds in a band across North America, from western Canada across to the east. Overwinters in Central America, down to Panama.

IT IS GENERALLY not easy to distinguish the *Empidonax* flycatchers, although the Yellow-bellied has a distinctive olive suffusion on the chest, quite apart from the yellow plumage on the lower underparts. These particular flycatchers seek out dense vegetation, staying close to the ground in such surroundings. Their diet consists mainly of flying insects.

PLUMAGE The white wing bars often appear rather grayish in the fall, being much brighter following the annual molt that occurs in the winter, after migration.

Western (Cordilleran) Flycatcher

FAMILY Tyrannidae

SPECIES *Empidonax occidentalis*

LENGTH 5½ in (14 cm)

HABITAT Coniferous forest

CLUTCH SIZE 3–4

DISTRIBUTION Found in woodland areas of southwestern Canada southward through the western part of the United States down into northern Mexico. Overwinters in southern Mexico.

THE CONFUSED STATE of the taxonomy in the case of members of this genus is illustrated by the fact that the Cordilleran Flycatcher and the Pacific Coast Flycatcher (*Empidonax difficilis*) now tend to be separated, although in reality, they are essentially identical in appearance. Even the calls of these flycatchers are so similar that it is virtually impossible to tell them apart, and they can only be distinguished by their distribution. Their breeding details too are the same, with the hen laying in a cup-shaped nest made of twigs and other vegetation, and lined with moss. This is usually positioned quite low down, in sites as variable as the upturned roots of a dead tree to the eaves of a mountain cabin. The chicks will hatch after a period of two weeks and will leave the nest after a similar interval.

BEHAVIOR These flycatchers are quite bold, often being seen near buildings. They start to fly south in August.

Hammond's Flycatcher

FAMILY Tyrannidae

SPECIES *Empidonax hammondii*

LENGTH 5½ in (14 cm)

HABITAT Coniferous woodland

CLUTCH SIZE 3–5

DISTRIBUTION Ranges in the summer from Alaska down the west coast of Canada to the southern United States. Overwinters in Central America as far as Nicaragua.

IN COMMON WITH other related flycatchers, Hammond's is a restless species, flicking its wings and tail regularly in a jaunty manner, even when seemingly resting. It is always on the lookout for invertebrates, darting off to seize a passing meal at every opportunity. A pair will often choose to nest at some considerable height off the ground, building in trees at heights of 60 ft (18 m) or more off the ground. They are quieter by nature than related species, but can be distinguished by having a very distinctive pip sounding call. Their plumage tends to be at its brightest in the fall.

DIFFERENCES Hammond's Flycatcher has relatively long primary feathers on the wings compared with related species, a rather shorter tail, and a smaller bill.

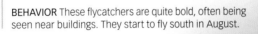

Least Flycatcher

FAMILY Tyrannidae
SPECIES *Empidonax minimus*
LENGTH 5¼ in (13 cm)
HABITAT Woodland/parks
CLUTCH SIZE 3–5

DISTRIBUTION Summer visitor, extending from northeastern Canada to southern Newfoundland, and to northern parts of the United States. Overwinters in southern Florida, but mainly in Central America.

IT IS NOT EASY to distinguish the various species of *Empidonax* flycatchers, especially because they are not very conspicious. The upperparts are olive, with two whitish bars across each wing. There is a white area on the throat, and white plumage also encircles the eyes.

SONGSTER The Least Flycatcher is quite vocal, with its song most likely to be heard in spring.

Dusky Flycatcher

FAMILY Tyrannidae
SPECIES *Empidonax oberholseri*
LENGTH 5¾ in (14 cm)
HABITAT Woodland/undergrowth
CLUTCH SIZE 3–5

DISTRIBUTION From southern Yukon Territory through western United States to southern California, Arizona, and New Mexico. Overwinters in Mexico.

GRAYISH-OLIVE coloration predominates on the upperparts, with the throat being whitish and the lower underparts having a pale yellowish tinge. The sexes are identical in appearance. As their name suggests, these birds hunt flies and other insects, catching their prey in flight. Dusky Flycatchers tend to be seen at lower altitudes in the more mountainous areas of the west.

APPEARANCE The tail of the Dusky Flycatcher is relatively long, with the bill being dark in color, matching that of the legs and feet.

Willow Flycatcher

FAMILY Tyrannidae

SPECIES *Empidonax traillii*

LENGTH 5¾ in (14 cm)

HABITAT Damp areas/ montane pastures

CLUTCH SIZE 3–4

DISTRIBUTION Broadly distributed from southern Canada, extending to southern California, Arizona, and New Mexico in the summer. Overwinters in Central America and northern South America.

AS ITS NAME SUGGESTS, the Willow Flycatcher often frequents areas where willow is common. Midges and similar flying insects are often found in such areas, particularly in the summer, providing a ready source of food for these summer visitors. It is usually possible to gain some idea of the identity of the members of this genus from the habitat in which they are to be found. Their call notes can also assist, as these differ between species, but an experienced ear is necessary to separate them on this basis. When breeding, Willow Flycatchers construct a nest relatively close to the ground, usually in a bush.

VARIATION The Willow Flycatcher's color varies through its range. Those from the west have darker heads and are browner than birds occurring in the east.

Acadian Flycatcher

FAMILY Tyrannidae

SPECIES *Empidonax virescens*

LENGTH 5¾ in (14 cm)

HABITAT Woodland/swamps

CLUTCH SIZE 3–5

DISTRIBUTION Southeastern United States in the summer, from the southern Great Lakes, to central Texas and Florida. Overwinters in south Central America and North America.

THE SONG OF these birds aids their identification, sounding rather like "PEE-tah," although in terms of their appearance, they are quite similar to other related species. Pairs will breed at some considerable height, building their nest as high as 25 ft (8 m) off the ground in a suitable tree. The nest itself is made from plant fibers, including small twigs and moss, with the incubation period lasting for about 14 days. The young flycatchers then fledge after a similar period. Their upperparts are brownish rather than olive at first.

CAMOUFLAGE The coloration of these flycatchers blends very effectively against their background.

Olive-sided Flycatcher

FAMILY Tyrannidae
SPECIES *Contopus cooperi*
LENGTH 7½ in (19 cm)
HABITAT Coniferous forest
CLUTCH SIZE 3–4

DISTRIBUTION Breeds on the north and western side of the continent, extending to Newfoundland and down to the Mexican border. Overwinters in Central and South America.

AS THEIR NAME SUGGESTS, these flycatchers have olive-gray flanks, with this coloration being separated by a narrow band of white plumage on the chest. They hunt by resting high up in a tree and use the perch here as a vantage point, venturing forth to grab flying insects.

DISTINCTIVE FEATURES Olive-sided Flycatchers are stocky birds, with long wings and a rather short tail.

Eastern Wood-pewee

FAMILY Tyrannidae
SPECIES *Contopus virens*
LENGTH 6¼ in (16 cm)
HABITAT Woodland
CLUTCH SIZE 3–4

DISTRIBUTION Breeds from Nova Scotia south to central Texas and east to Saskatchewan in Canada. Absent from southern Florida. Overwinters in Central America.

THEIR RESPECTIVE distributions help to separate the Eastern from the Western Wood-pewee, as they are actually very similar in appearance. Their upperparts are dark olive-gray with the breast being slightly paler. In profile, Eastern Wood-pewees have a slender body shape, reinforced by their relatively long tail feathers. The chin area is pale and there are two buff-gray wing bars evident on each wing.

CAMOUFLAGE The subdued coloration of these flycatchers means they are not conspicuous, even when perching in the open on a branch.

Western Wood-pewee

FAMILY Tyrannidae
SPECIES *Contopus sordidulus*
LENGTH 6¼ in (16 cm)
HABITAT Woodland
CLUTCH SIZE 3–4

DISTRIBUTION Summer range extends from southern Alaska down through western Canada to California and western Texas, extending across the Mexican border. Overwinters in northern South America.

THE UNUSUAL NAME of Wood-pewee describes the sound of the calls of these birds in their woodland setting. They have a very distinctive method of hunting, being patient and watchful. Western Wood-pewees have favored perches within their territory, often in exposed positions where they wait, swooping to seize flies and other similar insects that come within their reach. When nesting, a pair will choose a horizontal branch high up in a tree, about 20 ft (6 m) or more above ground level. Here they will construct a tightly woven nest of plant matter and feathers. The hen lays her clutch of white, spotted eggs within, and the incubation period lasts approximately two weeks.

CHICKS IN THE NEST These young Western Wood-pewees will leave the nest by the time they are about 18 days old.

Black Phoebe

FAMILY Tyrannidae
SPECIES *Sayornis nigricans*
LENGTH 6¾ in (17 cm)
HABITAT Woodland
CLUTCH SIZE 3–6

DISTRIBUTION Occurs in the western United States to Oregon, with the range here expanding northward. Withdraws southward to Baja California and western Mexico in the winter.

ALTHOUGH IT OCCURS in areas where trees are present, the Black Phoebe is most likely to be seen close to ponds and other stretches of water. It is here that flying insects that form its prey are most likely to be encountered during the warm days of summer. They are territorial by nature, and an established individual will chase away any would-be intruder. These flycatchers are slate-black overall, as their name suggests, with just their lower underparts being white. Young birds in contrast are much browner in terms of their coloration. The Black Phoebe can also be identified by its rather elongated body shape, emphasized by the bird's upright stance.

PROTECTION When breeding, the Black Phoebe builds its nest on a suitable ledge, perhaps under a bridge where it will be relatively safe from predators.

Eastern Phoebe

FAMILY Tyrannidae
SPECIES *Sayornis phoebe*
LENGTH 7 in (18 cm)
HABITAT Woodland
CLUTCH SIZE 3–8

DISTRIBUTION From central Canada southeastward across the United States up to Nova Scotia. Overwinters from North Carolina, through Florida and around the Gulf states to Mexico.

THIS PARTICULAR PHOEBE is often seen in fairly suburban locations, often close to streams and other stretches of water. It collects damp mud when breeding, combining this with moss to build a cup-shaped nest that will be lined with soft down feathers. From a distance, its blackish head and white underparts, sometimes with a pale yellow suffusion in the fall, serve to identify this species. Its bill is black too, and it moves in a jaunty fashion, wagging its tail, and also fanning these feathers as part of a display.

ON WATCH Phoebes are very alert and lively birds by nature, always on the look-out for potential prey. They feed on invertebrates.

Say's Phoebe

FAMILY Tyrannidae
SPECIES *Sayornis saya*
LENGTH 7½ in (19 cm)
HABITAT Arid country
CLUTCH SIZE 4–5

DISTRIBUTION Ranges from northern Alaska in the summer down the western side of North America. May overwinter in southern California and into southern Mexico.

THERE IS SOME VARIATION in the depth of coloration in Say's Phoebe through its range, with certain individuals being more brightly colored than others. The head is grayish-brown, becoming paler and grayer on the chest, with a rusty-orange belly and lower underparts. The tail is black and the wings too are blackish, as is the fairly narrow bill. Young birds are browner in terms of their overall coloration, with a pair of cinnamon wing bars being evident. Say's Phoebe has a slender profile, with relatively long wings. When breeding, a cliff face may be used as a site for the nest, or alternatively, these birds may move inside a building such as a barn, constructing their nest on a ledge here. The hen incubates the eggs, with hatching occurring after approximately two weeks. The young phoebes will then fledge after a similar interval. Invertebrates feature prominently in their diet, but these flycatchers will also eat berries occasionally.

EXPOSED Occurring in open stretches of country, Say's Phoebe can be seen in the open, perching on exposed branches or boulders.

Ash-throated Flycatcher

FAMILY Tyrannidae
SPECIES *Myiarchus cinerascens*
LENGTH 8½ in (22 cm)
HABITAT Open country
CLUTCH SIZE 3–5

DISTRIBUTION Summer range includes much of southwestern and southern central parts of the United States, overwintering along the western part of the Gulf Coast and southward into Mexico.

ASH-GRAY UNDERPARTS merging into pale yellow plumage on the belly help to identify this species. These flycatchers perch on the edge of clearings, or in large solitary trees, swooping down on flying insects. Pairs also nest in tree hollows, lining the nesting chamber with vegetation.

DISTINCTIVE HEAD The plumage on the head does not lie flat, but creates what in effect is a small crest.

Great Crested Flycatcher

FAMILY Tyrannidae
SPECIES *Myiarchus crinitus*
LENGTH 8 in (20 cm)
HABITAT Open woodland
CLUTCH SIZE 3–7

DISTRIBUTION Eastern North America up to the Great Lakes and to southern Nova Scotia. Overwinters in southern Florida and from southeastern Mexico to northern South America.

AS ITS NAME SUGGESTS, the Great Crested Flycatcher is a relatively large bird. The plumage on its head is olive-gray, with grayish-brown upperparts, while the lower underparts are pale yellow. The tail and flight feathers are reddish-cinnamon, with white barring evident on each wing. Its powerful, pointed bill enables it to grab flying insects easily, although it may eat berries too.

WAITING GAME Great Crested Flycatchers hunt for invertebrates in open woodland, watching and waiting for prey to come within their reach.

Dusky-capped Flycatcher

FAMILY Tyrannidae

SPECIES *Myiarchus tuberculifer*

LENGTH 7¼ in (18 cm)

HABITAT Wooded upland

CLUTCH SIZE 4–5

DISTRIBUTION Southern Arizona and New Mexico, also may breed in Texas. Migrates south for the winter to Mexico in Central America, reaching the vicinity of Oxaca.

DISTINGUISHING BETWEEN the various *Myiarchus* flycatchers can be difficult. This species has olive-brown upperparts, with a pale gray throat and upper breast, becoming yellow lower down. A diagnostic feature of the Dusky-capped, however, is the reddish edging around the secondary feathers on the wings.

HABITAT These flycatchers inhabit more densely wooded areas than related species, and may hover over vegetation, looking for invertebrates.

Brown-crested Flycatcher

FAMILY Tyrannidae

SPECIES *Myiarchus tyrannulus*

LENGTH 8¾ in (22 cm)

HABITAT Arid country

CLUTCH SIZE 3–5

DISTRIBUTION Breeds in the southwestern United States, as far east as southern Texas with its range extending down through Mexico to Guatemala, Belize, and Honduras.

RANGING INTO semi-desert areas where trees are scarce, Brown-crested Flycatchers may instead nest in holes in saguaro cactus, which may have been bored by woodpeckers. They line the nesting chamber with feathers, making a soft lining for the eggs. Incubation takes approximately three weeks, and the young flycatchers develop quickly, leaving the nest at just 16 days old.

PLUMAGE The crest of these flycatchers has a bushy appearance. The tail feathers are cinnamon in color, ending in darker tips.

Vermilion Flycatcher

FAMILY Tyrannidae

SPECIES *Pyrocephalus rubinus*

LENGTH 6 in (15 cm)

HABITAT Woodland

CLUTCH SIZE 2–3

DISTRIBUTION Summer visitor to the southern United States, generally overwintering to the south in Mexico but may be seen over a wider area in the early fall.

THE STUNNING, VIBRANT coloration of the male Vermilion Flycatcher is instantly recognizable. Hens, in contrast, are much duller, with streaked white markings on the underparts, and a hint of an orange-red wash on the belly itself. Young birds of both sexes resemble the hen, but have a yellower tone to the belly. Immature males start to molt into their adult plumage by the middle of their first winter. The upperparts are a paler shade of brown, compared with the more glossy black appearance of the cock bird. This species is quite common in the United States, although its range is centered mainly on Central America. These birds are usually seen close to water.

SIGHTINGS Vermilion Flycatchers are naturally tame, and quite conspicuous making them easy to spot as they are frequently observed in the open, on a tree stump or fence post.

Couch's Kingbird

FAMILY Tyrannidae
SPECIES *Tyrannus couchii*
LENGTH 9¼ in (24 cm)
HABITAT Woodland
CLUTCH SIZE 3–5

DISTRIBUTION Range in North America is restricted to southern Texas in the summer, extending down as far as northern Guatemala and Belize. Overwinters also in Central America.

THIS IS ANOTHER relatively colorful insectivorous species with a thick bill, a grayish head and breast, and yellow underparts. It frequents areas close to water, where insects will be numerous during the summer months. The stronghold of Couch's Kingbird is in the Rio Grande Valley, although it is not a particularly conspicuous species, perching quietly high up in trees and darting out only occasionally to catch a passing insect. The cup-shaped nest is located high up, often more than 20 ft (6 m) above the ground, and is also not usually apparent from here. Young birds are similar to, but not as brightly colored as, the adults when they fledge.

FEEDING Although insects form the bulk of the diet of Couch's Kingbird, it will also eat berries during the colder months of the year.

Scissor-tailed Flycatcher

FAMILY Tyrannidae
SPECIES *Tyrannus forficatus*
LENGTH 13 in (33 cm)
HABITAT Open country
CLUTCH SIZE 4–6

DISTRIBUTION Summer breeding range is in southern-central parts of the United States, with these birds flying as far south as western Panama in Central America to overwinter.

THE VERY LONG, forked tail is characteristic of this flycatcher, offset against its grayish head and body, with pale pink suffusion on the flanks. The wings are blackish-brown. Females can be recognized by their shorter tails, and young birds of both sexes also have shorter tails when they leave the nest. This takes the form of a shallow cup, built some 30 ft (9 m) or so off the ground. The incubation period lasts for approximately 14 days, with the young fledging after a similar interval.

DIET These flycatchers catch insects in flight, but will also hunt on the ground for grasshoppers. Berries also feature in their diet.

MALE VERMILION FLYCATCHERS (*see* p. 246) These birds usually catch the insects that they feed on in flight, and are lively birds, not infrequently twitching their tail feathers up and down, even when perched.

Eastern Kingbird

FAMILY Tyrannidae
SPECIES *Tyrannus tyrannus*
LENGTH 8½ in (22 cm)
HABITAT Woodland
CLUTCH SIZE 3–5

DISTRIBUTION Occurs widely through much of North America, up to the Yukon and southern Alaska, with individuals overwintering as far away as Ecuador, Peru, and Brazil.

WHITE UNDERPARTS offset against a dark grayish-black head and wings, with white tips to the tail feathers, help to identify this kingbird. The bill is black, too, and quite stocky. There may be a red area of feathering running across the crown, but this is not generally obvious. These kingbirds are common and conspicuous, often perching in the open. They use this vantage point to look for insects that attract their attention, swooping down to catch any that are within reach. Eastern Kingbirds are highly territorial by nature, and will readily defend an area from incursions by other members of their species, and will also turn on larger birds that may seek to drive them away from a chosen spot. They build relatively bulky nests, made up of vegetable matter, usually high off the ground in a tree. The incubation period lasts from two weeks and the young kingbirds will leave the nest after a similar interval.

FEEDING HABITS It is not just flying insects that will be caught by kingbirds. This particular bird has seized a grasshopper in its long, pointed bill.

Western Kingbird

FAMILY Tyrannidae
SPECIES *Tyrannus verticalis*
LENGTH 8¾ in (22 cm)
HABITAT Open country
CLUTCH SIZE 3–6

DISTRIBUTION Summer visitor to western North America, overwintering in Central America, being found in an area here extending from southern Mexico to Costa Rica and Panama.

A GRAY HEAD, with a grayish-olive tone over the back and wings are characteristics of the Western Kingbird. Its belly is bright yellow in contrast. Young birds can be distinguished by being less brightly colored, with their underparts being more of an olive shade.

BEHAVIOR This kingbird is often seen in the vicinity of cattle, catching insects disturbed by the herd as they graze.

Cassin's Kingbird

FAMILY Tyrannidae
SPECIES *Tyrannus vociferans*
LENGTH 9 in (23 cm)
HABITAT Woodland
CLUTCH SIZE 3–5

DISTRIBUTION Southwestern United States, extending across the border to central Mexico. Birds may overwinter in Honduras, although some remain in southern California.

THIS KINGBIRD is fairly adaptable in its habits, being encountered in a range of different environments, although it tends to be most common in relatively open country where there are trees that can serve as vantage points. Its white throat contrasts with the dark gray head and yellow underparts. The tail is quite short in comparison with the length of the wings.

MIGRANTS These kingbirds are summertime visitors to the United States, being driven south by a shortage of insects over the winter.

Northern Shrike

FAMILY Laniidae

SPECIES *Lanius excubitor*

LENGTH 10 in (25 cm)

HABITAT Open country

CLUTCH SIZE 3–9

DISTRIBUTION Found from Alaska through northern British Columbia and Alberta eastward, and in winter from Quebec and northern Ontario to the northeastern United States. Also occurs widely in Europe and Asia.

THE NORTHERN SHRIKE is a migratory species, but it spends its winters rather than summers in the United States. In the summer, these shrikes are found in the tundra region where they nest. When hunting, they will perch and then swoop down on small vertebrates such as mice.

ADAPTATION The stout, hooked bill of the Northern Shrike helps it to catch its prey easily. Young birds, in contrast to adults, are brownish in color.

Loggerhead Shrike

FAMILY Laniidae

SPECIES *Lanius ludovicianus*

LENGTH 9 in (23 cm)

HABITAT Open country

CLUTCH SIZE 3–8

DISTRIBUTION Summertime visitor in parts of Canada, up to Alberta and Saskatchewan, resident across the United States, down to Florida. May overwinter in Central America.

THE UPPERPARTS of the Loggerhead Shrike are gray, with a prominent black stripe running back from the bill through the eyes on each side of the face; the underparts are white, with a hint of barring. Young birds display more barring on their underparts. The nest itself is built in a tree or bush, with thorny plants being preferred for this purpose.

DIET Feeding largely on insects, Loggerhead Shrikes impale surplus prey on thorns, creating what is known as a larder, where they can return and feed.

Bell's Vireo

FAMILY Vireonidae
SPECIES *Vireo bellii*
LENGTH 4¾ in (12 cm)
HABITAT Woodland
CLUTCH SIZE 3–5

DISTRIBUTION Occurs quite widely in central parts of the United States, as far north as Lake Michigan. More localized in the southwest, with birds overwintering in Central America.

THE NONDESCRIPT PLUMAGE of Bell's Vireo means that it can be hard to spot, especially as it is quite shy. The chicks will leave the nest when they are about 13 days old, and it is not uncommon for a pair to nest twice over the summer.

SHOW OFF Bell's Vireo is a talented songster, and its long tail feathers are used to form part of a jaunty display.

Cassin's Vireo

FAMILY Vireonidae
SPECIES *Vireo cassinii*
LENGTH 5 in (13 cm)
HABITAT Woodland
CLUTCH SIZE 3–5

DISTRIBUTION From southern British Columbia through the western coastal United States to northern Baja California. Birds overwinter in Central America, down to Guatemala.

THIS SPECIES is closely related to both the Plumbeous and Blue-headed Vireos (*see* p. 257), and used to be grouped together with them as a single species. Its head is pale gray, with olive upperparts, and white plumage on the underside of the body. Cassin's Vireo is most likely to be observed either in oak or coniferous woodland.

SIMILAR APPEARANCE In the case of Cassin's Vireo, it is not possible to distinguish between the sexes on the basis of any difference in plumage.

Yellow-throated Vireo

FAMILY Vireonidae
SPECIES *Vireo flavifrons*
LENGTH 5½ in (14 cm)
HABITAT Woodland
CLUTCH SIZE 3–5

DISTRIBUTION Ranges over much of North America during the summer, from the United States, Gulf states north to just beyond the Great Lakes, reaching eastern Canada.

THESE SMALL VIREOS fly long distances from their wintering grounds, which may lie as far away as Venezuela in South America, arriving in southern parts of the United States by mid-March, and reaching Canada by May. Some birds winter through the Caribbean region and in Central America too.

INACCESSIBLE It is not easy to spot this colorful vireo because it lives high up in the trees.

White-eyed Vireo

FAMILY Vireonidae
SPECIES *Vireo griseus*
LENGTH 5 in (13 cm)
HABITAT Wooded scrubland
CLUTCH SIZE 3–5

DISTRIBUTION Central and eastern parts of the United States during the summer, withdrawing to the coastal area of the Gulf states in the winter, also being resident in Florida.

THIS VIREO is most likely to betray its presence by a sudden burst of its loud song, which consists of up to seven notes, usually beginning and ending with a harsh "chick" sound. In western areas, the population of the White-eyed Vireo seems to be falling, and this has been blamed on cowbirds (*see* p. 356) laying in its nest, preventing the vireos from rearing their own brood. Those birds that do migrate spend the winter in Mexico or in the Caribbean, although individuals have been recorded as far north as Ontario in December.

DIFFERENCES There are slight variations in the appearance of these vireos through their range, reflecting the fact that four distinctive North American races are recognized.

Warbling Vireo

FAMILY Vireonidae

SPECIES *Vireo gilvus*

LENGTH 5½ in (14 cm)

HABITAT Woodland

CLUTCH SIZE 3–5

DISTRIBUTION Occurs very widely throughout North America, virtually from Alaska in a southeasterly direction right across to the east coast, but absent from the southeast.

THIS VIREO IS ONE of the most plainly colored members of its family, with no contrasting wing bars, although with a paler stripe above each eye. It is a dedicated songster, however, singing on occasion for hours at a time, from a suitable perch high up in a tree. Various different song patterns have been recorded in Warbling Vireos from different parts of their range. Those occurring in eastern areas are considered to be the most musical. The cup-shaped nest is woven from plant fibers, and held together in part by the gossamer of spiders' webs. This species is essentially only a summertime visitor to North America. It withdraws back to Central America each fall, with the overwintering area varying according to the subspecies. The westerly race *Vireo gilvus swainsonii*, for example, flies down to El Salvador, whereas the nominate race is found in northeastern Costa Rica during this period, and others are to be found in Mexico.

FEEDING This young vireo is begging for food. Its flight feathers are already emerging. Chicks grow very rapidly on a diet comprised mainly of invertebrates.

Hutton's Vireo

FAMILY Vireonidae

SPECIES *Vireo huttoni*

LENGTH 5 in (13 cm)

HABITAT Woodland

CLUTCH SIZE 3–5

DISTRIBUTION The western side of North America, from British Columbia southward through California down to Arizona, New Mexico, and Texas. Also occurs in Mexico and Guatemala.

IT CAN BE RATHER confusing trying to identify this vireo, since it resembles the Ruby-crowned Kinglet (*see* p. 289) both in terms of its behavior and appearance. Hutton's Vireo twitches its wings when resting just like a kinglet, but can be identified by its lack of a ruby crown and the absence of a dark area below the lower wing bar, but these features may not be evident when looking up into the canopy from ground level. It is slightly bigger overall than a kinglet, however, and has a noticeably thicker bill.

HIGH LIVING Hutton's Vireo builds its suspended nest often 35 ft (11 m) or more off the ground.

Red-eyed Vireo

FAMILY Vireonidae

SPECIES *Vireo olivaceus*

LENGTH 6 in (15 cm)

HABITAT Woodland

CLUTCH SIZE 3–4

DISTRIBUTION Occurs over a broad area of North America, extending from the west to the east coasts. Ranges from Canada down to the Gulf states.

THE DISTINCTIVE red irises of these vireos are striking, when seen at close quarters. Unfortunately, like other members of the family, they are not easy to spot, in spite of their relatively large size as their coloration enables them to merge effectively in among vegetation. Red-eyed Vireos are actually quite common, though, and have extended their range into Oregon in the west and Newfoundland in the east, over the course of the past 50 years. In the fall, they fly south again, overwintering in Central America and parts of the Caribbean.

NESTING BEHAVIOR Invertebrates of various types feature prominently in the diet of nestlings. These birds also eat fruit and berries.

Plumbeous Vireo

FAMILY Vireonidae
SPECIES *Vireo plumbeus*
LENGTH 5¼ in (13 cm)
HABITAT Woodland
CLUTCH SIZE 3–5

DISTRIBUTION Western North America, from the Rocky Mountains in the northern United States southward to northwestern Mexico, which is where this particular race overwinters. Others occur in Central America.

THESE VIREOS SING regularly, even when they are not nesting, but their calls are not as clear and musical as in the case of some other species. Sometimes occurring in groups, they move through the woodland canopy in search of insects, favoring pine and oak forests.

DISTINCTIVE FEATURE The white ring around the eye, which extends to run forward over the bill, helps to identify this vireo.

Blue-headed Vireo

FAMILY Vireonidae
SPECIES *Vireo solitarius*
LENGTH 5 in (13 cm)
HABITAT Woodland
CLUTCH SIZE 3–5

DISTRIBUTION Breeds from northeastern British Columbia, southeast across the continent. Overwinters in the southeastern United States, Central America, and the Caribbean.

THIS VIREO is so-called thanks to the distinctive area of bluish-gray plumage on the crown and sides of the head. Even so, it is not always easy to distinguish from Cassin's Vireo (*see* p. 253) in particular, especially as their songs are similar. It flies south relatively late during the fall, rarely being seen in Florida or the Gulf states until October.

EARLY VISITOR The Blue-headed is generally the first vireo to arrive in the summer, reaching the northern extremities of its range by May.

Blue Jay

FAMILY Corvidae
SPECIES *Cyanocitta cristata*
LENGTH 11 in (28 cm)
HABITAT Woodland/suburbs
CLUTCH SIZE 3–5

DISTRIBUTION Central and eastern United States to southern Texas; further north in summer in western areas. Year-round in Newfoundland.

EGG THIEF Blue Jays are predatory birds, and may raid the nests of songbirds, stealing eggs and young chicks.

THIS IS A COMMON species through its wide range, being conspicuous in part due to its loud calls, although some birds learn the calls of other species as well as their own. They may often be encountered in small groups, in parks and other similar areas of woodland quite close to human habitation. They are often attracted to backyard bird tables in such areas. The Blue Jay's upperparts are bluish, with areas of white in the wings, and a crest. The sides of the face are white, with a black collar extending down and around the chest; the rest of the underparts are grayish-white. The stout bill is black, as are the legs and feet. These jays eat a wide variety of foods, taking seeds and nuts, as well as larger invertebrates. When nesting, a pair of birds build a platform-type nest of sticks and other material high up in a tree. The incubation period lasts about 17 days on average.

Steller's Jay

FAMILY Corvidae

SPECIES *Cyanopsitta stelleri*

LENGTH 11½ in (29 cm)

HABITAT Coniferous/mixed forest

CLUTCH SIZE 3–5

DISTRIBUTION Resident in the northwest, from Alaska south to California, western Texas, and Mexico. Also offshore such as on Queen Charlotte Islands.

DARK IN COLOR, Steller's Jay has black plumage extending over the head and down on to the chest and upper back, sometimes with some paler streaks and spotting in this area. The lower parts of the body are blue, including the wings and tail. There is a prominent crest on the head, although this may not always be evident. Essentially woodland birds, Steller's Jays will nevertheless congregate at bird table feeders on occasions, especially during the winter when other sources of food may be in short supply. Acorns may be a natural mainstay of the diet during this period. This is the largest jay species to be found in North America, with an extensive range. Conifer trees are usually selected for nesting, with the hen incubating the eggs on her own.

SHOCK OF BLUE When Steller's Jay is in flight the tall crest at the back of its head is obscured—the feathers lie flat and streamlined.

Gray Jay

FAMILY Corvidae

SPECIES *Perisoreus canadensis*

LENGTH 11½ in (29 cm)

HABITAT Mountain forest

CLUTCH SIZE 3–5

DISTRIBUTION Occurs across northern areas, from Alaska to Newfoundland, through the western United States, inland to Arizona and New Mexico.

THESE JAYS ARE well-known to campers in northern areas, as they will often descend to seek food, sometimes proving to be remarkably tame. Their forehead and cheeks are whitish; the upperparts of the body are dark gray shades while the underparts are pale gray. There are regional variations in appearance that are recognized through their range. Young birds are entirely slate-gray, apart from a white streak around the bill, resembling a mustache. Gray Jays will cache surplus food in trees, returning to these stores when they are hungry.

CANADA JAY One of the most conspicuous features of this jay, which used to be known as the Canada Jay, is its short bill.

BLUE JAY (*see* p. 258) These striking birds are relatively common in urban areas of the eastern United States, but often appear simply as a flash of blue as they fly past, moving from one tree to the next.

Pinyon Jay

FAMILY Corvidae

SPECIES *Gymnorhinus cyanocephalus*

LENGTH 10½ in (27 cm)

HABITAT Coniferous mountain forest

CLUTCH SIZE 3–4

DISTRIBUTION Western-central parts of the United States. A shortage of food may take it outside its usual range.

COMMUNITY SPIRIT Pinyon Jays can sometimes be observed in flocks numbering hundreds of individuals. They may forage for food on the forest floor.

THE COLORATION of these jays is distinctive: They are a grayish-blue, slightly darker on the head and occasionally with white flecking on the throat. The bill is black, quite narrow in shape, and elongated. Pinyon Jays feed mainly on pine nuts in the pinyon pine and juniper woodland that is their favored habitat. They will bury pine nuts during the fall as a store to provide food during the colder months. The cock bird in particular returns to these supplies in the late winter, by which time, the hen will already be incubating her eggs. He feeds her using these stores of food, so she does not have to leave the nest in search of food, exposing the eggs to the cold.

Western Scrub-jay

FAMILY Corvidae

SPECIES *Aphelocoma californica*

LENGTH 11 in (28 cm)

HABITAT Woodland/parks

CLUTCH SIZE 3–6

DISTRIBUTION From British Columbia south to California and inland, southeaster to Texas and into Mexico. Largely resident throughout the year.

THESE JAYS ARE surprisingly bold, and are seen increasingly in backyards and parks, although their natural habitat is scrub oak and pinyon pine and juniper woodland. They have bright blue coloration extending from above the bill over the head, and down the back. There is a blue area on the chest, broken by white markings, and the underparts are grayish-white. Birds from coastal populations tend to be more brightly colored than those occurring further east. Western Scrub-jays may associate in small groups, but are not seen in large flocks. When breeding, a pair choose a well-concealed site for a nest, usually in bushy areas rather than in trees.

BOTH THE SAME Male and female Western Scrub-jays cannot be identified by means of plumage distinctions.

Green Jay

FAMILY Corvidae

SPECIES *Cyanocorax yncas*

LENGTH 10½ in (27 cm)

HABITAT Brushland

CLUTCH SIZE 3–5

DISTRIBUTION Occurs in a restricted area across the Mexican border into central-southern Texas, in the Lower Rio Grande Valley, north to Live Oak County, and west to Laredo.

THIS JAY IS UNMISTAKABLE, thanks to its plumage: Blue feathering extends back over the crown, and is also evident on the sides of the face. There is a black bib that has a paler yellowish border, and the rest of the body and wings are green, while the underside of the tail is yellow. The loud calls of these jays attract attention, particularly as they tend to associate in small and inevitably noisy groups. They are omnivorous in their feeding habits, taking fruit, berries, and seeds, as well as invertebrates and small animals, even raiding the nests of other birds. They build a platform-style nest and their young fledge at around three and a half weeks old.

RARE BEAUTY This is an uncommon species in North America, with its main area of distribution lying further south.

Mexican Jay

FAMILY Corvidae

SPECIES *Aphelocoma ultramarina*

LENGTH 11½ in (29 cm)

HABITAT Pine-oak woodland

CLUTCH SIZE 4–5

DISTRIBUTION Mainly Central America, but resident in the United States in east Arizona and adjacent New Mexico; also in southwestern Texas.

THE DISTRIBUTION of the Mexican Jay is centered on Central rather than North America, where it only occurs in the oak woods to the north of the Mexican border. The coloration is subtle. The head is bluish-gray, the back and wings are also gray, while the underparts are a paler shade of gray. Acorns feature prominently in their diet, but they are omnivorous and opportunistic in their feeding habits, like most corvids. Mexican Jays live in family groups, with all members of the flock helping to provide food when the adult pair have chicks.

A YOUNG MEXICAN JAY The pale color of the bill reveals that this is a young bird. The bill is jet black in adults.

Clark's Nutcracker

FAMILY Corvidae

SPECIES *Nucifraga columbiana*

LENGTH 12 in (30 cm)

HABITAT Coniferous mountain forest

CLUTCH SIZE 2–6

DISTRIBUTION Resident in western and central North America, from British Columbia to New Mexico and Arizona. Present in parts of California.

PALE GRAY COLORATION with a whitish area around the eyes and bill is characteristic of these corvids. There is black plumage evident on the wings and tail. The bill is relatively long, terminating in a sharp point. Clark's Nutcracker uses its bill to crack open pine nuts, which feature prominently in its diet, although these birds often beg extra rations from hikers and campers. They also store pine nuts for the winter.

SEASONAL POPULATIONS In years when pine nuts are in short supply, Clark's Nutcrackers are forced to seek alternative food supplies elsewhere, resulting in seasonal population irruptions.

Black-billed Magpie

FAMILY Corvidae

SPECIES *Pica pica*

LENGTH 19 in (48 cm)

HABITAT Woodland

CLUTCH SIZE 7–9

DISTRIBUTION Resident from the Aleutian Islands and southern Alaska down through central and western parts of the United States, as far south as northern Arizona.

THESE MAGPIES are easily recognizable, thanks partly to the black coloration of their bills. They are lively birds, with distinctive cackling calls. Several pairs may associate together, and breed communally. They construct bulky nests in trees, and descend to the ground to forage.

RAIDERS Magpies may visit suburban bird tables and harry small songbirds, taking their eggs and chicks.

American Crow

FAMILY Corvidae

SPECIES *Corvus brachyrhynchos*

LENGTH 17½ in (44 cm)

HABITAT Open country

CLUTCH SIZE 3–6

DISTRIBUTION Found across Canada in summer, but only in southern parts and the United States over the winter; absent from the extreme south.

LARGEST CROW The American Crow is the largest of the crows in North America. Their jet black plumage has a glossy hue, especially on the wings.

LARGE IN SIZE and black in color, the American Crow is a common sight over much of North America, especially during the summer months. It has adapted remarkably well to changes in the landscape resulting from human activity, and even benefited from them, extending its range as a consequence. These crows used to be found essentially in forested areas, but now they have adapted to thrive in areas of open farmland, and at the same time, are now becoming increasingly common in cities, being seen particularly in the vicinity of municipal parks. Social by nature, they tend to nest in colonies, although the number of birds breeding together varies considerably. There may be several hundred in a large colony, which will create a considerable noise, thanks to the loud cawing of these large birds. It is difficult to approach them undetected, as American Crows are very watchful, and call to each other at any hint of danger. Their young are reared on a nest of sticks, with incubation lasting for around 17 days. The young crows will fledge once they are about five weeks old.

Common Raven

FAMILY Corvidae
SPECIES *Corvus corax*
LENGTH 24 in (61 cm)
HABITAT Mountain/desert
CLUTCH SIZE 4–7

DISTRIBUTION Resident all through the far north, right up to Greenland, and down the western side of the United States into Central America.

THE MOST OBVIOUS point of distinction between crows and ravens is in their bill shape and size, as those of ravens are much thicker and heavier. The Common Raven is also much larger overall. It has black plumage, with a glossy hue especially evident over the wings, although this is less apparent in young birds. The feathering in the throat area is relatively long, forming a ruff when it is raised. In terms of its calls, the Common Raven tends to utter a deep "craak," which is a further point of distinction with crows, but it can also display a more varied vocal range. Breeding birds form a life-long pair bond. These corvids occur in a wide range of habitats, and are now becoming increasingly common in cities. Although cliffs are still used as nest sites in some areas, Common Ravens may also build their nests in trees in parks or even adopt a high building for nesting purposes.

NOISE MAKERS These ravens are quite noisy. This one is calling and showing the longer feathering present under the throat.

Chihuahuan Raven

FAMILY Corvidae
SPECIES *Corvus cryptoleucus*
LENGTH 19½ in (49 cm)
HABITAT Arid country
CLUTCH SIZE 4–8

DISTRIBUTION Summer visitor to southeastern Kansas and southwestern Missouri; resident from Arizona west to Texas and south into Mexico.

NAMED AFTER the Mexican province of Chihuahua, this raven is far more common south of the border, but it is seen in parts of the United States. It lives in large flocks that number hundreds of individuals after the breeding season. Although the Chihuahuan Raven is mainly black, the feathers on the neck have white bases, to the extent that this bird was once called the White-necked Raven. However, this feature is not always apparent. When breeding, a pair builds a large nest of sticks and similar material, high off the ground typically in a tree, but sometimes on top of a utility pole.

IDENTICAL The sexes appear identical in the Chihuahuan Raven. These are adaptable birds, and eat a range of plant and animal matter

Fish Crow

FAMILY Corvidae
SPECIES *Corvus ossifragus*
LENGTH 15½ in (39 cm)
HABITAT Near water
CLUTCH SIZE 4–5

DISTRIBUTION Resident in the southeastern United States; extending its range northward. Found along the Gulf Coast as far as eastern Texas.

AS ITS NAME SUGGESTS, the Fish Crow is most likely to be seen in coastal areas. It wades through the shallows in search of fish and crustaceans, which form the basis of its diet, and also patrols the shoreline for carrion that may have washed up. This species may also be seen occasionally further inland in salty marshland or near rivers, that also offer good feeding opportunities. It may associate with its larger relative, the American Crow, forming mixed flocks. They look virtually identical but the Fish Crow's call is different, sounding like "ca-hah," which helps to distinguish the two species.

BREEDING CONDTIONS Fish Crows breed in a similar fashion to other members of the family, but may use seaweed in their nests.

Horned Lark

FAMILY Alaudidae
SPECIES *Eremophila alpestris*
LENGTH 7¾ in (20 cm)
HABITAT Open country
CLUTCH SIZE 3–5

DISTRIBUTION Through Alaska and much of Canada in the summer, except for central areas. Largely resident further south, but absent from Florida and the adjacent Gulf Coast.

THE PROMINENT BLACK feathering on the head of cock birds looks rather like horns, hence the common name. There are yellow areas evident here too, and a black band across the upper chest. The underparts are whitish, broken by chestnut speckling. Hens are duller in coloration than their mates. The Horned Lark is the only species of lark occurring in North America, being found over almost the entire continent. They forage for food on the ground, seeking seeds as well as invertebrates, and may sometimes be seen close to buildings, including airport terminals. Pairs also nest in these surroundings, with the eggs being laid in a scrape, lined with vegetation. The hen sits alone, and the young hatch in 12 days, and fledge after a similar period. Groups of these larks often congregate during the fall, forming large flocks over the winter in some areas.

GROUND BIRD The Horned Lark spends much of its time on the ground, sometimes running in pursuit of invertebrate prey.

Tree Swallow

FAMILY Hirundinidae
SPECIES *Tachycineta bicolor*
LENGTH 5¾ in (14 cm)
HABITAT Woodland near water
CLUTCH SIZE 4–6

DISTRIBUTION Breeds across northern and central North America; tends to be absent in the south. Overwinters by the coast. Resident in California.

THE METALLIC BLUISH-BLACK coloration of the Tree Swallow is very evident on the head and upperparts, contrasting with the pure white on the throat and underparts. The wings are both broad and very long, reaching beyond the tip of the tail. These birds nest widely across much of North America, breeding in natural tree hollows, adopting the abandoned nests of a woodpecker, or even occupying nestboxes. Each fall, large flocks of these swallows congregate before undertaking the journey to their southern wintering grounds.

SELECTION OF PERCHES Tree Swallows may be seen perching on wire fences as here, or on telephone lines. They hunt invertebrates, but will eat berries occasionally.

Purple Martin

FAMILY Hirundinidae
SPECIES *Progne subis*
LENGTH 7½ in (19 cm)
HABITAT Woodland/suburbs
CLUTCH SIZE 3–6

DISTRIBUTION Summer visitor from Canada to Florida. Sporadic elsewhere, seen especially in southwestern states and on the west coast. Overwinters in northern South America.

RELATIVELY DULL IN COLOR, in spite of its name, the Purple Martin is the largest species of swallow occurring in North America. Cock birds display glossy bluish-black upperparts, with the iridescence being greatest over the head. Hens resemble young birds of both sexes, being dusky black above and a lighter, grayish shade below. They hunt invertebrates in flight, flying fast and then gliding in short bursts. Purple Martins may be seen quite commonly in urban areas, often nesting under the eaves of buildings, although hollow trees are more traditional. The hen incubates the eggs alone, with hatching occurring after about 16 days. The young martins fledge at about a month old.

URBAN HOMES Manmade structures, such as this purpose-built martin house, provide these birds with suburban nesting opportunities.

Northern Rough-winged Swallow

FAMILY Hirundinidae
SPECIES *Stelgidopteryx serripennis*
LENGTH 5 in (13 cm)
HABITAT Cliffs/riverbanks
CLUTCH SIZE 4–8

DISTRIBUTION All over North America, from British Columbia south, in summer. Overwinters in southern Florida. Resident on the southern Texas border.

THESE SWALLOWS are so-called because of the small rough hooks present on the leading outer edge of each of the longest flight feathers, the function of which is unclear. The sexes are similar in appearance and dull in coloration: The upperparts are brown, while the underparts are paler, with a grayish-brown suffusion across the chest. They migrate in small groups, rather than as large flocks.

SHORT TAILS This swallow species has a very short, square tail. The sexes are similar in appearance but young birds have cinnamon wing bars.

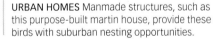

Violet-green Swallow

FAMILY Hirundinidae

SPECIES *Tachycineta thalassina*

LENGTH 5¼ in (13 cm)

HABITAT Woodland

CLUTCH SIZE 4–5

DISTRIBUTION In summer seen in western North America from Alaska to New Mexico, into Mexico. Overwinters from California to Central America.

SUBURBAN BIRDS Violet-green Swallows often perch on buildings, and they may also choose to use them as nesting sites. Pairs may even adopt nestboxes.

THESE SWALLOWS display a metallic bronze-green coloration over their backs, combined with an iridescent violet area on their rump and tail. There is a white streak above each eye, broadening over the cheeks down on to the white underparts. Young birds are much duller in coloration, having a dusky-colored face, and grayish-brown upperparts. Violet-green Swallows breed in colonies in woodland areas during the summer. They construct a nest of vegetation and feathers, sometimes in trees or even under the eaves of a building. Their chicks grow very rapidly, leaving the nest before they are two weeks old, and then begin to build up their flight muscles to head south for the winter.

Cliff Swallow

FAMILY Hirundinidae

SPECIES *Hirundo pyrrhonota*

LENGTH 5½ in (14 cm)

HABITAT Cliffs

CLUTCH SIZE 4–6

DISTRIBUTION Summer visitor over the entire North American continent, apart from the far north and northeast, plus the southeast, including Florida. Overwinters in South America.

IN SPITE OF ITS wide range in the summer, the Cliff Swallow is seen significantly less often in eastern areas, compared with the west, where the species is common. They may nest here in large colonies, with the birds returning annually to their traditional cliff sites. Their nests are built using mud, and typically lined with feathers and grass. Increasingly, as urbanization has occurred, so these swallows have adapted too, to the extent of attaching their nests to the undersides of bridges and other buildings. The incubation period lasts just two weeks, with the young swallows fledging at around three weeks old.

CHESTNUT MARKINGS The Cliff Swallow has a chestnut throat and cheeks, which helps in its identification. These markings are clearly evident in this individual. The crown area and back are bluish-black.

Barn Swallow

FAMILY Hirundinidae

SPECIES *Hirundo rustica*

LENGTH 6¾ in (17 cm)

HABITAT Buildings

CLUTCH SIZE 3–6

DISTRIBUTION Ranges from southern Alaska southeastward and south, over virtually the whole continent. Absent in parts of the extreme southwest and southern Florida.

OUT OF ALL the swallows, it is this species that has become most closely identified with human settlements in North America. The Barn Swallow breeds in colonies, attaching its nest of mud and dry grass to a vertical surface such as the wall of a building or a bridge. In the past, these birds used to nest in hollow trees, but buildings are now used far more frequently. It is impossible to distinguish the sexes by sight, but the appearance of the Barn Swallow is such that it cannot be confused with any other swallow species. The wings are long, as is the deeply forked tail, which may sometimes appear just as a single streamer if the tail feathers are kept closed.

ON THE WING Barn Swallows are a glossy bluish-black shade and have a small chestnut area above the bill.

Bank Swallow

FAMILY Hirundinidae

SPECIES *Riparia riparia*

LENGTH 4¾ in (12 cm)

HABITAT Riverbanks

CLUTCH SIZE 4–6

DISTRIBUTION From Alaska to Newfoundland and south across much of the northern United States; generally absent from the south, with the exception of the southern Texan border.

THE COLORATION of the Bank Swallow is quite plain, with the upperparts being brown, and the lowerparts white, apart from a dark brown band across the chest. This is also the smallest North American swallow, and is usually associated with river banks, where it nests in large colonies. Instead of building a nest, these swallows tunnel into the soft earth, to construct a burrow that enlarges into a nesting chamber at its end. This chamber is lined with feathers and vegetation. Swallow pairs return to the same nesting areas every year.

RIVERSIDE HOME The chicks spend three weeks in the nest. When they emerge, they can be distinguished at first by buff wing bars.

NESTING INDOORS Barn Swallows nest in buildings, which insures their young have some security and protection from the elements. Thanks to their flying abilities, feeding time creates no problems.

Black-capped Chickadee

FAMILY Paridae
SPECIES *Parus atricapillus*
LENGTH 5¼ in (13 cm)
HABITAT Woodland
CLUTCH SIZE 4–8

DISTRIBUTION Resident in a southeasterly direction across the continent to Newfoundland, south to northern California in the west, and as far south as northern New Mexico.

THIS IS NOT THE ONLY chickadee with a black cap on its head; where their distribution overlaps, it is difficult to distinguish this species and the Carolina Chickadee by appearance only. It is possible on the basis of size, however, since the Black-capped Chickadee is larger. Another point of distinction, particularly after the molt, is the white edging that this species has on its secondary wing feathers. Active by nature, Black-capped Chickadees often visit backyard feeders, with sunflower seed kernels being a particular favorite. They breed in tree holes, and sometimes adopt nestboxes. An assortment of plant matter and feathers is used to line the interior of the nest.

BLACK AND WHITE The black throat patch and white face of the Black-capped Chickadee are clearly evident from this angle. The underparts of the body are a creamy shade.

Tufted Titmouse

FAMILY Paridae
SPECIES *Parus bicolor*
LENGTH 6½ in (17 cm)
HABITAT Woodland
CLUTCH SIZE 5–8

DISTRIBUTION Found year-round in southeastern parts, from the area around the Great Lakes westward to Oklahoma and through eastern Texas. Absent from southern Florida.

THIS SPECIES can vary in the color of its tufted crest and its forehead. Some individuals have a gray crest with a black area above the bill, while others have a blackish crest and much paler forehead coloration. The underparts are always whitish, with a slight buffy hue apparent on the flanks. The Tufted Titmouse is social by nature, sometimes seen foraging in mixed groups alongside other similar species, looking for invertebrates in among the branches of trees and shrubs.

BIRDSONG The cock bird of this species is a very talented songster, with a surprisingly varied range of different song patterns.

Carolina Chickadee

FAMILY Paridae

SPECIES *Parus carolinesis*

LENGTH 4¾ in (12 cm)

HABITAT Woodland

CLUTCH SIZE 4–8

DISTRIBUTION Present from the vicinity of Delaware through the southeast. Absent from southern Florida, and parts of the Gulf Coast. Range extends into central Texas.

THIS BIRD'S BLACK plumage extends over the top of the head, and is also present on the throat, with an intervening area of white running back from the sides of the small, black bill and broadening out over the sides of the face. The flanks are buff in color, and the tail is relatively long. Carolina Chickadees are very common within their area of distribution, and conspicuous too, in spite of their small size. They are frequently seen in backyards, particularly if there are trees nearby where they can hunt for insects, and also nest in suitable hollows. Persistent pecking with their stocky bill allows chickadees to excavate a hole for this purpose in rotten wood if necessary. The sexes are identical in appearance, and pairs remain in close contact with each other in the backyard setting, even when visiting bird feeders. Their nesting period corresponds to that of the Black-capped Chickadee, with small insects being particularly important in the diet of the adult birds when they have young to rear in the nest. Incubation lasts for two weeks, and the chicks will stay in the nest until they are approximately 16 days old.

PART OF THE FLOCK Chickadees may be seen in loose flocks after the breeding season, from the fall on through the winter.

Mountain Chickadee

FAMILY Paridae
SPECIES *Parus gambeli*
LENGTH 5¼ in (13 cm)
HABITAT Upland forest
CLUTCH SIZE 6–8

DISTRIBUTION Occurs in southern British Columbia extending south and east; southern range ends near the Mexican border in western Texas. Also found in California.

THE POINT OF distinction that separates the Mountain Chickadee from related species is the white stripe that is present above its eye on each side of the head. As its name suggests, this chickadee is found in mountain forests throughout its range, but it may be seen at lower altitudes as well, particularly during the winter months when food may be harder to find.

ALERT AND AGILE Chickadees are very agile birds, darting quickly from branch to branch. This allows them to seize insects that might otherwise escape.

Boreal Chickadee

FAMILY Paridae
SPECIES *Parus hudsonicus*
LENGTH 5½ in (14 cm)
HABITAT Coniferous forest
CLUTCH SIZE 6–9

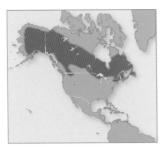

DISTRIBUTION Mainly occurs in the far north, from Alaska to Newfoundland, in Canada, but can be found on the United States' side of the border, in Washington and elsewhere.

THIS PARTICULAR CHICKADEE is not as well-known as some other members of the group because it is closely allied with dense forest where it can be hard to observe, although these birds are quite bold by nature. A dark brown cap, with grayish-brown upperparts, helps to identify this species. Boreal Chickadees feed mainly on various invertebrates, with caterpillars being a particular favorite, although they also eat seeds. They may even store food during the early fall, hiding seed, for example, behind the bark of trees within their territory so they can return here to feed in the winter when food is likely to be much scarcer in this environment.

FOREST PERCH This chickadee is sitting on a conifer branch. The species has a black throat stripe; the cheeks and underparts are white; there is a pale rust suffusion on the flanks.

Bridled Titmouse

FAMILY Paridae
SPECIES *Parus wollweberi*
LENGTH 5¼ in (13 cm)
HABITAT Oak woodland
CLUTCH SIZE 5–8

DISTRIBUTION Restricted to central-eastern Arizona and the adjacent southwestern area of New Mexico, being resident here throughout the year. Extends into Mexico.

SECOND HOME These titmice naturally use a hollow tree for nesting and sometimes take over an abandoned chamber created by a woodpecker.

THE CREST of the Bridled Titmouse is especially evident, curving forward and being black and gray in color. There is a prominent white collar around the back of the neck. The common name of these birds comes from the black stripes on the face, said to resemble a horse's bridle in appearance. The underparts are a pale shade of gray, with the upperparts being more grayish-green. The tail is quite long, relative to the body. These titmice are quite bold by nature, sometimes joining with other forest-dwelling species to harry potential predators, such as corvids or birds of prey, which may intrude on to their territory.

Juniper Titmouse

FAMILY Paridae
SPECIES *Baeolophus griseus*
LENGTH 5¼ in (13 cm)
HABITAT Juniper-pine woods
CLUTCH SIZE 4–8

DISTRIBUTION Widely found in the southwestern United States, ranging from Oregon and Idaho in the north to Oklahoma in the east. Isolated populations occur in California.

THE COLORATION of these titmice is very plain, which is why for a period, this species used to be called the Plain Titmouse, until it was separated from the Oak Titmouse (*see* p. 278). The Juniper Titmouse is essentially grayish in color, sometimes displaying a brownish hue that is particularly evident over the wings; their underparts are paler in color. They also have a small crest. Unlike most other titmice, the Juniper Titmouse does not associate in flocks even outside the nesting period, being seen either singly or in pairs.

NESTING IN BOXES Naturally breeding in tree holes, for which they create a cup-like lining, Juniper Titmice may also settle for a nestbox.

Oak Titmouse

FAMILY Paridae
SPECIES *Baeolophus inornatus*
LENGTH 5 in (13 cm)
HABITAT Oak woodland
CLUTCH SIZE 4–8

DISTRIBUTION Resident over a small range from southern Oregon, south to California, in areas of suitable oak-type woodland, into Baja California.

THIS BIRD LOOKS VERY SIMILAR to the Juniper Titmouse (*see* p. 277), but is slightly smaller in size, browner, and darker overall in color. It also frequents a different type of woodland, although the habits of both species are very similar. Invertebrates are prominent in their diet.

IDENTICAL The two sexes are identical in appearance. Incubation lasts approximately two weeks.

Bushtit

FAMILY Aegithalidae
SPECIES *Psaltriparus minimus*
LENGTH 4½ in (11 cm)
HABITAT Woodland/parks
CLUTCH SIZE 5–14

DISTRIBUTION Southernmost parts of British Columbia, across the United States to western Texas. Generally resident, but these birds may overwinter in New Mexico too.

THESE SMALL BIRDS are generally gray, and lighter gray on their underparts, but there is a population in Texas with black patches behind the eyes, known as Black-eared Bushtits. Highly social by nature, Bushtits live in areas of deciduous woodland, and flocks of them comb the trees in search of a wide variety of invertebrates, which are the mainstay of their diet, although they also eat small berries.

NEST CONSTRUCTION Breeding pairs of Bushtits construct their nest from plant fibers, making the entrance near the top.

Verdin

FAMILY Remizidae
SPECIES *Auriparus flaviceps*
LENGTH 4½ in (11 cm)
HABITAT Arid country
CLUTCH SIZE 3–5

DISTRIBUTION Occurs in the southeast, from southeastern California spreading in an easterly direction via Nevada and across into Texas. Extends across the border into Mexico.

THE NARROW BILL of these birds, although not especially long, allows them to probe flowers for nectar. They are also able to feed on nectar present in backyard hummingbird feeders. The Verdin appears to be common through its range. When breeding, the pair construct a large ball-shaped nest of twigs, siting this in a safe location such as on a large cactus. The incubation period is short, typically lasting as little as 11 days. The young grow quite rapidly and will leave the nest for the first time when they are about three weeks old. At this stage, the young birds are wholly gray in color.

YELLOW HEAD The Verdin has a very distinctive yellowish head and chestnut wing patches. It has pale gray underparts and darker gray upperparts.

Red-breasted Nuthatch

FAMILY Sittidae

SPECIES *Sitta canadensis*

LENGTH 4½ in (11 cm)

HABITAT Woodland

CLUTCH SIZE 5–8

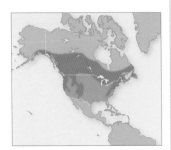

DISTRIBUTION Occurs in southern Canada, breeding further north in the summer. It can be seen virtually anywhere in the United States in winter but is absent from Florida.

NUTHATCHES ARE FOUND in woodland areas, scurrying up and down the trunk with remarkable agility. The Red-breasted Nuthatch tends to favor coniferous forest. It is possible to distinguish the sexes by their appearance. Cock birds have a black cap, with white stripes beneath, running above the eye. There is a black stripe across the eyes; the underparts are rusty-red, and the back and wings are bluish-gray. Hens have a slate-gray rather than a black cap; this coloration is also seen in young birds of both sexes. Pairs of this species may breed in tree hollows up to 100 ft (30 m) off the ground.

NOT ONLY NUTS These nuthatches feed on conifer seeds, which form a major part of their diet over the winter, and invertebrates.

White-breasted Nuthatch

FAMILY Sittidae

SPECIES *Sitta carolinensis*

LENGTH 5¾ in (14 cm)

HABITAT Woodland

CLUTCH SIZE 5–9

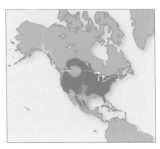

DISTRIBUTION Resident in southern Canada, and western parts of the United States. Also occurs widely in the eastern United States, but absent from Florida and the Gulf Coast.

SHARP PROBE The narrow beak of the White-breasted Nuthatch allows it to probe small holes in the bark and seize its prey without difficulty.

THIS PARTICULAR nuthatch can be identified quite easily, as it is the only species with a white face. This coloration also extends down on to the underparts. The crown and nape are black, with the back and wings being bluish-gray. It has a wide distribution, and is found in both broadleaf and coniferous woodland, although it generally inhabits mature trees. In common with other nuthatches, the agile White-breasted Nuthatch hunts invertebrates partly by pausing at regular intervals, to watch for any signs of movement in its vicinity.

Brown-headed Nuthatch

FAMILY Sittidae
SPECIES *Sitta pusilla*
LENGTH 4½ in (11 cm)
HABITAT Coniferous woodland
CLUTCH SIZE 4–9

DISTRIBUTION From Delaware to Mississippi; not in southern Florida. A separate population occurs in southwest Oklahoma and eastern Texas, western Arkansas, and Louisiana.

THE BROWN CAP on the head helps to distinguish this nuthatch, with a white spot usually being evident on the nape of the neck too. There is a blackish line running back from the bill toward the eyes, while the underparts are a creamy shade of buff. Like woodpeckers, nuthatches are able to move vertically up the tree; they can also head down the trunk in a similar fashion. Their tail feathers are not reinforced to help them stay securely in place when moving around, but instead, nuthatches rely on their strong toes to anchor themselves as they climb on the lookout for invertebrates.

CAMOUFLAGE Like other species, the wings of the Brown-headed Nuthatch are bluish-gray, helping these birds to blend into the colors of the forest against the bark of the trees.

Pygmy Nuthatch

FAMILY Sittidae
SPECIES *Sitta pygmaea*
LENGTH 4¼ in (11 cm)
HABITAT Coniferous forest
CLUTCH SIZE 5–9

DISTRIBUTION Western areas from Washington to California. A separate population extends from Wyoming to Arizona and New Mexico, and into western Texas. Sporadic elsewhere.

THE PYGMY NUTHATCH has relatively dull plumage. Its head, from the bill down to the level of the eyes, is grayish, as are the back and wings, while the underparts are a creamy shade. In common with other species, the Pygmy Nuthatch starts to build up stores of food within its territory from late summer onward, relying on this to sustain itself over the winter, when food otherwise becomes increasingly hard to find. These food stores may be kept in small holes or tucked behind bark.

COMMUNAL LIVING Pigmy Nuthatches use tree holes not just for nesting purposes, but also to roost communally; they also form flocks during the daytime.

Bewick's Wren

FAMILY Troglodytidae
SPECIES *Thryomanes bewickii*
LENGTH 5¼ in (13 cm)
HABITAT Undergrowth
CLUTCH SIZE 4–9

DISTRIBUTION From southern British Columbia to California along the coast and inland to Missouri and Arkansas, through Oklahoma and Texas; extends further west in winter.

THE MOST OBVIOUS feature of Bewick's Wren is its long, barred tail, which it flicks in a very distinctive fashion from side to side slowly, and then up and down. The white tips are only apparent when the tail feathers are fanned. The upperparts of this wren are brownish in color, with a creamy stripe extending back down the neck from above the eye. The underparts are pale. These wrens usually breed in small tree holes, although they will use nestboxes as well. Their nest is made from moss and leaves, and then lined with feathers to create a snug interior. It will be two weeks before the young chicks hatch, and they then spend a similar period in the nest. On occasions, it is not unusual for a breeding pair to have more than one round of chicks during the summer period.

LOSS OF HABITAT It is thought likely that loss of nesting habitat is the cause of the decline in numbers of Bewick's Wrens in the eastern parts of its range.

Brown Creeper

FAMILY Certhidae

SPECIES *Certhia americana*

LENGTH 5¼ in (13 cm)

HABITAT Woodland

CLUTCH SIZE 4–8

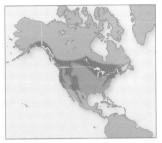

DISTRIBUTION From southern Alaska via Arizona and New Mexico into Mexico. Breeds across southern Canada; resident east of the Great Lakes. Widespread over winter.

THE MOTTLED PLUMAGE on the back and wings of the Brown Creeper enables it to blend very effectively against the bark of most trees. The tail feathers are quite rigid at their tips, tapering to a point, and they help to support these birds when they are climbing up tree trunks. Just as with woodpeckers, however, this characteristic prevents them from moving head-first downward.

NARROW BILL The Brown Creeper has a narrow, down-curving bill, allowing it to probe into cracks in the bark and extract invertebrates easily.

Carolina Wren

FAMILY Troglodytidae

SPECIES *Thryothorus ludovicianus*

LENGTH 5½ in (14 cm)

HABITAT Swampy woodland

CLUTCH SIZE 4–8

DISTRIBUTION Southeastern area of the United States, north to southern Maine. Western boundary of their range extends via southern Iowa, eastern Kansas, and eastern Texas into Mexico.

A RICH SHADE of rusty-brown allows the Carolina Wren to be distinguished from Bewick's Wren. This species is found in vegetation in wetland areas, where it will be relatively inconspicuous. Their numbers can fall quite severely during a bad winter, when food is scarce.

LOOKING THE SAME Both sexes of this jaunty little bird are identical in appearance.

Rock Wren

FAMILY Troglodytidae

SPECIES *Salpinctes obsoletus*

LENGTH 6 in (15 cm)

HABITAT Arid country

CLUTCH SIZE 4–7

DISTRIBUTION Resident from California southeast to Texas. Breeds to the north and east of this, reaching southwestern Canada and south through the Dakotas to Oklahoma.

ROCKY TERRAIN The typical habitat for these wrens is rocky scrubland or desert areas where there are boulders. Their coloration helps them to blend in.

ROCK WRENS are quite conspicuous birds, they are often seen out in the open and usually bobbing up and down along the ground. The bill is long, narrow, and curves down slightly toward the tip, allowing these wrens to reach invertebrates concealed under rocks or in small crevices. A breeding pair will often choose to nest in a rocky outcrop too, constructing their nest using dry vegetation and other items such as wool or hair, and then lining the structure with soft feathers. The hen sits alone, while the cock bird may build a path of small stones leading to the nest, revealing its location for reasons that are unclear.

Canyon Wren

FAMILY Troglodytidae

SPECIES *Catherpes mexicanus*

LENGTH 5¾ in (14 cm)

HABITAT Canyons

CLUTCH SIZE 4–6

DISTRIBUTION Resident from southern British Columbia through the western United States into Mexico. Most common in coastal California, east from Arizona to Texas.

THE COLORATION of the Canyon Wren helps to conceal its presence in the canyons where it is likely to be encountered. The head is dark and speckled, with the throat and chest being white. The back and wings, as well as the underparts, are chestnut-brown, with black spots and bars. The two sexes are identical in appearance. The bill of these wrens is particularly long, increasing their ability to extract invertebrates from cracks in the rocks. A pair often chooses to breed within the rocks too, building a snug nest.

CANYON DWELLERS As their name suggests, Canyon Wrens frequent steep-sided areas of countryside. However, they will sometimes nest in buildings, often on stone walls.

Cactus Wren

FAMILY Troglodytidae

SPECIES *Campylorhynchus brunneicapillus*

LENGTH 8½ in (22 cm)

HABITAT Desert

CLUTCH SIZE 4–7

DISTRIBUTION Resident from Nevada, Utah, and southern California into Arizona and New Mexico, across the Mexican border. Also extends eastward into the western parts of Texas.

THE CHATTER OF THESE wrens draws attention to their presence in an area. They usually occur in groups and, as their name suggests, they like to construct their nest in a cactus, or sometimes a yucca. They use the nest not just for breeding, however, but also for roosting purposes through the year. Cactus Wrens can easily be distinguished from other wren species, partly by their large size: They rank as the biggest of the North American wrens. The back and wings are dark brown and mottled paler; the chest is dark too. The underparts are a pale-reddish brown near the vent, again mottled with darker brown patterning.

INDIVIDUAL MARKINGS The markings of these wrens are quite distinctive, which enables many of the individuals in an area to be recognized.

Marsh Wren

FAMILY Troglodytidae
SPECIES *Cistothorus palustris*
LENGTH 5 in (13 cm)
HABITAT Marshland
CLUTCH SIZE 5–9

DISTRIBUTION Resident in the west; absent from central and eastern United States; spends winter in the south. Breeds from western Canada east via the Great Lakes to Nova Scotia.

ALTHOUGH SMALL and also quite inconspicuous birds in terms of their coloration, Marsh Wrens have a powerful song that belies their size, as in the case of many wrens. They may often be heard singing from the depths of a reed bed, but pinpointing their location can be difficult. Marsh Wrens are predominantly brown in color. They have a prominent brown cap with a white stripe running back above the eye; the underparts are pale in color. The back and wings are blackish, with white striping. The sexes are identical in appearance. Marsh Wrens hunt midges and other invertebrates living in their damp habitat, sometimes catching their prey on the surface of the water. Pairs build a ball-shaped nest of reeds, anchored just above the waterline.

COCKED TAIL Many wren species typically perch with their tail feathers vertical, as shown here by this Marsh Wren.

Sedge Wren

FAMILY Troglodytidae
SPECIES *Cistothorus platensis*
LENGTH 4½ in (11 cm)
HABITAT Sedge meadow
CLUTCH SIZE 3–8

DISTRIBUTION Breeds from northwest of the Great Lakes eastward to Quebec and south to Illinois. Overwinters from Delaware through Florida to eastern Texas.

IN CONTRAST TO THE Marsh Wren, this species displays much greater barring over its upperparts, with its underparts tending to be more of a buff shade. The Sedge Wren is also not easy to observe, partly due to its secretive nature, but also because it is not particularly common through its range. In addition, there are fears that it may be declining in some areas, as the result of habitat change. In its northern breeding grounds, it nests just above the waterline, constructing a ball-shaped chamber using mainly sedges, although grass may be incorporated as well. The birds enter through a side entrance. Incubation is carried out by the hen; it takes two weeks for the young wrens to hatch, and they will leave the nest after a similar interval.

PERILOUS PERCH Their agility means these birds can easily dart away out of sight.

House Wren

FAMILY Troglodytidae
SPECIES *Troglodytes aedon*
LENGTH 4¾ in (12 cm)
HABITAT Buildings/parks
CLUTCH SIZE 3–6

DISTRIBUTION Breeds across southern Canada and most of the United States. Resident in California and from Alabama east to North Carolina. Spends winter in the southern states.

THIS IS ONE of the most conspicuous wrens, as it often occurs in backyards and city areas. It has a rich, bubbling song that often emanates from undergrowth without the bird being visible. Its upperparts are grayish-brown, with this coloration extending down on both sides of the head to the vicinity of the throat; just the hint of an eyebrow stripe is evident.

TASTY MEAL House Wrens forage for invertebrates in gardens and parks. They breed in nestboxes, tree hollows, or holes in walls.

Winter Wren

FAMILY Troglodytidae

SPECIES *Troglodytes troglodytes*

LENGTH 4 in (10 cm)

HABITAT Woodland

CLUTCH SIZE 4–7

DISTRIBUTION Resident on western coasts, south from the Aleutian Islands. In summer found east to Newfoundland. Overwinters in the southeast.

FEEDING THE BROOD This Winter Wren is returning to the nest with food for the chicks, which spend about two weeks in the nest.

THESE WRENS RANGE over a wide area through the year, occurring further north than most related species in the winter. They have the unmistakable profile of a wren, being small, with a jaunty tail and a short, pointed bill that is used to catch invertebrates. Their coloration varies somewhat through their range, with individuals from the northwest of their range, which extends into southern Alaska, being slightly bigger in terms of their overall size, as well as being paler in color than those found elsewhere. Their basic coloration is reddish-brown, with evident barring on the flanks and underparts and across the wings. The chest is a slightly paler shade, and there is a buff-colored stripe above each eye. Winter Wrens tend to favor forest areas, but they are always hard to spot as they prefer dense undergrowth.

American Dipper

FAMILY Cinclidae
SPECIES *Cinclus mexicanus*
LENGTH 7½ in (19 cm)
HABITAT Mountain streams
CLUTCH SIZE 3–6

DISTRIBUTION Occurs down the western side of North America extending from Alaska south to California. Found as far south as Panama in Central America in suitable habitat.

WADING IN WATER Even when not in water, these birds walk in a jaunty manner; water runs off their plumage readily.

THE AMERICAN DIPPER is only ever likely to be encountered in the vicinity of fast-flowing streams in mountain areas. It has a somewhat stocky appearance, and is slate-gray in color overall, with yellow legs and a relatively dark bill. Its name comes partly from the way it moves in and out of the water, often traveling on foot, hopping from one partially submerged rock to another along the stream, even in proximity to a waterfall. American Dippers are solitary birds by nature, with pairs only coming together to nest in the spring. The nest is well-concealed, sometimes being built under a manmade structure, such as a bridge. The hen sits alone on the eggs for just over two weeks, with the young dippers fledging when they are just over three weeks old.

Ruby-crowned Kinglet

FAMILY Regulidae
SPECIES *Regulus calendula*
LENGTH 4¼ in (11 cm)
HABITAT Woodland
CLUTCH SIZE 5–11

DISTRIBUTION This is a summer visitor from Alaska via Hudson Bay to the east coast. It overwinters in central, western, and southern areas, down into Central America.

ONLY THE COCK BIRD displays the bright red area on the crown that typifies this kinglet, and this area will only be evident if these feathers are raised. Ruby-crowned Kinglets are not easy birds to observe, partly because of their rather subdued coloration, but also because they live high up in the trees, largely out of sight from the ground.

HARD WINTERS Kinglets may struggle to find insects, which form the basis of their diet, in winter. They are more likely to be seen at this time.

AT HOME IN WATER American Dippers are rarely found far from water. These agile birds can scramble easily over slippery rocks in fast-flowing streams. In addition to wading, they swim well and will dive for invertebrate prey.

Golden-crowned Kinglet

FAMILY Regulidae
SPECIES *Regulus satrapa*
LENGTH 4 in (10 cm)
HABITAT Coniferous woodland
CLUTCH SIZE 5–11

DISTRIBUTION Breeds from Alaska eastward to northern Newfoundland. Resident in the west and east. Overwinters in areas through the United States.

A GOLDEN-YELLOW crown surrounded by a black border characterizes this kinglet, with this area being a more intense orange shade in cock birds. Golden-crowned Kinglets are often seen in mixed flocks, joining up with parties of other small birds and feeding communally in the dense woodlands that they inhabit. They feed on small invertebrates, often clinging on to the underside of branches to find any that may be hidden beneath leaves. Breeding pairs nest at a considerable height, often 100 ft (30 m) off the ground. The nest itself is constructed using a variety of lichens and moss, and is suspended off a branch. It has an entry hole at the top.

BRIGHT-EYED The lively nature of these small birds can draw attention to their presence, although their coloration also enables them to merge very effectively into the background.

Arctic Warbler

FAMILY Sylviidae
SPECIES *Phylloscopus borealis*
LENGTH 5 in (13 cm)
HABITAT Tundra
CLUTCH SIZE 5–7

DISTRIBUTION This is a summer resident in western and central Alaska, migrating to overwinter in Asia after the breeding season. Also recorded in the Aleutian Islands.

THE ORIGINS OF THIS warbler lie in Asia rather than in the Americas, with these small birds migrating back and forth across the Bering Sea each year, to reach their favored Alaskan breeding grounds. They are grayish-olive in color above, with prominent pale lemon stripes above each eye; their underparts are whitish. The sexes are identical in appearance. Although they may be seen moving around in areas of willow and other low-growing shrubs that grow on the tundra, pairs will nest on the ground, creating a dome-shaped cup nest.

WINTER SUN This species normally leaves North America in the fall, but has been seen wintering in California on a couple of occasions.

Blue-gray Gnatcatcher

FAMILY Polioptilidae

SPECIES *Polioptila caerulea*

LENGTH 4¼ in (11 cm)

HABITAT Woodland

CLUTCH SIZE 4–5

DISTRIBUTION Extends across most of the United States in summer, but absent from the northwest and center. Resident in the southeast and California. Overwinters south into Mexico.

THE BLUE-GRAY GNATCATCHER is a relatively stocky bird, with a long tail. It is very active by nature, constantly on the search for invertebrates and flicking its tail frequently when on the move. Their upperparts are bluish-gray, being bluer in cock birds than in hens; their underparts are pale. When in breeding plumage, the sexes can be distinguished thanks to the male's black eye stripes. They create a woven nest, using grasses and other vegetation, siting this in the fork of a tree branch high off the ground.

EYE RINGS The white eye rings of the Blue-gray Gnatcatcher aid its identification; the eyes are black and relatively large.

Black-tailed Gnatcatcher

FAMILY Polioptilidae

SPECIES *Polioptila melanura*

LENGTH 4 in (10 cm)

HABITAT Arid country

CLUTCH SIZE 4–6

DISTRIBUTION Resident in the southwest, from Nevada and southeastern California, across Arizona, southern New Mexico to southwestern Texas; also across the border in Mexico.

A LONG BLACK TAIL helps to identify this species, hence the common name. Cock birds molt at the start of the breeding season, when the gray plumage on the crown is replaced by black. Pairs usually nest in bushes, with the incubation period lasting for about two weeks.

NEST IN SCRUB In this breeding pair, it is the male that is perched on their tall-sided, cup-shaped nest.

Varied Thrush

FAMILY Turdidae

SPECIES *Ixoreus naevius*

LENGTH 9½ in (24 cm)

HABITAT Dense woodland

CLUTCH SIZE 3–5

DISTRIBUTION Breeds in Alaska east and south through British Columbia. Resident in coastal areas here, right down to California. Overwinters further to the southeast.

WINTER SEARCH This cock bird is seeking food on the ground in the snow. When food is scarce, such thrushes may be more conspicuous.

THE COCK VARIED THRUSH is especially colorful, with a bright yellowish-orange stripe over the eyes and similar coloration evident on its underparts, broken by a black band across the chest. The top of the body—the head, back, and tail—is mainly grayish. Hens are not as brightly colored. Varied Thrushes are not easy birds to observe, however, as they inhabit forested areas, being particularly associated with coniferous woodland. The eggs are laid in a large, cup-shaped nest, with the chicks hatching after a period of two weeks.

Wood Thrush

FAMILY Turdidae

SPECIES *Hylocichla mustelina*

LENGTH 7¾ in (20 cm)

HABITAT Woodland

CLUTCH SIZE 2–5

DISTRIBUTION Summer visitor from Nova Scotia west via the Great Lakes into Oklahoma and eastern Texas. Absent from southern Florida. Overwinters in Central America.

GARDEN VISITOR Wood Thrushes may be seen in open areas, often in gardens, but typically where there is woodland in the vicinity.

THE RELATIVELY LARGE SIZE of the Wood Thrush helps to distinguish it from similar species that also have spotted plumage on their underparts. The upperparts are reddish-brown, becoming browner lower down on the back and tail. The sexes appear very similar to each other. These thrushes eat a wide selection of invertebrates, including snails and earthworms, as well as berries of various types. At the start of the breeding season a pair build a cup-shaped nest, using vegetation anchored together by mud. This is usually located high up in a tree.

American Robin

FAMILY Turdidae

SPECIES *Turdus migratorius*

LENGTH 10 in (25 cm)

HABITAT Woodland

CLUTCH SIZE 3–4

DISTRIBUTION Breeding range extends through Canada, and it is resident through the United States. Winters in Florida and in southern California and Texas.

THE BEAUTIFUL COLORATION of the American Robin helps to make these members of the thrush family easy to identify. The reddish-orange of the underparts contrasts with the grayish-brown upperparts. There is white plumage around the eyes, and streaking on the throat, with the plumage on the head being of a blackish shade. As is often the case, the hens are less brightly colored. The American Robin is a very adaptable species, and bold by nature, being observed in a range of different habitats. These birds are common backyard visitors, being attracted by bird-table offerings during the winter months, and may also hunt for worms on the lawn. When breeding, they often choose a forked branch on which they construct a cup-shaped nest, but may sometimes use an accessible shelf in an outbuilding instead.

BERRY FEAST In the fall, berries feature prominently in the diet of American Robins. The seach for this food can draw birds into gardens at this time of year.

Veery

FAMILY Turdidae
SPECIES *Catharus fuscescens*
LENGTH 7 in (18 cm)
HABITAT Woodland
CLUTCH SIZE 3–5

DISTRIBUTION Breeds in a band across most of North America, occurring in southern Canada and northern parts of the United States. Overwinters as far south as Brazil.

THE VEERY IS A SHY BIRD by nature, and as it chooses to live in dense woodland habitats, it is hard to locate, even though it is not a rare species. It lives largely on the ground, where it survives by hunting for invertebrates, although it will also feed on berries when these are available.

VEERY SONG This bird's unusual name is a reflection of the sound of its calls, as well as that of its song.

Hermit Thrush

FAMILY Turdidae
SPECIES *Catharus guttatus*
LENGTH 6¾ in (17 cm)
HABITAT Woodland
CLUTCH SIZE 3–5

DISTRIBUTION Breeds from Alaska east to Newfoundland, and south to Texas. Resident on west and east coasts. Spends winter across the south and southeast to Central America.

THE HERMIT THRUSH is a common species, but it is more likely to be noticed by the sound of its song emanating from undergrowth rather than by being seen. Its upperparts are olive-brown, with blackish-brown spotting across its pale chest, with these markings fading over the abdomen. The flanks have a grayish suffusion, helping to distinguish this species from other similarly marked thrushes.

FEEDING YOUNG An adult feeds three nestlings with invertebrates. The Hermit Thrush builds its cup-shaped nest close to the ground.

VARIED DIET Hermit Thrushes eat berries, as well as hunting for earthworms, spiders, and similar creatures on or near the forest floor. Although it is stocky with short wings, this thrush flies long distances to breed.

Gray-cheeked Thrush

FAMILY Turdidae
SPECIES *Catharus minimus*
LENGTH 7¼ in (18 cm)
HABITAT Woodland
CLUTCH SIZE 3–5

DISTRIBUTION This species spends summer on its breeding grounds in Alaska and northern Canada. It overwinters in northern South America, occurring as far south as Brazil.

THE GRAY MARKINGS on the face and throat of this thrush can help to distinguish it from similar thrush species; the upperparts of its body are olive-brown. The two sexes are very similar in appearance. The Gray-cheeked Thrush is a summer visitor to the far north of Canada, inhabiting woodland where it will build its nest close to the ground. The eggs take two weeks to hatch, with the chicks then remaining in the nest for a similar period of time before fledging.

FEEDING HABITS Thrushes usually feed largely on invertebrates such as earthworms, but will also eat berries.

Swainson's Thrush

FAMILY Turdidae
SPECIES *Catharus ustulatus*
LENGTH 7 in (18 cm)
HABITAT Woodland
CLUTCH SIZE 3–5

DISTRIBUTION Breeds from Alaska across Canada, down to California in the west, and the vicinity of the Great Lakes in the east. Overwinters in northern South America.

THESE THRUSHES ARE relatively common through their range in North America during the summer breeding season, frequenting damp woodland areas. When they head south for winter, they generally migrate under cover of darkness rather than during the day. This species is similar in appearance to other members of the genus, but it is olive-brown overall, with those individuals from western areas being of a more reddish-brown shade. They feed on the ground, sometimes turning over vegetation with their bills in search of invertebrates.

SONGBIRD Like many thrushes, Swainson's Thrush has an attractive song. Cock birds sing most frequently at the start of the nesting period.

Townsend's Solitaire

FAMILY Turdidae
SPECIES *Myadestes*
townsendi
LENGTH 8½ in (22 cm)
HABITAT Mountainous forest
CLUTCH SIZE 3–4

DISTRIBUTION Main breeding range extends from Alaska to British Columbia. Overwinters to the southeast and south. Resident to New Mexico and into Central America.

GRAY COLORATION, slightly darker on the upperparts, helps to identify this species, which also has bright white rings of plumage around the eyes. There is a white wing patch, which is most visible in flight. The two sexes are identical in appearance. Young birds can be distinguished by their mottled plumage—a combination of gray and white. Townsend's Solitaire occurs in a range of woodland areas, but invariably at high altitude, although it may move to lower levels and even more arid country over the winter period. These thrushes are not seen in flocks, tending to be solitary by nature as reflected by their common name.

GROUNDED Townsend's Solitaire spends much of its time on or close to the ground, seeking food and it also builds its cup-shaped nest in vegetation close to the ground.

Wrentit

FAMILY Sylviidae
SPECIES *Chamaea fasciata*
LENGTH 6½ in (17 cm)
HABITAT Chaparral/brushland
CLUTCH SIZE 3–5

DISTRIBUTION Found in western coastal areas, from Oregon south to California, and into Baja California. Closely associated with chaparral or huckleberry-salal vegetation.

THIS SPECIES is the only member of the Old World warbler family permanently resident in the New World. It has a jaunty manner, as reflected by the movements of its tail feathers. Wrentits are brown with white eyes and there is slight streaking evident on the breast. Populations remain localized and there is some regional variation, since those from northern parts of the range are a more reddish-brown shade. Wrentits are not conspicuous birds, and they prefer to remain concealed in vegetation rather than emerging into the open.

SECLUDED HOME Wrentits use spiders' webs to help hold their cup-shaped nests together. They make them well-concealed in vegetation.

Mountain Bluebird

FAMILY Turdidae

SPECIES *Sialia currucoides*

LENGTH 7¼ in (18 cm)

HABITAT Upland areas

CLUTCH SIZE 4–6

DISTRIBUTION Breeds in the west in Canada and the United States to California. Resident from Oregon to New Mexico. Overwinters in the south.

MOUNTAIN BLUEBIRDS are found in fairly open areas of country in the summer, but always where there are trees nearby for roosting and breeding. The sexes can be determined easily: The cock bird has sky-blue upperparts and the breast area is a paler shade of blue, while the belly is white. Hens are not as brightly colored, being grayer with a brown suffusion and having a white belly. The upperparts have more of a bluish-gray hue. Young birds resemble hens, but can be recognized by their spotted underparts. Pairs will breed in tree cavities, sometimes taking over a nest site created by a pair of woodpeckers. The incubation period lasts for two weeks, with the young emerging from the nest after a similar interval. Insects feature prominently in the diet of these bluebirds, although they will also eat berries.

LEAVING HOME This cock bird is emerging from its nest in the hollow of a tree. These bluebirds tend to move to lower altitudes during the winter.

Western Bluebird

FAMILY Turdidae

SPECIES *Sialia mexicana*

LENGTH 7 in (18 cm)

HABITAT Woodland/open
country

CLUTCH SIZE 4–6

DISTRIBUTION Breeds in southern British Columbia into California, and in Colorado. Overwinters over a broad area: Arizona, New Mexico, and Texas.

A DEEP BLUE COLOR is characteristic of the Western Bluebird male, which has chestnut areas on the underparts and sides of the body and a bluish-gray belly. Hens are not so brightly colored, being brownish-gray above, with a grayish throat, and a chestnut suffusion on the chest. Especially after the breeding season, Western Bluebirds can be seen large flocks.

MUSICAL SONG Like related species, these bluebirds have an attractive song, heard most often at the start of the breeding season. This is a male.

Eastern Bluebird

FAMILY Turdidae

SPECIES *Sialia sialis*

LENGTH 7 in (18 cm)

HABITAT Woodland/open
country

CLUTCH SIZE 2–7

DISTRIBUTION Breeds in the north, to southeastern Canada. Resident from Maine to north Texas. Overwinters further to the southeast, and in southern Arizona. Not in southern Florida.

THESE BLUEBIRDS ARE SIMILAR in appearance to related species; rusty upperparts and a white belly are identifying features of the cock bird. Pairs will often adopt nestboxes, although they traditionally breed in tree holes, creating a cup-shaped nest made largely with grass.

VARIED MENU Eastern bluebirds hunt insects and also visit bird tables. Young birds are brownish in color.

Gray Catbird

FAMILY Mimidae

SPECIES *Dumetella carolinensis*

LENGTH 8½ in (22 cm)

HABITAT Woodland/shrubland

CLUTCH SIZE 3–5

DISTRIBUTION Eastern United States in the summer, north to Yukon and Nova Scotia. Resident down the east coast and across the southern states, wintering on the Gulf coast.

GOOD MIMIC Although the Gray Catbird is a common summer visitor over a wide area of North America, its unusual calls may mean that its presence is sometimes overlooked.

GRAY COLORING predominates in this species and overall its appearance is very subdued, although it has a black area on the head, contrasting with the surrounding gray plumage, and chestnut-red undertail coverts. What sets it apart, however, is the sound of its calls. These are like the miaowing of a cat, which can create considerable confusion in the suburban areas where it often occurs. In addition, the aptly named Gray Catbird is also able to mimic the sounds of other birds in its immediate environment, potentially resulting in further confusion. During the breeding season, pairs nest in a suitable thicket, building a cup-shaped nest.

Northern Mockingbird

FAMILY Mimidae

SPECIES *Mimus polyglottos*

LENGTH 10 in (25 cm)

HABITAT Woodland/shrubland

CLUTCH SIZE 3–5

DISTRIBUTION Resident across many of the southern states, from Nova Scotia to New Mexico and west to California. Also breeds further north in midwestern states.

THE NATURAL SOUND of the Northern Mockingbird's song is attractive and loud, although these birds also prove to be talented mimics, picking up the calls of other species with ease. Their plumage is quite dull in color, with gray upperparts and white underparts. The white areas in the wings are evident when they are in flight. They can also be seen when these birds are foraging, as they often flash their wings during their search for invertebrates. They have adapted well to the suburbs, where there are trees and shrubs to serve as nest sites, and feeding opportunities on the lawn.

COCKED TAIL As with wrens, this mocking bird often raises its long tail feathers when on the move, revealing the white feathers underneath.

Bendire's Thrasher

FAMILY Mimidae
SPECIES *Toxostoma bendirei*
LENGTH 9¾ in (25 cm)
HABITAT Open country
CLUTCH SIZE 3–4

DISTRIBUTION Breeding range extends to California and southern Utah, and westward into New Mexico from northern Arizona. Resident in southern Arizona and into Mexico.

THE LONG, down-curving bill of Bendire's Thrasher aids its identification. It is brown in terms of its overall coloration, with paler underparts and small, arrow-shaped markings on the breast. Sexes are similar in appearance. These birds tend to be found in fairly arid areas, nesting close to the ground, using a bush or sometimes even a cactus for this purpose.

ON THE RUN This bird tends to live close to the ground, where it hunts for insects. If disturbed, they often prefer to run away through the brush, rather than fly.

Crissal Thrasher

FAMILY Mimidae
SPECIES *Toxostoma crissale*
LENGTH 11½ in (29 cm)
HABITAT Thicket
CLUTCH SIZE 2–4

DISTRIBUTION Resident in the southeast, from southern parts of Nevada and Utah to southeastern California, and from Arizona, New Mexico, and southwest Texas into Mexico.

A LONG TAIL HELPS to identify this species. Crissal Thrashers are brown on the upperparts, with a grayer tone to the underparts and a pale throat. The bill is long and black, curving down toward its tip. They use their bills to turn over leaves searching for food on the ground and also spend most of their time at ground level, hiding in brush and thickets.

HIDDEN NESTS Crissal Thrashers build a large bowl-shaped nest, well-hidden within a bush. Incubation lasts about two weeks.

Curve-billed Thrasher

FAMILY Mimidae

SPECIES *Toxostoma curvirostre*

LENGTH 11 in (28 cm)

HABITAT Brushland

CLUTCH SIZE 2-4

DISTRIBUTION Southwestern United States, from southern Colorado and Kansas extending south into Central America.

THRASHERS AS A GROUP are so-called because of the way in which they feed, picking up and throwing down vegetation, in the hope of uncovering invertebrates beneath. The Curve-billed Thrasher displays the typically curved bill shape associated with members of this genus; young birds have straighter, shorter bills. Predominantly brown in color, with speckling on the breast that is especially pronounced in young birds, the Curve-billed Thrasher also has bright yellow eyes, another feature associated with many thrashers. Their plain coloration helps them to blend into the background in the arid areas where they live. The song of these thrashers is most likely to be heard in the early morning or at dusk, when they are most active. Unlike some related species, the Curve-billed Thrasher remains in its range throughout the year. They inhabit desert areas, breeding among the cactus, with pairs constructing a bulky nest of vegetation, often quite high up in the arm of one of these plants, as much as 12 ft (4 m) off the ground. Both male and female adult birds incubate the eggs, with the young birds hatching after an interval of approximately two weeks. They remain in the nest for a similar period of time before fledging.

PRICKLY PERCH This thrasher perches on top of a cactus. These plants provide the birds with both feeding and nesting opportunities.

Long-billed Thrasher

FAMILY Mimidae

SPECIES *Toxostoma longirostre*

LENGTH 11½ in (29 cm)

HABITAT Thicket

CLUTCH SIZE 2–5

DISTRIBUTION Restricted to southern parts of Texas, being resident throughout the year, with a range that extends over the border to Central America.

GRAYISH-BROWN UPPERPARTS and white underparts with elongated dark streaking help to identify this species. The streaking patterns are sufficiently distinctive to allow individual birds to be recognized. The bill is black, and curves along its length. The Long-billed Thrasher is not

THRUSHLIKE The speckling and overall body shape of this thrasher are reminiscent of the thrush.

easy to spot, as it spends much of its time hiding in undergrowth, but it is likely to be more obvious at the start of the breeding season, when cock birds sing frequently.

California Thrasher

FAMILY Mimidae

SPECIES *Toxostoma redivivum*

LENGTH 12 in (30 cm)

HABITAT Scrubland

CLUTCH SIZE 2–4

DISTRIBUTION Confined to California, in the southwestern United States, occurring in the chaparral region along the coast and in the Sierra Nevada. Ranges down to Baja California.

THE DARK BILL of these thrashers is strongly curved, down toward its tip. They are brown in color, but with fine white streaking on the sides of the face and a pale throat. California Thrashers are not very conspicuous, spending most of their time on the ground hidden in vegetation. Although they have a restricted range, they are not uncommon within this area.

BOTH ALIKE It is impossible to tell male and female California Thrashers apart. Pairs construct a nest using twigs and similar vegetation.

Brown Thrasher

FAMILY Mimidae

SPECIES *Toxostoma rufum*

LENGTH 11½ in (29 cm)

HABITAT Thicket/woodland

CLUTCH SIZE 2–4

DISTRIBUTION Eastern half of the United States, northwest to Alberta in Canada during the summer. Resident along the eastern coast and through the southeastern United States.

UNLIKE MANY THRASHERS, this species has a comparatively short and stocky bill. The upperparts are reddish-brown with two white bars with darker edging above running across each wing. There are pale areas around the eyes as well, with thin streaking on the sides of the face. Elongated dark blotches are evident on the white underparts. Cock birds can be distinguished by their song at the start of the breeding season, often singing from a conspicuous branch. The nest itself is built on or near the ground.

BRAVE FORAGER This species can be bold, venturing into backyards where they forage for berries.

Sage Thrasher

FAMILY Mimidae

SPECIES *Oreoscoptes montanus*

LENGTH 8½ in (22 cm)

HABITAT Sagebrush/juniper

CLUTCH SIZE 4–5

DISTRIBUTION Southwestern Canada to northern Arizona and New Mexico. Overwinters in California and further south to Texas and Mexico.

RELATIVELY SMALL IN SIZE, with a short black bill, the Sage Thrasher spends its summers in the sagebrush flats where it breeds. It usually lives close to the ground, flying or running back to cover when startled or disturbed. Its upperparts are grayish-brown, with the underparts being grayish-white, broken by brownish speckling. During the winter, it inhabits juniper woodland.

SAGE AND JUNIPER This thrasher is linked with specific habitats through the year, although it may also be observed in backyards.

American Pipit

FAMILY Motacillidae

SPECIES *Anthus rubescens*

LENGTH 6½ in (17 cm)

HABITAT Tundra/open country

CLUTCH SIZE 3–7

DISTRIBUTION Breeds in Alaska and northern Canada, as well as southwestern parts of the United States to central Arizona. Overwinters in the southern states, into Mexico.

THE AMERICAN PIPIT spends much of its time on the ground, walking rather than hopping. Its long tail twitches up and down as it moves in this way. Their appearance varies through the year. They have grayish-brown upperparts when they are on their breeding grounds in the far north, with only faint streaking on the underparts; they become browner in color and display more conspicuous markings on their underparts in winter, when they are most likely to be encountered in flocks in open country, and sometimes venture into coastal areas. Pairs nest on the ground, lining a scrape with soft material as insulation for their brown-speckled, whitish eggs. The hen sits alone, with the young hatching after two weeks and fledging after a similar period.

DIET OF BUGS The short, slender bill of the American Pipit is used to catch the small invertebrates that form its diet.

European Starling

FAMILY Sturnidae

SPECIES *Sturnus vulgaris*

LENGTH 8½ in (22 cm)

HABITAT Urban areas/ farmland

CLUTCH SIZE 5–6

DISTRIBUTION Throughout the United States and much of Canada, being a summer visitor to northern parts. One of the most widely distributed birds.

THIS HIGHLY ADAPTABLE species was first brought to the United States in the 1890s, being liberated in New York. Since then, European Starlings have spread right across the continent and up into the far north. Their appearance is unmistakable, as they have blackish plumage with greenish-purple iridescence and brownish speckling, becoming duller over the winter. Young birds are grayish-brown overall.

NOT FUSSY Berries, insects, and bird-table fare are all readily consumed by European Starlings, which may sometimes form large flocks.

BRAVERY The Brown Thrasher's (*see* p. 306) coloration makes it hard to spot, but it reveals its presence by its powerful song in the spring. These small birds can prove surprisingly aggressive in defense of their nests.

Cedar Waxwing

FAMILY Bombycillidae
SPECIES *Bombycilla cedrorum*
LENGTH 7¼ in (18 cm)
HABITAT Woodland
CLUTCH SIZE 3–6

DISTRIBUTION Seen in summer across southern Canada, resident across the northern half of the United States, also overwintering further south, down into Central America as far as Panama.

WAXWINGS ARE so-called because of the reddish areas at the back of the wings, which resemble sealing wax in appearance. They feed mainly on berries, and breed relatively late in the year for this reason. Although traditionally associated with woodlands, Cedar Waxwings are now being seen increasingly in backyards, being attracted here to feed on the berries of exotic plants. They can be sexed on the basis of the black plumage present under the bill—this is more extensive in cock birds. Young Cedar Waxwings can be recognized by their streaked underparts and duller appearance overall. Social by nature, these waxwings may be seen in large flocks over the fall and winter.

FEEDING Waxwings will pluck individual berries using their pointed bill, and swallow each one in turn. They also catch invertebrates on occasions, and may eat flowers.

Bohemian Waxwing

FAMILY Bombycillidae
SPECIES *Bombycilla garrulus*
LENGTH 8¼ in (21 cm)
HABITAT Woodland
CLUTCH SIZE 4–6

DISTRIBUTION Summer visitor, from Alaska southeast to Hudson Bay. Resident further south in Canada, and seen in western areas of the United States over the winter.

THE CREST FEATHERS of the Bohemian Waxwing may trail back low over the head, only being raised when the individual is alert. This species is larger than the Cedar Waxwing, and has gray rather than yellowish underparts. Pairs may rear their chicks as high as 50 ft (15 m) up in a conifer, using a horizontal branch to help in supporting the nest. This is made from twigs, with the interior being lined with softer material such as moss. The incubation and fledging periods will both last approximately two weeks.

DIET The Bohemian Waxwing no longer relies just on native North American plants, eating the berries of introduced backyard plants, too.

Phainopepla

FAMILY Ptilogonatidae

SPECIES *Phainopepla nitens*

LENGTH 7¾ in (20 cm)

HABITAT Woodland/mesquite brushland

CLUTCH SIZE 2–4

DISTRIBUTION Resident in central and southern California eastward to western Texas, occurring further north.

THE PHAINOPEPLA is the only member of its family regularly occurring on the North American continent. Ptilogonatids all have soft plumage and hunt invertebrates in flight, and so they are also known as Silky Flycatchers. The name of this particular species comes from Greek for "shining robe," reflecting its glossy plumage. In summer, they eat invertebrates, but in winter, they feed on mistletoe berries.

IDENTIFICATION A cock Phainopepla is shown here; hens are grayish overall.

Golden-winged Warbler

FAMILY Parulidae

SPECIES *Vermivora chrysoptera*

LENGTH 4¾ in (12 cm)

HABITAT Woodland/swamp

CLUTCH SIZE 4–7

DISTRIBUTION Summer visitor extending north to Manitoba in Canada, occurring around the Great Lakes and south as far as northern Georgia. Overwinters mainly in Central America.

THE COLORATION OF the Golden-winged Warbler varies, partly because in some areas, it hybridizes regularly with the Blue-winged Warbler (*Vermivora pinus*). The offspring of such crosses are broadly divided into Lawrence's Warbler and the more common Brewster's Warbler, although they are not true species.

PLUMAGE The bright yellow crown of this individual shows that it is a cock bird. Hens are duller in coloration.

Northern Parula

FAMILY Parulidae

SPECIES *Parula americana*

LENGTH 4½ in (11 cm)

HABITAT Woodland near water

CLUTCH SIZE 3–6

DISTRIBUTION Summer visitor to southeastern Canada. Mainly absent in an area south of the Great Lakes, but seen through the southeastern United States.

THERE IS SOME DISPUTE over the status of this species, which is very similar to the Tropical Parula (*Parula pitiayumi*), whose distribution is centered on Central America. These species are sometimes considered to be conspecific, meaning they are essentially the same. While the Northern Parula has a wide distribution over the continent, overwintering mainly in Central America, the Tropical Parula is only seen in southern Texas, and mainly during the summer months. These warblers can be distinguished quite easily, however, by the fact that the Northern Parula has narrow white rings around the eyes. In addition, it has dark banding across the chest that is absent in the case of its Tropical cousin, although this feature is not clearly defined in hens or young

INCONSPICUOUS Its small size means that the Northern Parula is not easy to spot in woodland.

Northern Parulas. The head is bluish-gray, with a greenish area on the upper back and two white wing bars running across each wing. Yellow plumage extends down from the bill to the breast, with the belly being white. Northern Parulas are more likely to be heard rather than seen, as they will often sing high up in the trees, from where they sally out to catch invertebrates in flight or hunt them among the leaves. They nest well off the ground, in among lichens or other epiphytic plants growing on the trees, weaving a ball-shaped nest where the hen will incubate the eggs on her own.

Prothonotary Warbler

FAMILY Parulidae

SPECIES *Protonotaria citrea*

LENGTH 5½ in (14 cm)

HABITAT Swampy woodland

CLUTCH SIZE 3–7

DISTRIBUTION Seen in summer mainly to the south of the Great Lakes, across southeastern parts of the United States to central Texas in the west, and central Florida.

THE COCK BIRD HAS a bright yellow head and underparts. The hen displays more subdued coloration, with a greenish hue on the head, as do young birds of both sexes. Prothonotary Warblers seek insects close to water, overwintering often in mangrove areas in Central America.

BEHAVIOR The Prothonotary is one of only two North American warblers to nest in tree holes.

Black-throated Blue Warbler

FAMILY Parulidae

SPECIES *Dendroica caerulescens*

LENGTH 5¼ in (13 cm)

HABITAT Deciduous forest

CLUTCH SIZE 3–5

DISTRIBUTION Summer range, to the northwest and west of the Great Lakes. Winters in southern Florida, the Greater Antilles, and the Bahamas.

THERE IS A very marked difference in appearance between the sexes of these wood-warblers, with only cock birds displaying blue feathering. They frequent areas of dense cover, and are not easy to spot in their woodland habitat. A pair will nest close to the ground, foraging for insects here in the understorey. The incubation period lasts about 12 days.

GENDER DIFFERENCES This is a cock Black-throated Blue Warbler. Hens in contrast are greenish-gray above, with dusky ear coverts, and buff-colored underparts.

Cerulean Warbler

FAMILY Parulidae

SPECIES *Dendroica cerulea*

LENGTH 4¾ in (12 cm)

HABITAT Woodland near water

CLUTCH SIZE 4–5

DISTRIBUTION Summer visitor to the area of the Great Lakes southward, reaching Alabama, and west to eastern Oklahoma. Winters across northwestern South America to Bolivia.

THESE WOOD-WARBLERS live high up in tall trees where they hunt invertebrates, sometimes catching them in the air. Their breeding habits are hard to observe, as a pair may construct their nest at a height of up to 100 ft (30 m) above the ground. The hen incubates alone, with young Cerulean Warblers of both sexes resembling hens on fledging.

COLOR DIFFERENCES The cock Cerulean Warbler has vivid sky-blue plumage on the head and upperparts, in contrast to the greenish-blue coloration of hens.

Yellow-rumped Warbler

FAMILY Parulidae

SPECIES *Dendroica coronata*

LENGTH 5½ in (14 cm)

HABITAT Woodland/parks

CLUTCH SIZE 4–5

DISTRIBUTION Widely distributed from Alaska across Canada to Newfoundland. Resident in areas of the west coast and southwest. Overwinters in the southeast and southern parts.

AS WITH A NUMBER of the warblers, there has been much debate about the correct taxonomy for this species. The Yellow-rumped Warbler is the result of interbreeding between two separate species, occurring widely across the continent and known as the Myrtle Warbler and Audubon's Warbler.

PLUMAGE Both cock and hen birds in breeding condition display the characteristic yellow plumage on the rump.

Prairie Warbler

FAMILY Parulidae

SPECIES *Dendroica discolor*

LENGTH 5½ in (14 cm)

HABITAT Scrubland/swamps

CLUTCH SIZE 4–5

DISTRIBUTION Occurs widely through the southeastern United States in the summer and resident around the coast of Florida. Overwinters mainly in the Caribbean.

THE NAME OF THIS warbler is rather misleading, because it occurs in scrub and will also be encountered in mangrove swamps, rather than on the prairies. The cock bird is more brightly colored than the hen, whose face is greenish, blending in with the back and wings. Yellow plumage here is restricted to a small area around the eyes. There are variable black markings on the flanks of both sexes. Pairs nest quite close to the ground in a variety of locations, typically in a bush. The cup-shaped nest itself is made of small twigs, grass, and similar material. The eggs, which are a pale shade of green with variable brown spots, will take about 14 days to hatch, being incubated by the hen on her own. The young Prairie Warblers will then leave the nest after a similar period.

DISTINCTIVE The adult cock bird can be distinguished easily by the black plumage on the face.

Yellow-throated Warbler

FAMILY Parulidae
SPECIES *Dendroica dominica*
LENGTH 5½ in (14 cm)
HABITAT Woodland
CLUTCH SIZE 4–5

DISTRIBUTION Eastern United States, south of the Great Lakes in summer. Resident on the Gulf coast and Florida, overwintering in southern Florida, the Caribbean, and Central America.

THESE WARBLERS are found primarily in sycamore woods and pine-oak forests. They breed high up in the treetops, and have an unusual way of foraging for food here. Yellow-throated Warblers will probe the bark for invertebrates using their long bill, and move slowly along the branches, to catch their prey unawares. Various localized races are recognized through their range, with birds from western areas tending to have a pure white stripe above the eyes.

COLORATION
The bright yellow plumage of this species extends down on to the underparts, while the back is grayish.

Blackburnian Warbler

FAMILY Parulidae
SPECIES *Dendroica fusca*
LENGTH 5 in (13 cm)
HABITAT Woodland
CLUTCH SIZE 4–5

DISTRIBUTION Ranges from central-eastern Alberta across to Nova Scotia, down along the Atlantic coast south to Georgia. Winters mainly in northern South America.

THE APPEARANCE of these warblers varies through the year, with the yellow seen on the heads of cock birds being transformed to a fiery orange during the breeding period. Hens are less brightly colored, with orange restricted to the throat. They frequent conifer woodlands, breeding high up, up to 80 ft (24 m) off the ground. Pairs build a tight cup-shaped nest, along a branch extending from the main trunk, using twigs, lichens, and other vegetation. Incubation lasts about 12 days and the chicks then fledge after a similar period.

WIDE RANGING These warblers often wander widely outside their traditional range, especially into western areas of the United States.

Magnolia Warbler

FAMILY Parulidae

SPECIES *Dendroica magnolia*

LENGTH 5 in (13 cm)

HABITAT Coniferous woodland

CLUTCH SIZE 3–5

DISTRIBUTION Across much of Canada from eastern parts of Yukon Territory and British Columbia to Newfoundland and southward into the eastern United States. Overwinters in the Caribbean.

THE UNUSUAL NAME of this warbler simply commemorates the fact that the first example described was seen perched in a magnolia tree. Males in breeding plumage have a gray crown with a prominent white stripe beneath and black plumage on the sides of the face extending over the back. They then molt so the plumage here on the head is predominantly grayish-olive. The eggs are laid in a cup-shaped nest, constructed at a relatively low height in a conifer.

VARIABLE MARKINGS This male Magnolia Warbler is in breeding plumage. The extent of dark flecking on the flanks varies between individuals, but is less pronounced in adult hens.

Black-throated Gray Warbler

FAMILY Parulidae

SPECIES *Dendroica nigrescens*

LENGTH 5 in (13 cm)

HABITAT Woodland/chaparral

CLUTCH SIZE 3–5

DISTRIBUTION Breeds in summer from southern British Columbia, down the coast to California, inland to Colorado and New Mexico. Overwinters from southern California to Mexico.

THESE WARBLERS are a combination of black, gray, and white. They can also be recognized by the lack of any yellow plumage on their bodies, aside from a small yellow spot evident near the base of the bill, on each side of the head. The sexes are quite similar in appearance, except that the throat area is solid black in the case of the cock bird, and hens also have grayer heads. They hunt a variety of invertebrates, including small caterpillars, and build their nests in dense bushes.

RAISING CHICKS The nest of the Black-throated Gray Warbler is a well-camouflaged, cup-shaped structure made out of a variety of vegetation.

Palm Warbler

FAMILY Parulidae
SPECIES *Dendroica palmarum*
LENGTH 5½ in (14 cm)
HABITAT Brush/open country
CLUTCH SIZE 4–5

DISTRIBUTION Breeds in Canada, from eastern Yukon to Newfoundland, and south to the Great Lakes. Overwinters in the southeast United States from Virginia to eastern Texas.

IN SPITE OF ITS NAME, this warbler breeds in northern latitudes, only being seen in warm southern areas over winter, when both sexes are predominantly brown in color. Their feeding pattern on the ground is quite distinctive, as they move along with their tail bobbing up and down.

SUMMER STATE This male is in breeding condition with a chestnut cap, and yellow eye streaks and underparts.

Yellow Warbler

FAMILY Parulidae
SPECIES *Dendroica petechia*
LENGTH 5 in (13 cm)
HABITAT Willow/wet woodland
CLUTCH SIZE 4–5

DISTRIBUTION Through much of North America including the south and southeastern United States. Overwinters in the south, down to Brazil.

YELLOW PLUMAGE predominates in this species, with the wings and tail being more of an olive shade. Cock birds are more brightly colored than hens, with chestnut stripes on the breast and flanks. Yellow Warblers breed across much of North America in the summer months and are likely to be seen in areas of open woodland, usually close to water. Here they move through the foliage in search of invertebrates. When breeding, they build a deep cup-shaped nest for their eggs, which usually hatch after 10 days or so.

DISTANT TRAVELS These birds may fly long distances every year from their southern winter homes to their breeding grounds.

Chestnut-sided Warbler

FAMILY Parulidae

SPECIES *Dendroica pensylvanica*

LENGTH 5 in (13 cm)

HABITAT Deciduous woodland

CLUTCH SIZE 3–5

DISTRIBUTION Breeds in the east, from southern Alberta to Nova Scotia to Arkansas and Georgia. Spends the winters in Central America.

ONLY COCK BIRDS have the distinctive chestnut coloration on the flanks at the start of the breeding season. They also have a yellow crown, with white cheeks and underparts, as well as a distinctive white collar. There is a black stripe running through the eye and a broader stripe running down from each side of the bill. Hens in their breeding plumage can be easily recognized by their green crown. Outside of the breeding season, the sexes are hard to distinguish: Their upperparts are green and they have two parallel yellow bars extending across each wing. Their facial feathering is pale gray with white eye rings. Although Chestnut-sided

Warblers forage for invertebrates hopping from branch to branch quite close to the ground, they may also fly out and capture insects in flight. They eat berries and may take seeds as well.

LOUD SONG At the start of the nesting period a cock bird will sing quite loudly to lay claim to his territory.

BIG VOICE The Palm Warbler (*see* p. 318) has a powerful song that belies its small size. This consists of a rather repetitive trill, but these warblers also utter a much sharper warning note if alarmed.

Pine Warbler

FAMILY Parulidae

SPECIES *Dendroica pinus*

LENGTH 5½ in (14 cm)

HABITAT Coniferous/mixed woodland

CLUTCH SIZE 4–5

DISTRIBUTION Breeds from the Great Lakes, south along the coast, and generally resident in the Gulf states. Winter range includes southeastern Texas.

AS THEIR NAME SUGGESTS, these warblers frequent pine forests in northern areas, breeding here in the summer, and then overwintering in more southerly latitudes in mixed deciduous and coniferous woodland. Some Pine Warblers remain and breed in the southeast each year. The nest is built at the end of a branch, being virtually impossible to spot from the ground as it can be up to 80 ft (24 m) high, and it is usually well-concealed by the pine needles. Pine needles and bark are used in its construction, with a softer lining of feathers or moss acting as a cushion for the eggs. The Pine Warblers comb the branches of the pines looking for invertebrates, which are used for rearing their offspring. Seeds and berries feature more prominently in their diet over the winter. The cock bird has a yellowish throat and chest, becoming whitish on the lower underparts. The head, back, and wings are olive-green, with two white bars running across each wing. Hens have much plainer coloration and young birds vary widely in terms of their appearance, from being predominantly grayish-white through to being quite yellow.

HIDING PLACES Pine Warblers can conceal their presence easily within the branches of pine trees.

Cape May Warbler

FAMILY Parulidae
SPECIES *Dendroica tigrina*
LENGTH 5 in (13 cm)
HABITAT Spruce forest
CLUTCH SIZE 6–8

DISTRIBUTION Breeds from southeastern Yukon and British Columbia east to southwestern Newfoundland and south to the Great Lakes. In southern Florida and the Caribbean for winter.

THE BLACK CAP of the cock Cape May Warbler is only apparent during the breeding period. Pairs nest in spruce trees, with hens having a duller, grayer appearance overall. Cape May Warblers may often be seen in parts of the eastern United States when they are migrating.

YELLOW FACE Cock birds have yellow faces, with a dark stripe running between the bill and the eyes.

Black-throated Green Warbler

FAMILY Parulidae
SPECIES *Dendroica virens*
LENGTH 5 in (13 cm)
HABITAT Coniferous/mixed
woodland
CLUTCH SIZE 4–5

DISTRIBUTION Summer range is eastern British Columbia to Newfoundland, Nova Scotia, and Alabama. Overwintering areas include southern Florida.

THIS WARBLER can be distinguished from other Black-throated species by its olive-green upperparts. It is seen not just in forests, but also wanders into areas of cypress swamp in eastern parts of its range, breeding here as well. Hens can be identified by the white area on the throat, which is a characteristic shared with juveniles of both sexes.

GREEN SPOT On each side of this warbler's face, behind the eyes, is a characteristic green spot.

Black-and-white Warbler

FAMILY Parulidae

SPECIES *Mniotilta varia*

LENGTH 5½ in (14 cm)

HABITAT Woodland

CLUTCH SIZE 4–5

DISTRIBUTION Widespread across central North America and southeast to Texas. Seen in coastal areas of the southeast in winter, through Central America and the Caribbean.

IN THE BREEDING season, the male of this species is characterized by his pied plumage. The throat and cheeks are black; the chin becomes white during the winter. Hens have buffy-colored plumage on their flanks, with gray streaking being apparent here as well. These warblers are unusual in that they will search for invertebrates on tree trunks, not just on branches.

INSECT-LOVER This species tends to be less active than other warblers, using its long bill to probe in bark for invertebrates of various types.

Ovenbird

FAMILY Parulidae

SPECIES *Seiurus aurocapillus*

LENGTH 6 in (15 cm)

HABITAT Forest

CLUTCH SIZE 4–6

DISTRIBUTION Occurs in the southeast across central North America into northern Alabama and Georgia. Overwinters in southern Florida and southern Texas southward.

THE UNUSUAL NAME of the Ovenbird results from the dome-shaped nest that it builds, in a concealed area on the forest floor. These birds are largely terrestrial in their habits, walking with their tail feathers held in a semi-vertical posture. They live mainly on invertebrates.

PLUMAGE The Ovenbird has a black stripe on each side of the head, bordering the rusty-orange crown.

Louisiana Waterthrush

FAMILY Parulidae
SPECIES *Seiurus motacilla*
LENGTH 6 in (15 cm)
HABITAT Woodland streams
CLUTCH SIZE 4–6

DISTRIBUTION Breeding is centered on the southeastern United States, but not along the coast or in Florida. Overwinters further south.

THIS SPECIES OCCURS in dense woodland, being found in the vicinity of fast-flowing mountain streams. These waterthrushes feed along the edges of such streams, looking for invertebrates of various types, which may be lurking here, either in the water or under fallen leaves. As they walk, so their short tail bobs up and down. Louisiana Waterthrushes are not easy to observe, partly because of the relative inaccessibility of the terrain in which they are found, quite apart from their rather shy nature. Their appearance also helps to conceal their presence, with the brown coloration over the back and wings merging very effectively into a muddy background. A pair will breed in among the roots of a tree, close to water, creating a cup-shaped nest from vegetation, and lining the interior with moss.

LONG LEGS The Louisiana Waterthrush has long legs that help it to wade through the shallows, and its powerful bill means it can catch a variety of prey.

Northern Waterthrush

FAMILY Parulidae
SPECIES *Seiurus noveboracensis*
LENGTH 5¾ in (14 cm)
HABITAT Woodland swamps
CLUTCH SIZE 4–6

DISTRIBUTION Breeds across much of Alaska and Canada to Newfoundland in the east, and Wyoming in the south. May overwinter in southern Florida.

UNLIKE ITS LOUISIANA relative, the Northern Waterthrush is found in boggy areas and swampland, rather than in the vicinity of fast-flowing water, although it forages in a similar way. In this species, both sexes are identical in appearance. Breeding occurs throughout the far north, and pairs stay close to water, creating a cup-shaped nest where the hen can lay her clutch of white eggs, which have variable gray-brown spotting. In the fall, the Northern Waterthrush will migrate south for the winter, with some birds flying as far as Peru.

DARK LEGS The Northern Waterthrush has dark legs and feet, which distinguishes it from the pink-legged Louisiana Waterthrush.

Kentucky Warbler

FAMILY Parulidae

SPECIES *Oporornis formosus*

LENGTH 5¼ in (13 cm)

HABITAT Damp woodland

CLUTCH SIZE 3–6

DISTRIBUTION Breeds through the southeast United States, south of the Great Lakes; absent from Florida, but extends west to eastern Texas. Overwinters down to South America.

SECRETIVE BY NATURE and hard to observe, the Kentucky Warbler has a stocky body and a short tail. These birds are quite colorful, with a black crown and cheek patches, and intervening areas of yellow plumage that extend to the underparts. They live mainly on the ground, hunting for invertebrates and hiding away in undergrowth if danger threatens. Pairs nest on the ground too, building a cup-shaped nest of vegetation for this purpose.

COMMONPLACE Although rarely seen, these warblers are quite common within much of their breeding range in the United States.

MacGillivray's Warbler

FAMILY Parulidae

SPECIES *Oporornis tolmiei*

LENGTH 5¼ in (13 cm)

HABITAT Dense undergrowth

CLUTCH SIZE 3–5

DISTRIBUTION Breeds from southern Yukon in Canada south as far as Arizona and New Mexico. Overwinters from Baja California and Mexico, southward as far as Panama.

IN COMMON WITH the Kentucky Warbler, this is another rarely observed summer visitor to North America. MacGillivray's Warbler can be identified by the gray area on its head and a broken white eye ring. The dark olive upperparts help to hide its presence; the underparts are yellow. When breeding, these warblers choose a site at or close to the ground. The cup-shaped nest is made from a variety of vegetation, such as leaves and grasses. The hen alone is responsible for the task of incubation, with the chicks hatching after a period of 13 days.

BLACK MARKS This male bird is seen here in nesting time, as revealed by the black area of plumage on the lower breast.

Mourning Warbler

FAMILY Parulidae

SPECIES *Oporornis philadelphia*

LENGTH 5¼ in (13 cm)

HABITAT Dense undergrowth

CLUTCH SIZE 3–5

DISTRIBUTION Only breeds in North America. Ranges from south Yukon to Newfoundland, down to the Great Lakes. Overwinters south to Ecuador.

THE MOURNING WARBLER is a shy species, inhabiting dense and often more-or-less impenetrable undergrowth. Cock birds may emerge from their seclusion at the start of the breeding season, however, when they become more conspicuous, singing loudly to lay claim to their territory and attract a mate. They can also be distinguished by their plumage. They have a gray hood, which is of a darker shade than seen in the hen, with a variable area of black plumage across the breast. The lower underparts are yellow, with the upperparts being olive-green. Aside from their paler overall coloration, hens can also be recognized by the incomplete white rings of feathering encircling the eyes, which is a feature also associated with immature birds. Young Mourning Warblers also have yellow throats. Invertebrates of various types form the diet of this warbler, and they catch these on or near the ground, where these birds also nest. Pairs use a variety of materials to construct their cup-shaped nest, and it will be about 12 days from egg-laying until the young warblers hatch.

SUMMER ONLY This warbler is only resident in North America over the summer period when it is nesting.

Hooded Warbler

FAMILY Parulidae

SPECIES *Wilsonia citrina*

LENGTH 5¼ in (13 cm)

HABITAT Dense wet woodland

CLUTCH SIZE 3–5

DISTRIBUTION Breeds in the southeast from the Great Lakes south; absent from all but the north of Florida. Overwinters into northern South America.

THE BLACK HOOD that covers the top of the head of the cock bird, extending down around the neck to the throat, helps to identify this warbler. Adult hens may display some trace of black feathering on the sides of the head but this is not seen in young birds. The sexes can also be distinguished through observing their feeding habits, since cock birds are more likely to catch flies of various types while they are in flight, whereas hens prefer to forage near the ground.

GROUP TRAVEL Hooded Warblers breed each summer in the deciduous forests of the southeastern United States. When migrating, these small birds travel in large flocks, often joining up with other species.

Canada Warbler

FAMILY Parulidae

SPECIES *Wilsonia canadensis*

LENGTH 5¼ in (13 cm)

HABITAT Dense woodland

CLUTCH SIZE 3–5

DISTRIBUTION Occurs from southeastern Yukon across to southwest Newfoundland and around the Great Lakes, south as far as northern Georgia. Overwinters south to Peru.

IN SPITE OF ITS NAME, this warbler is not simply confined to Canada. It prefers to occupy the lower storey of vegetation within a forest, often being seen quite close to water sources. When they are on the move, these small birds can be seen to be constantly twitching their tails.

NECKLACE The male has more distinctive black markings across the chest area than the hen.

Wilson's Warbler

FAMILY Parulidae
SPECIES *Wilsonia pusilla*
LENGTH 4¾ in (12 cm)
HABITAT Dense woodland
CLUTCH SIZE 3–6

DISTRIBUTION Breeds from Alaska to Newfoundland, north of the Great Lakes in the east, and down to California. Overwinters along the Gulf coast into Central America.

THESE WARBLERS ARE characterized in part by their long, narrow tail and short, quite slender bill. Yellow predominates in their plumage, and the cock bird has a black cap. While the facial area is yellow, and the underparts have a decidedly yellowish tone, the upperparts, from the neck down over the back, wings, and rump to the tail are olive. Adult hens may sometimes display some black feathering on the head, but this is never as extensive as it is in the cock bird. Wilson's Warblers are lively by nature, and certainly not as shy as a number of other warblers. They forage on the branches of trees and shrubs and will also catch insects in flight. Despite this, like other warblers, they nest close to the ground, with the nest being a relatively large structure made from a variety of vegetation.

SUMMER VISITOR This warbler is most commonly seen in western areas of North America over summer.

American Redstart

FAMILY Parulidae

SPECIES *Setophaga ruticilla*

LENGTH 5¼ in (13 cm)

HABITAT Woodland

CLUTCH SIZE 3–5

DISTRIBUTION Breeds from northwestern Canada east, and across the southeastern United States, but absent from Florida and the Gulf coast.

THE CHARACTERISTIC COLORATION of these warblers helps to distinguish them from similar species. There is a very marked difference in appearance between the sexes. The cock bird is very bright, with his overall coloration being black, but with reddish-orange areas of plumage on the wings and flanks, as well as the outer tail feathers; the abdominal area is whitish. The reddish-orange areas are particularly apparent in flight, or when the cock bird is displaying, which he does by fanning his tail feathers and wings. The almost constant movements of the cock bird have led to the species being called "candelita," in parts of Central America, likening their movements to that of a candle flame. They often fly out from a perch to catch flying insects. Hens in contrast are grayish, being

of a darker shade on the head compared to the underparts of the body, while their back and wings are brown. Pairs will frequently nest high up in trees, up to 75 ft (23 m) off the ground, building a cup-shaped nest. The hen incubates the eggs on her own, with the young hatching after about 12 days. Juvenile birds of both sexes resemble hens when they fledge, which is at about three weeks old. The American Redstart overwinters in southern Florida, down to Peru.

IN THE NEST This American Redstart hen is sitting on her bulky nest, built from a wide variety of material and securely sited in the fork of a tree.

Yellow-breasted Chat

FAMILY Parulidae
SPECIES *Icteria virens*
LENGTH 7½ in (19 cm)
HABITAT Dense thicket
CLUTCH SIZE 3–5

DISTRIBUTION Breeds from southern Canada across the United States. Present south of the Great Lakes in the east, but absent from most of Florida. Winters in Central America.

THE LARGE SIZE of these chats helps to identify them. Although they are the biggest of the warblers occurring in North America, their shyness means they can be difficult to observe. In both sexes, the head is gray, with white stripes on either side that run above and encircle the eyes,

WELL-HIDDEN NEST These chats conceal their nests well, often quite close to the ground.

as well as extending from the bill, separated by an intervening area of black feathering. The upperparts of the body are olive-brown; the underside is yellow.

Common Yellowthroat

FAMILY Parulidae
SPECIES *Geothlypis trichas*
LENGTH 5 in (13 cm)
HABITAT Grassland/marshland
CLUTCH SIZE 3–6

DISTRIBUTION Breeds over most of North America, apart from the far north. Resident in southern areas, occurring further south in winter.

THESE WIDELY distributed warblers tend to favor open areas of country, often grassland, where they feed on invertebrates. Even so, the birds are not very conspicuous, although the cock will usually choose to sing from a prominent position, especially at the start of the breeding period. The hen is more of a brownish shade than her mate above, with buff rather than white underparts.

BLACK MASK The male Common Yellowthroat is distinguished by having a black mask and a white streak across the head.

Hepatic Tanager

FAMILY Thraupidae
SPECIES *Piranga flava*
LENGTH 8 in (20 cm)
HABITAT Mountain forest
CLUTCH SIZE 3–5

DISTRIBUTION Breeds from Colorado via New Mexico to western Texas, also California and Arizona. Winters in the extreme south of Arizona, and through Central America.

THERE IS A MARKED DIFFERENCE in appearance between the sexes in this species, with only cock birds displaying the bright reddish-orange feathering. Hens have olive-green upperparts and deep yellow underparts. Young birds of both sexes are similar to hens in overall coloration, but can be distinguished by streaking on their underparts. Pairs nest in areas of pine and oak woodland, building cup-shaped nests, as high as 30 ft (9 m) above the ground.

DIET These tanagers feed their young mostly on invertebrates. However, the adults will also eat fruit.

Western Tanager

FAMILY Thraupidae
SPECIES *Piranga ludoviciana*
LENGTH 7½ in (19 cm)
HABITAT Coniferous forest
CLUTCH SIZE 3–5

DISTRIBUTION Breeds in western North America, from southern Northwest Territories into western Texas. Sometimes overwinters in south California, generally in Central America.

THESE BRIGHTLY colored tanagers often seek invertebrates in the upper branches of trees. They are sufficiently agile to catch insects in flight, although fruit and berries also feature in their diet on a regular basis. Pairs usually rear their chicks well away from the ground, sometimes choosing a nest site up to 65 ft (20 m) high in a conifer.

BRIGHT MALE This is a male Western Tanager. The hen has yellow-green upperparts, and is yellow beneath, with similar wing bars to the cock.

Scarlet Tanager

FAMILY Thraupidae
SPECIES *Piranga olivacea*
LENGTH 7 in (18 cm)
HABITAT Deciduous forest
CLUTCH SIZE 3–5

DISTRIBUTION Breeding range lies in eastern North America, from Nova Scotia to the west of the Great Lakes down to Oklahoma. Overwinters in northern South America.

BRILLIANT RED PLUMAGE over much of the body contrasts with the black wings and tail of the male Scarlet Tanager in breeding plumage. The hen is easily distinguished by her greenish-yellow coloring; again the wings and tail are darker. Outside the nesting season, cocks resemble hens. Their brilliant coloration means that these tanagers are conspicuous when they are migrating, being reported over a much wider area of the country, south of their breeding haunts as they travel to their wintering grounds. They may even visit suburban areas at this stage, eating invertebrate pests, although they tend to seek food much higher in the canopy when nesting. The hen alone is responsible for incubating the eggs. These should hatch after a period of about two weeks, with the chicks fledging after a similar interval.

RED FOOD The bright coloration of the Scarlet Tanager stems from pigments ingested in its diet.

Summer Tanager

FAMILY Thraupidae
SPECIES *Piranga rubra*
LENGTH 7¾ in (20 cm)
HABITAT Pine-oak woodland/ cottonwood
CLUTCH SIZE 3–4

DISTRIBUTION Breeds in the southeast, west to Iowa, central Florida, and the Mexican border. Winters in southern Florida and into Central America.

THE HEN Summer Tanager can be easily distinguished from her mate by her orange-yellow underparts, and a greener area under the tail. The upperparts are an olive-shade. Birds from western parts of their range may be grayer, and are generally larger in size. Young birds of both sexes display a combination of red and yellow feathering at first.

ROSE COLOR The male Summer Tanager is rosy-red. As with related species, these birds have a stout bill, which reflects their varied diet.

Green-tailed Towhee

FAMILY Emberizidae
SPECIES *Pipilo chlorurus*
LENGTH 7¼ in (18 cm)
HABITAT Brushland/chaparral
CLUTCH SIZE 4

DISTRIBUTION Breeds in the western United States north to Montana, into New Mexico and California. Overwinters from California across to central Texas and into Central America.

INDISTINGUISHABLE It is not possible to distinguish between the sexes by differences in their plumage. Towhees have particularly long tails.

THE RUSTY-RED FEATHERING on the head, which can be raised to form a small crest, helps to identify these towhees. The back and wings are olive-green and the breast is gray. There is some darker blackish plumage on the sides of the face, while the throat area is white. Green-tailed Towhees tend not to stray too far from cover, seeking food on the ground and around vegetation. They have a varied diet of invertebrates, seeds, and berries. Pairs nest low down as well, creating a deep, cup-shaped receptacle for the eggs. Their young have streaking on their underparts, and lack the distinctive cap.

House Sparrow

F/ Passeridae
ES *Passer domesticus*
GTH 6¼ in (16 cm)
HABITAT Urban areas
CLUTCH SIZE 5–6

DISTRIBUTION Resident throughout the United States, as far north as the Northwest Territories in Canada. Also occurs on the south and eastern side of Newfoundland.

THESE SPARROWS were brought to North America from Europe, with the first birds being released during 1850, in Central Park, New York. The aim was to establish this lively, familiar species as a reminder of home for settlers from Europe. The House Sparrow settled in well, and started to breed, with its numbers increasing rapidly and soon forming into small flocks. Pairs will nest in a variety of locations in buildings, under the eaves for example, constructing an untidy nest, as well as breeding in tree holes in parks.

PLUMAGE This is a male with chestnut coloration prominent over the wings, and gray feathering on the crown. Hens are mainly pale brown.

Spotted Towhee

FAMILY Emberizidae

SPECIES *Pipilo maculatus*

LENGTH 7½ in (19 cm)

HABITAT Chaparral/woodland

CLUTCH SIZE 2–6

DISTRIBUTION Resident largely in southwestern parts, from British Columbia into western Texas. Breeding range extends to the northeast. Winters from Idaho southward.

THE SPOTTED TOWHEE has a completely black head with variable white spotting over the back and wings. It is chestnut-red on the flanks and the rest of the underparts are white. Hens can sometimes be recognized by the grayer tone to this white feathering. Young birds lack the colorful flank markings, and are browner overall with pronounced streaking over the body.

CUP-SHAPED NESTS The Spotted Towhee builds a nest on the ground. It will take two weeks for their eggs to hatch.

Eurasian Tree Sparrow

FAMILY Passeridae

SPECIES *Passer montanus*

LENGTH 6 in (15 cm)

HABITAT Parks/farmland

CLUTCH SIZE 2–6

DISTRIBUTION Restricted to western Illinois, southeastern Minnesota, and northeastern Iowa, not having spread far from where the species was originally introduced.

LIKE THE HOUSE SPARROW, this species is not native to North America, but is now well-established on the continent. It was introduced later than the House Sparrow, during the 1870s when some of these birds were released in the vicinity of St Louis. Pairs nest in cavities in trees, and the incubation and fledging periods each last for two weeks.

BLACK EAR PATCHES This species can be distinguished from its relatives by black ear patches.

EURASIAN TREE SPARROWS These birds are not found in city centers, but frequently nest in suburbs. Large flocks may form in agricultural areas when food is plentiful. They feed largely on seeds, but invertebrates are also important.

Golden-crowned Sparrow

FAMILY Emberizidae

SPECIES *Zonotrichia atricapilla*

LENGTH 7 in (18 cm)

HABITAT Tundra/woodland

CLUTCH SIZE 4–5

THE HABITAT OF THESE sparrows varies markedly though the year. They breed in tundra and then overwinter in woodland, with their plumage being duller in overall coloration at this time. Golden-crowned Sparrows may form flocks with other sparrows outside the breeding season.

DISTINCTIVE This species is identified by its gold crown, edged with black feathering on each side.

DISTRIBUTION Breeds from Alaska to the Aleutian Islands, south to British Columbia and western Alberta. Overwinters further south, from southern British Columbia into California.

White-throated Sparrow

FAMILY Emberizidae

SPECIES *Zonotrichia albicollis*

LENGTH 6¾ in (17 cm)

HABITAT Woodland/parks

CLUTCH SIZE 3–5

THE UPPERPARTS of the White-throated Sparrow are chestnut-brown, with two white bars running across each wing. The throat is white as the name of the species suggests, and the sexes are identical in appearance. Young birds are duller, displaying brown and buff coloring on the crown, with streaking on the breast. These sparrows can be seen in a range of habitats, not just woods but also in the vicinity of people, such as in backyards, where they may visit bird tables for food, as well as in parks.

DISTRIBUTION Breeds from the Northwestern Territories to Newfoundland. Overwinters down the western coast and across much of the southeast, except in southern Florida.

STRIPED CROWN The head of this species is streaked with alternating black and white feathering, with a yellow spot behind the bill.

White-crowned Sparrow

FAMILY Emberizidae

SPECIES *Zonotrichia leucophrys*

LENGTH 7 in (18 cm)

HABITAT Woodland/grassland

CLUTCH SIZE 3–5

DISTRIBUTION Breeds across the north to Newfoundland, and southwest to Colorado. Overwinters over a wide area.

THE WHITE-CROWNED SPARROW is somewhat similar in appearance to the White-throated Sparrow, and the two species overlap in some parts of their range throughout the year. It is possible to distinguish the White-crowned Sparrow, however, because its underparts are much grayer. The upperparts also tend to be grayish-brown in color. The bill coloration is a further point of distinction, being either yellow or pinkish in this species. Young birds are not as brightly colored as the adults, with their crown coloration also being less distinctive. When breeding, White-crowned Sparrows may build their nests at a various heights, sometimes quite high off the ground. The nest takes the form of a carefully woven cup of grass, which is well-hidden from potential

SUBURBAN BIRDS The White-crowned Sparrow is not an uncommon winter visitor in the suburbs. It will avoid areas of dense woodland.

predators. Their eggs are pale blue in color, with variable reddish-brown spots, and are incubated by the hen on her own. It will take about two weeks for hatching to occur, and then the young White-crowned Sparrows will spend a further two weeks in the nest before fledging. When the young leave the nest, the cock bird assumes the duty of caring for his offspring until they are fully independent, which is likely to take another couple of weeks. Meanwhile in some areas, the hen may start to nest again, rearing a second round of chicks.

Baird's Sparrow

FAMILY Emberizidae

SPECIES *Ammodramus bairdii*

LENGTH 5½ in (14 cm)

HABITAT Open country

CLUTCH SIZE 4–5

DISTRIBUTION Breeds in southwestern Canada, Montana, and the Dakotas. Overwinters in Arizona and New Mexico, across into Mexico and in southwestern Texas.

VARIABLE BROWNISH striping on the upperparts helps to identify Baird's Sparrow. The underparts are whitish, with a necklace of dark streaking on the breast. The sexes are identical in appearance. This shy species is not commonly observed. Although they live in open countryside, these particular sparrows are reluctant to fly away when confronted by potential danger. Instead, they will try to slip away through the vegetation where they are hiding. Cock birds tend to be the most conspicuous, singing loudly at the start of the breeding period.

NESTING Only the female Baird's Sparrow incubates the eggs. These are laid in a cup-shaped nest built of grasses on the ground.

Seaside Sparrow

FAMILY Emberizidae

SPECIES *Ammodramus maritimus*

LENGTH 6 in (15 cm)

HABITAT Grassy tidal marshland

CLUTCH SIZE 3–5

DISTRIBUTION Summer range north to New Hampshire, and resident from here down to north Florida. Also at the tip of Florida and along the Gulf Coast.

THIS IS ONE OF THE most highly specialized members of the sparrow family, and is found in a relatively small area, leaving it facing the threat of extinction. They feed on both seeds and small invertebrates. The appearance of these sparrows is variable, especially in coloration: Some are significantly darker than others. Overall, Seaside Sparrows are generally a dark olive-brown shade on the upperparts, with yellow stripes on the face, and a white throat, becoming buff-white on the underparts. Young birds are duller and browner in color.

DISTINCTIVE The dark bill of the Seaside Sparrow is longer and more sharply pointed than in similar species.

Grasshopper Sparrow

FAMILY Emberizidae

SPECIES *Ammodramus savannarum*

LENGTH 5 in (13 cm)

HABITAT Grassland

CLUTCH SIZE 4–5

DISTRIBUTION Found in the eastern United States in the summer, northwest to southern Canada. Resident in the Gulf states and along the Mexican border, overwintering more widely here.

THIS IS ANOTHER species that spends much of its time concealed in grassland. The coloration of these sparrows helps to disguise their presence here, being a mottled shade of brown, with a buff-colored breast and a whitish belly. There is a dark brown area on the crown, with a pale central stripe running down in the direction of the bill. Solitary by nature, the Grasshopper Sparrow nests on the ground as well, creating a cup-shaped nest using grass and other material. The chicks should hatch after a period of about 12 days.

BEHAVIOR The cock Grasshopper Sparrow sings loudly to attract a mate. These sparrows feed largely on seeds and also hunt for invertebrates.

Song Sparrow

FAMILY Emberizidae

SPECIES *Melospiza melodia*

LENGTH 6 in (15 cm)

HABITAT Thicket/urban areas

CLUTCH SIZE 3–6

DISTRIBUTION Resident from southern Alaska right down the west coast. Breeds across southern Canada; resident in northern parts of the United States. Overwinters in the south.

HEAVY STREAKING on the underparts helps to identify these sparrows, along with the reddish-brown streaking over the back and wings. They are the most widespread of the North American species, although they are not always very conspicuous, retreating into vegetation at any hint of danger.

BACKYARD VISITOR Song Sparrows are often drawn into backyards in search of bird-table fare during spells of harsh weather.

Lapland Longspur

FAMILY Emberizidae
SPECIES *Calcarius lapponicus*
LENGTH 6¼ in (16 cm)
HABITAT Tundra/open country
CLUTCH SIZE 4–7

DISTRIBUTION Breeds in the far north, including the Greenland coast. Overwinters in the United States, down to east Texas along to Alabama, and north over the Canadian border.

THESE BIRDS are known as longspurs because of the elongated hind claw on each foot, which may help them to stay upright when they are running across boggy ground. In the winter, they often form large mixed flocks with other species such as Snow Buntings.

COLORATION A male Lapland Longspur in breeding plumage displays black feathering on the head and a broad chestnut collar.

McCown's Longspur

FAMILY Emberizidae
SPECIES *Calcarius mccownii*
LENGTH 6 in (15 cm)
HABITAT Grassland/open country
CLUTCH SIZE 4–7

DISTRIBUTION Summer range from Alberta and Saskatchewan to Montana, and south to Colorado and eastern Kansas. Overwinters mainly in Texas.

THE BREEDING GROUNDS of McCown's Longspur are on the open plains, but then in the fall, they move into cultivated fields and grassland, feeding on a diet of seeds and invertebrates. The cock bird in breeding condition is distinguished by the black areas on the head. There is a rust-colored wing bar, with the back and wings being streaked.

NESTING Pairs of McCown's Longspurs nest on the ground, often using a shallow scrape in the soil, which they line with some grass.

Chestnut-collared Longspur

FAMILY Emberizidae

SPECIES *Calcarius ornatus*

LENGTH 6 in (15 cm)

HABITAT Prairie/grassland

CLUTCH SIZE 3–5

DISTRIBUTION Southern Alberta east to Manitoba in Canada. Southward through Montana and the Dakotas to Colorado. Overwinters from southern Kansas down through Texas, west to Arizona.

THE COCK BIRD in breeding condition has a prominent chestnut area of plumage on the nape of the neck, with a black crown and alternating black and white striping on the sides of the face. It has a yellow area on the throat and cheeks. The underparts are black, with mottled brown plumage over the wings. Hens in comparison are much duller in coloration, being grayish-brown overall. In flight, however, the black triangular patch on the tail feathers is usually seen. Chestnut-collared Longspurs tend to favor longer grass than the McGowan's Longspur, where their distributions overlap. They are not especially conspicuous as a result, remaining largely hidden out of sight, but cock birds will reveal their presence by their song, flying up out of the grass when displaying, and sometimes perching in the open. The nest is simply a shallow depression on the ground lined with grass, and usually partly concealed near a shrub. Their eggs are well-camouflaged as well, thanks to their speckled green coloration, with the incubation period lasting for about two weeks. After the breeding period, as the fall approaches, the longspurs will then fly south to their wintering grounds.

FEEDING HABITS Chestnut-collared Longspurs feed mainly on the ground, taking a varied diet of seeds and small invertebrates.

Dark-eyed Junco

FAMILY Emberizidae
SPECIES *Junco hyemalis*
LENGTH 6¼ in (16 cm)
HABITAT Coniferous woodland/thicket
CLUTCH SIZE 3–6

DISTRIBUTION Breeds across Canada; resident over much of the western and eastern areas of the United States. Overwinters in other parts.

THE DISTINCTIVE BLACK coloration of the eyes of this species are accentuated by the presence of dark surrounding feathering here. Its plumage coloration overall is variable, and reflects the area of an individual's origin, with six distinctive variations having been identified across its range. Birds of these different colors breed separately but may be seen overwintering together in mixed flocks.

VARIATION This is the Pink-sided form of the Dark-eyed Junco, distinguishable by the pinkish-cinnamon coloration on the sides of its body.

Yellow-eyed Junco

FAMILY Emberizidae
SPECIES *Junco phaeonotus*
LENGTH 6¼ in (16 cm)
HABITAT Coniferous or pine-oak forest
CLUTCH SIZE 3–4

DISTRIBUTION Resident within the United States in southeastern Arizona and southwestern New Mexico only, but occurs further south through Mexico down to Guatemala in Central America.

THE BRIGHT YELLOW eyes of this species are quite distinctive, but the sexes are identical in appearance. These juncos forage for food on the ground, tending to walk in a rather deliberate fashion, and also nest here. They eat a variety of seeds, invertebrates, and berries.

PLUMAGE A gray head with rust-red coloration over the back and wings, and paler gray underparts characterize this species.

Snow Bunting

FAMILY Emberizidae

SPECIES *Plectrophenax nivalis*

LENGTH 6¾ in (17 cm)

HABITAT Tundra/open country

CLUTCH SIZE 4–6

DISTRIBUTION Breeds throughout the far north, including on Greenland. Resident in coastal areas of western and southern Alaska. Overwinters across southern Canada and the northern United States.

THESE BUNTINGS vary significantly in appearance through the year. It is harder to tell the sexes apart in the winter, when the black areas in the cock's plumage are replaced by buffy-brown feathering. The crown is also similarly colored at this stage, with corresponding ear patches too. Hens have more of a rusty-tan appearance in these areas. Social by nature, it is not unusual to see Snow Buntings in mixed flocks, alongside species such as longspurs and Horned Larks (*see* p. 268). They are predominately terrestrial in their habits.

SEASONAL CHANGE A male Snow Bunting in breeding plumage is recognizable by his white head and underparts, and contrasting black wings.

Lark Bunting

FAMILY Emberizidae

SPECIES *Calamospiza melanocorys*

LENGTH 7 in (18 cm)

HABITAT Prairie/sagebrush

CLUTCH SIZE 4–5

DISTRIBUTION Summer range from north Texas to southern Alberta and Saskatchewan. Winters more widely in Texas, south New Mexico, and Arizona.

THE LARK BUNTING has a relatively large, conical bill, helping it to crack the seeds that form a significant part of its diet. The upperparts of both sexes are buff-brown with streaking in the winter, and their underparts are white, again broken by brown streaks. The tail feathers terminate in white tips. Their name reflects the song of the cock bird, uttered when displaying. The nest itself is well-concealed in a scrape on the ground, lined with grass. During the winter, these buntings occur in large flocks.

IDENTIFICATION The cock bird can be distinguished during the breeding period by its black plumage. They otherwise resemble hens.

Lazuli Bunting

FAMILY Cardinalidae
SPECIES *Passerina amoena*
LENGTH 5½ in (14 cm)
HABITAT Woodland/brushland
CLUTCH SIZE 3–4

DISTRIBUTION Breeds from southern British Columbia east to the Dakotas. Southern range extends beyond the California border and to northern New Mexico. Overwinters in Mexico.

THE REAL BEAUTY of the male Lazuli Bunting only becomes apparent at the start of the breeding season. This is when the brilliant turquoise feathering on the head becomes evident, extending down over the back to the rump. There are two parallel white bars running across each wing. The breast is a warm shade of cinnamon-brown, with the lower underparts being whitish in color. Outside the breeding season, the cock is much duller in coloration, being significantly browner. Hens can be identified by their grayish-brown upperparts, with their buff-colored underparts. They do display just a hint of blue, however, on the tips of their wings, as well as on the rump and tail. These buntings prefer to search for their food on the ground, taking a variety of invertebrates, as well as seeds. They build a cup-shaped nest in vegetation up to 10 ft (3 m) off the ground, where it will be well concealed. The hen incubates on her own, but will be brought food by her partner. The young buntings should hatch after approximately 12 days; they will fledge once they are about two weeks old.

SEASONAL VISITOR Lazuli Buntings are only likely to be seen in North America over the summer months.

Painted Bunting

FAMILY Cardinalidae
SPECIES *Passerina ciris*
LENGTH 5½ in (14 cm)
HABITAT Woodland/brushland
CLUTCH SIZE 3–4

DISTRIBUTION Resident over south-central parts of the United States and from North Carolina to Florida. Some birds overwinter in southern Florida but most go to Central America.

ALTHOUGH ONE OF the most vividly colored birds occuring in North America, the Varied Bunting is surprisingly hard to observe. It has a very shy nature, to the extent that cock birds will sing in undergrowth rather than emerging into the open at this stage. The sexes are easily distinguished, however, as the hen has lime-green upperparts, being yellowy-green on the underside of her body. Despite this bright coloration, there is no breeding plumage in this species.

SPECTACULAR The male has bright red feathering on the underparts and rump, contrasting with the green wings and blue head.

Indigo Bunting

FAMILY Cardinalidae
SPECIES *Passerina cyanea*
LENGTH 5½ in (14 cm)
HABITAT Woodland/brushland
CLUTCH SIZE 3–5

DISTRIBUTION Summer range extends west to southern Canada and Montana. Present in Arizona in the southwest. Overwinters in southern Florida, along the Gulf Coast to Mexico.

VIVID BLUE coloration predominates in the case of the male Indigo Bunting during the breeding season. Outside this period, their appearance is transformed to a dull brown with streaking on the chest and a hint of blue coloration remaining on the tail. It becomes impossible to distinguish the sexes at this time of year. The range of this species partly overlaps in western areas with that of the Lazuli Bunting, and it is not unknown for these birds to interbreed in this area, creating so-called hybrid offspring.

BEHAVIOR It is not uncommon for Indigo Buntings to be seen on farmland, where flocks forage for food on the ground.

Varied Bunting

FAMILY Cardinalidae

SPECIES *Passerina versicolor*

LENGTH 5½ in (14 cm)

HABITAT Thicket/canyons

CLUTCH SIZE 3–5

DISTRIBUTION Summer visitor to the United States, breeding in southeastern Arizona and adjacent New Mexico. Also along the Texan-Mexican border, with a small resident population.

THE BRILLIANT purple-red coloration of the cock bird is muted to a more brownish appearance in the fall, through until the start of the following breeding season. Hens in contrast are light brown in color throughout the year. This species inhabits relatively arid country, retreating to mesquite thickets but usually near water. A pair will create a woven cup-shaped nest for their eggs, choosing a well-concealed locality in a vine or a tree. The young hatch at 13 days, fledging after a similar period.

PLUMAGE VARIATION The coloration of the male Varied Bunting can differ quite markedly between individuals, with some birds tending to be of a bluer shade than others.

Northern Cardinal

FAMILY Cardinalidae

SPECIES *Cardinalis cardinalis*

LENGTH 8¾ in (22 cm)

HABITAT Woodland/backyards

CLUTCH SIZE 3–4

DISTRIBUTION Resident throughout the southeastern area of the United States into Mexico, and also westward to central Arizona. Northern range extends right up to Nova Scotia.

THIS SPECIES is often known as the Virginian Cardinal, having been adopted as that state's national symbol. The range of these cardinals continues to expand northward and westward, as has been the case for over a century, with the first Canadian record of their presence dating back to 1901. They occur in a wide range of different environments, wherever there is cover available. Northern Cardinals may therefore enliven city parks, as well as being regular visitors to backyard bird tables, although usually preferring to feed on the ground.

GENDER DIFFERENCES Only the cock Northern Cardinal is brightly colored. Hens are easily distinguished by their olive-buff body color.

Dickcissel

FAMILY Cardinalidae
SPECIES *Spiza americana*
LENGTH 6¼ in (16 cm)
HABITAT Prairie/meadow
CLUTCH SIZE 2–5

DISTRIBUTION Western Montana to western Ohio marks the typical northern boundaries, south to the Texan-Mexican border.

A SUMMER VISITOR to North America, the Dickcissel seeks out seeds in the grassland areas that it frequents, also hunting for invertebrates here. These become especially significant as a food for its nestlings. The Dickcissel may sometimes choose to breed on the ground, particularly in more remote areas where it is less likely to be disturbed. Elsewhere, pairs construct their nest in trees. In the fall, flocks head back to South America.

PLUMAGE The black bib and white chin seen here indicate a cock bird in breeding condition.

Pyrrhuloxia

FAMILY Cardinalidae
SPECIES *Cardinalis sinuatus*
LENGTH 8¾ in (22 cm)
HABITAT Woodland/brushland
CLUTCH SIZE 2–4

DISTRIBUTION Resident in southeastern Arizona, the adjacent area of New Mexico and along the Texan-Mexican border. May also overwinter slightly further north in New Mexico.

THE RELATIVELY LARGE size of this cardinal, its crest, and its color scheme aids its identification in the wild. In the case of the cock bird, the head and wings are a darker shade of gray, compared with the underparts. There is a highly individual blood-red area here, extending from around the bill down the center of the chest itself. The bill color itself varies through the year, being yellow through the summer and becoming a duller gray shade in the fall. This change is also seen in hens. They are recognizable by their predominantly buff coloration.

USEFUL DIET Within the cotton fields, Pyrrhuloxias are a biological means of controlling invertebrate pests.

Rose-breasted Grosbeak

FAMILY Cardinalidae

SPECIES *Pheucticus ludovicianus*

LENGTH 8 in (20 cm)

HABITAT Woodland near water

CLUTCH SIZE 3–5

DISTRIBUTION Breeds from southern parts of the Northwest Territories southeastward, to southern Newfoundland and south as far as Oklahoma and northern Georgia. Overwinters mainly in Mexico.

ADAPTATION The stout bill seen here is a characteristic feature of grosbeaks, helping them to crack thick-coated seeds that often feature prominently in their diet.

THE PROMINENT rose-red Y-shaped marking on the chest of cocks of this species during the summer makes them instantly recognizable, with the surrounding feathering being white. The entire head and upperparts are a glossy black color, with white markings across the wings and in the tail. The bill is a vibrant horn-color, with a dark tip. During the winter months, these birds will assume a much browner shade. Hens in contrast have dark brown upperparts throughout the year, with their underparts being dull white, broken by brownish streaking. They also have very distinctive white eyebrow streaks. These summer visitors are most likely to be seen in eastern areas, favoring woodlands where there are streams. Pairs construct a fairly shallow cup-shaped nest for their eggs, positioning this in a secluded spot in a bush or tree. Both the incubation and fledging periods are likely to last two weeks. Unlike a number of other members of the bunting family, these grosbeaks prefer to remain high up off the ground, being relatively inconspicuous here, although they are likely to be drawn down by the availability of food and may even visit backyard feeders.

Black-headed Grosbeak

FAMILY Cardinalidae

SPECIES *Pheucticus melanocephalus*

LENGTH 8¼ in (21 cm)

HABITAT Woodland

CLUTCH SIZE 3–5

DISTRIBUTION Ranges in the summer from British Columbia down through western parts of the United States, east to the Dakotas, Nebraska, and Kansas. Overwinters in Mexico.

ONLY THE COCK in this case displays black plumage on the head. Hens are brownish above, with buff-colored underparts. The Black-headed has a very stocky bill, enabling these birds to crack thick-shelled seeds easily to reach the kernel inside. When breeding, these birds become far

COCK BIRD The Black-headed Grosbeak nest has a relatively loose, flat, and quite fragile structure.

more insectivorous, rearing their young mainly on invertebrates. It is the hen rather than the cock bird who lays claims to the breeding territory, driving away rivals.

Blue Grosbeak

FAMILY Cardinalidae

SPECIES *Passerina caerulea*

LENGTH 6¾ in (17 cm)

HABITAT Woodland

CLUTCH SIZE 3–4

DISTRIBUTION Across the southern United States in summer, northward to southern South Dakota and Minnesota. Absent from southern Florida. Overwinters in Central America.

IT IS VERY EASY to distinguish between the sexes in this case, because only the cock bird displays the rich blue plumage with reddish-brown wing bars. Hens in contrast are predominantly brown in color. Cock birds are not just conspicuous because of their coloration, however, but also because they often sing in the open, perched on a suitable branch.

FEEDING CHICKS Young Blue Grosbeaks are reared largely on insects, particularly grasshoppers, which the adults forage for in fields and on roadside verges.

Red-winged Blackbird

FAMILY Icteridae
SPECIES *Agelaius phoeniceus*
LENGTH 8¾ in (22 cm)
HABITAT Marshland/fields
CLUTCH SIZE 3–5

DISTRIBUTION Summer range extends up to northern Canada, with the species being found over the entire continent to the south at this stage. Overwinters in Mexico.

THIS SPECIES is one of the most common birds in North America, with a population that may be approaching 200 million individuals. It favors damp areas of countryside, particularly reedbeds. Males are easily identified by the bright red shoulder patches, with yellowish edging, which will not be very apparent when the wing is folded. Birds from the area of Central California lack this yellowish edging, with this area being completely red. Hens are easily distinguished by their brown-streaked appearance, with buff eyebrows, and again have relatively short tail feathers. Juveniles of both sexes resemble hens. Pairs nest on their own, close to the ground often in reed beds, carefully weaving a nest that is firmly supported. The hen incubates the eggs by herself, with the chicks hatching after a period of about 12 days. They will then fledge when they are about two weeks old. After the breeding season, Red-winged Blackbirds will start to form large flocks, sometimes being seen in the company of other blackbirds at this stage. They feed on invertebrates, particularly during the summer when they are rearing their chicks, and also eat seeds.

DISPLAY Red-winged Blackbirds display with their wings held slightly away from their bodies, singing loudly.

Tricolored Blackbird

FAMILY Icteridae
SPECIES *Agelaius tricolor*
LENGTH 8¾ in (22 cm)
HABITAT Marshland/fields
CLUTCH SIZE 3–4

DISTRIBUTION Found during the summer in northern and eastern areas of California and also Oregon. Resident from the Californian coast inland, and south to Baja California.

BLACK FEATHERING predominates in the case of males of this species. In addition to the red plumage on its wings, there is a very evident white area below here too. Hens are of more of a grayish-brown shade, and the streaking on their underparts is not as pronounced as in the case of the Red-winged Blackbird.

UNDER THREAT The range of this species is small, and its numbers are falling, because of habitat loss, with marshland areas being drained.

Yellow-headed Blackbird

FAMILY Icteridae
SPECIES *Xanthocephalus xanthocephalus*
LENGTH 9½ in (24 cm)
HABITAT Marshland/fields
CLUTCH SIZE 3–5

DISTRIBUTION Western Canada, reaching Alberta and southeast to the Great Lakes. Inland down the west United States' coas;, resident in southern California. Overwinters in Arizona and New Mexico.

RICH YELLOW plumage on the head, extending down on to the breast, is characteristic of the male, whereas hen Yellow-headed Blackbirds have a dusky yellow area here. They are duller overall, with the glossy black of the male being replaced by brownish-black feathering. Young birds of both sexes are dark in color, with a buff-yellow plumage on the head.

BEHAVIOR Marshland areas are frequented by these blackbirds. Cocks undertake an elaborate courtship dance to attract mates at the start of the breeding season.

Bobolink

FAMILY Icteridae
SPECIES *Dolichonyx oryzivorus*
LENGTH 7 in (18 cm)
HABITAT Grassland/fields
CLUTCH SIZE 4–7

DISTRIBUTION Summer range extends from southern Canada east to Nova Scotia, south in a broad band across the United States as far as Kansas. Overwinters in South America.

THE COCK BOBOLINK in breeding condition has a jet-black face, with a white area on the nape of the neck, which has a yellowish hue. The rump is also white, with white edging to the wings and narrow white wing bars evident here too. It is impossible to distinguish the sexes outside the breeding season, as both then have a streaked appearance. Pairs breed on the ground in areas of grassland, constructing a cup-shaped nest here. It will take about two weeks before their eggs hatch, with the young leaving the nest after a similar period.

FALLING NUMBERS The Bobolink is not as common as it used to be in various parts of its range today.

Eastern Meadowlark

FAMILY Icteridae
SPECIES *Sturnella magna*
LENGTH 9½ in (24 cm)
HABITAT Meadow/fields
CLUTCH SIZE 3–7

DISTRIBUTION Summer range to Nova Scotia, and southwest across the United States to Arizona. Largely resident below the Great Lakes down through Texas, where some birds overwinter.

THE MARKINGS of these meadowlarks are individual. They have streaked upperparts, with prominent stripes above the eyes. There is some black on the throat, with the underparts being yellow. Markings vary between individuals, but the sexes cannot be distinguished by differences in plumage. The mottled patterning helps to conceal these birds very effectively in their grassland habitat. As their name suggests, meadowlarks are talented songsters, with cocks singing loudly in spring to attract mates. Their dome-shaped nest made of grass is well-concealed on the ground, and the hen incubates alone.

IDENTIFICATION A long, pointed bill and short tail are characteristic features of the Eastern Meadowlark, creating a rather dumpy appearance.

Western Meadowlark

FAMILY Icteridae

SPECIES *Sturnella neglecta*

LENGTH 9½ in (24 cm)

HABITAT Grassland/open
country

CLUTCH SIZE 3–7

DISTRIBUTION Summer visitor from British Columbia to the Great Lakes and the northern United States. Resident in the west and central parts. Overwinters eastward to Tennessee.

THE RANGE OF the Western Meadowlark overlaps in part with that of its Eastern cousin, to the extent that these birds may interbreed in some areas. They are very similar in appearance, although there is usually a distinction in their calls, with those of the Western species being rather like the notes of a flute. These meadowlarks are also effective mimics, however, so that in areas where the western species is present, Eastern Meadowlarks may mimic their song. They tend to occur in slightly different habitats though, with Western Meadowlarks favoring more open areas, where the grass is shorter. They spend much of their time on the ground, searching for invertebrates as well as seeds. When nesting, the hen incubates on her own, with the eggs taking approximately 14 days to hatch. The young meadowlarks will then leave the nest once they are about 12 days old. From some distance away, these birds can be identified by their shallow wing beats, fluttering in flight rather like a butterfly.

FEEDING Western Meadowlarks may be spotted in open country, often hunting for food on road verges.

Bronzed Cowbird

FAMILY Icteridae

SPECIES *Molothrus aeneus*

LENGTH 8¾ in (22 cm)

HABITAT Open country/farmland

CLUTCH SIZE 1 per nest

DISTRIBUTION Summertime visitor to southwestern parts of the United States. Resident population in Louisiana, and in Mexico.

COWBIRDS ARE so-called because of the way they associate with herds of cattle, catching invertebrates disturbed by their grazing activities or even pulling ticks directly off the cattle. The black plumage of the male has a very distinct bronze sheen, with hens being duller overall. Pairs do not actually rear their own chicks in this case. Instead, when the hen is ready to lay, she seeks out the nests of other birds, depositing a single egg in each one.

PARASITIC PARENTING Over 30 different species of birds are known to have reared Bronzed Cowbird chicks successfully. Hens often seem to prefer to lay in the nests of orioles and blackbirds.

Brown-headed Cowbird

FAMILY Icteridae

SPECIES *Molothrus ater*

LENGTH 7½ in (19 cm)

HABITAT Woodland/farmland

CLUTCH SIZE 1 per nest

DISTRIBUTION In summer from northwestern Canada east to southern Newfoundland, and south to northern Arizona and New Mexico. Overwinters across southern parts and down the west coast.

BROWN FEATHERING on the head and chest distinguishes the cock of this species, with hens being grayish-brown. This is another parasitic species, with hens seeking out and laying in the nests of small birds such as vireos and warblers. The hen will also destroy their eggs at this stage, and other eggs laid by her own species, preventing them from hatching. The foster parents will then put all their energy into raising the young cowbird chick when it hatches in due course. Hen Brown-headed Cowbirds may lay over 70 eggs in a breeding season.

DIET Brown-headed Cowbirds spend much of their time on the ground, hunting for invertebrates and seeds.

Rusty Blackbird

FAMILY Icteridae
SPECIES *Euphagus carolinus*
LENGTH 9 in (23 cm)
HABITAT Wet woodland
CLUTCH SIZE 4–5

DISTRIBUTION Breeds right across northern Canada, overwintering in the southeastern United States, south of the Great Lakes, typically east to South Dakota.

DURING THE BREEDING season, the cock bird is black with green iridescence on his plumage, while the female is slate-gray, with both having bright yellow eyes. Only during the winter do adult birds appear rusty-brown in color, with slight barring present on the underparts. Hens have a gray rump, and young birds resemble adults in winter plumage on fledging.

AQUATIC HABITAT This particular blackbird is usually seen close to water, and may even forage here for aquatic creatures ranging from shrimps to tadpoles.

Brewer's Blackbird

FAMILY Icteridae
SPECIES *Euphagus cyanocephalus*
LENGTH 9 in (23 cm)
HABITAT Open country/parks
CLUTCH SIZE 4–6

DISTRIBUTION Summer range extends across southwestern Canada, down to the Great Lakes, south to Colorado. Resident through much of the western United States, overwintering in the south.

AN IRIDESCENT PURPLISH head helps to identify the cock of this species, with the remainder of the body having more of a greenish tinge. During the winter months, however, this iridescence is less noticeable. Hens and young birds are grayish-brown. Nesting occurs in colonies.

ADAPTABLE Brewer's Blackbird is an adaptable species, often seen in city areas where pairs may nest in parks.

Boat-tailed Grackle

FAMILY Icteridae

SPECIES *Quiscalus major*

LENGTH 14–16 in (36–41 cm)

HABITAT Saltwater marshland/ lakes

CLUTCH SIZE 3–5

DISTRIBUTION Resident down the Atlantic seaboard of the United States, from southern New York state southward, being found throughout Florida and along the Gulf coast to Texas.

THE HEN IN THIS CASE is noticeably smaller than the cock, and can also be distinguished by her tawny-brown underparts. Boat-tailed Grackles tend to live in groups and breed colonially too. They build bulky nests, which are generally located high up in trees.

SUCCESSFUL This grackle's range has been expanding progressively out of the marshlands into adjacent areas of countryside for over a century.

Common Grackle

FAMILY Icteridae

SPECIES *Quiscalus quiscula*

LENGTH 12½ in (32 cm)

HABITAT Fields/backyards

CLUTCH SIZE 4–6

DISTRIBUTION Southern parts of the Northwestern Territories eastward to Nova Scotia and southeast to eastern New Mexico in summer. Resident in eastern parts of United States.

THE COMMON GRACKLE is a highly adaptable species, occurring in a wide range of different habitats. Cock birds may vary in appearance, with the most commonly seen form having a bronze hue on the lower part of its body, and blue on its head and breast, but there is also a purple form, which has suffusion of this color replacing the blue.

FEEDING These grackles may eat seeds, invertebrates, amphibians, and small fish. They will also raid nests of other birds for eggs and chicks.

Great-tailed Grackle

FAMILY Icteridae

SPECIES *Quiscalus mexicanus*

LENGTH 15–18 in (38–46 cm)

HABITAT Open country/ marshland

CLUTCH SIZE 3–5

DISTRIBUTION Occurs in the summer from Oregon to western Iowa, and resident from California and Nevada to Arizona, New Mexico, and Texas east to Missouri.

THESE LARGE AND SPECTACULAR grackles are social by nature, seen in flocks. They can be easily sexed, partly because hens are brown in color, with buff plumage above the eyes and on the underparts, while young birds resemble hens but may display some streaking here. Cock Great-tailed Grackles are black, with a purplish gloss on their plumage, and also discernible by their yellow rather than dark eyes. There is also a marked difference in size between the sexes, as cock birds are significantly larger. Great-tailed Grackles will eat a very varied diet, even scavenging on discarded food and garbage, as well as hunting for invertebrates and robbing the nests of other birds. When breeding, they create a bulky nest, often incorporating twigs along with grass and other vegetation. This may be well-concealed in a reed bed, or located in a tree, depending on the birds' environment. The eggs are incubated by the hen on her own for approximately 14 days, and then the young grackles will fledge once they are about three weeks old. The range of this species is presently increasing within the United States, both to the north and the west.

PLUMAGE The tail feathers of the Great-tailed Grackle increase in width toward their tips.

COMMON GRACKLE (*see* p. 358) Iridescence is a feature of the plumage of many icterids, particularly cock birds, as illustrated by this male Common Grackle. The eyes are often colorful too, being a pale yellow shade in this case.

Bullock's Oriole

FAMILY Icteridae

SPECIES *Icterus bullockii*

LENGTH 8¼ in (21 cm)

HABITAT Woodland near water

CLUTCH SIZE 3–6

DISTRIBUTION Ranges widely over western parts, from southern British Columbia to western North Dakota and south to Texas. Small resident coastal population in southern California.

THE BRIGHT YELLOWISH coloration that typifies cock orioles is evident in this species, with hens and young birds being duller in appearance. Their upperparts are olive-brown, with yellow plumage on the throat and breast becoming whiter over the belly. The white wing bars are apparent, offset against the dusky wing coloration. This species is closely related to the Baltimore Oriole and in areas where their distribution overlaps, they may often hybridize together. The bluish-white eggs, with darker scrawls over the surface, are laid in a nest that hangs down from the tip of a branch, carefully woven from plants fibers. The hen will incubate the clutch on her own, and the chicks should hatch after about two weeks. The young orioles will then leave the nest after a similar interval.

IDENTIFICATION The male Bullock's Oriole can be recognized by its black cap, black eye streak, and prominent white patches evident on the wings.

Hooded Oriole

FAMILY Icteridae

SPECIES *Icterus cucullatus*

LENGTH 8 in (20 cm)

HABITAT Woodland/ suburbs

CLUTCH SIZE 3–5

DISTRIBUTION Summertime visitor to southwestern United States, including California and Arizona, and southern areas of New Mexico and Texas.

THIS ORIOLE is a relatively common backyard visitor through its range, especially in areas where there are palms or trees nearby for breeding purposes. The hen bird is quite subdued in coloration compared with the cock, being olive-yellow on her head and underparts, with gray wings. The black bill curves slightly along its length, and this may assist these orioles in taking nectar from flowers. They may also be drawn to backyard hummingbird feeders, although fruit, berries, and invertebrates are usually the main items in their diet.

COLORATION The cock bird in this case has prominent black feathering on the throat, as well as on the back and wings.

Baltimore Oriole

FAMILY Icteridae
SPECIES *Icterus galbula*
LENGTH 8¼ in (21 cm)
HABITAT Deciduous woodland
CLUTCH SIZE 3–6

DISTRIBUTION Eastern British Columbia to Nova Scotia, but absent from the southeastern United States in summer. Overwinters from north Carolina through Florida to southern Louisiana and Texas.

THE LINKS BETWEEN this oriole and Bullock's Oriole are such that they are sometimes considered to be a single species, referred to as the Northern Oriole. Although cock birds do differ significantly in terms of their appearance, hens and juveniles are actually very similar. As in the case of other orioles, the cocks have an attractive song. Hens sometimes sing back in an apparent reply to their partner's call, a behavior that is known as duetting.

PLUMAGE Cocks have a black cap on the head, with orange-yellow underparts and a bar of similar coloring on each wing.

Scott's Oriole

FAMILY Icteridae
SPECIES *Icterus parisorum*
LENGTH 9 in (23 cm)
HABITAT Arid grassland/ light woodland
CLUTCH SIZE 3–5

DISTRIBUTION Summer range north to southern Idaho and Wyoming, east to Texas. Resident on the southern Californian border. Overwinters in Arizona.

THE MALE Scott's Oriole has black feathering on the head and chest, extending over the back to the wings. The underparts are yellow, with white wing bars clearly evident. Hens in comparison are duller, with olive-green upperparts. Occurring in relatively dry areas, they may nest not just in trees, but in yuccas as well, creating a typical hanging pouch-shaped nest. When young cock birds molt out of juvenile plumage, they usually start to develop black feathering on the chest and around the eyes initially.

GARDEN VISITORS Orioles can often be attracted to visit backyards regularly by putting up fruit, such as the sliced oranges, for them.

Black Rosy Finch

FAMILY Fringillidae

SPECIES *Leucosticte atrata*

LENGTH 6 in (15 cm)

HABITAT Montane areas

CLUTCH SIZE 3–5

DISTRIBUTION Summer visitor to eastern Oregon. Main range extends from Idaho and Montana down to Nevada in the west and New Mexico in the east.

THE NATURAL HAUNTS of these finches lie above the tree line, where they forage on the seeds of plants, as well as catching various invertebrates. They may move to lower altitudes when the weather becomes more severe in the winter. The body of the cock bird is blackish, with this area being more of a dark gray shade in hens. As the name implies, there is a very evident rosy suffusion on the wings and underparts in the cock, but again, these areas are paler in hens.

SEASONAL CHANGE The bill coloration of these finches changes according to the season, being blackish in the summer, as seen here, and changing to yellow over the winter period.

Gray-crowned Rosy Finch

FAMILY Fringillidae

SPECIES *Leucosticte tephrocotis*

LENGTH 5¾ in (14 cm)

HABITAT Montane areas

CLUTCH SIZE 3–6

DISTRIBUTION Summer visitor to much of Alaska south to British Columbia, and resident from here down to California. Main wintering area is to the east, to New Mexico.

THERE ARE TWO FORMS of the Gray-crowned Rosy Finch, with those occurring in the Rocky Mountains having brown plumage on the cheeks. The heads of birds from further north are mostly gray in color, aside from black plumage on the crown, the areas around the eyes, and on the chin. Hens are less brightly colored than cock birds. They nest in among rocks, constructing a bulky nest of moss and other vegetation here.

STANDING OUT The coloration of these rosy finches means they are quite conspicuous when seen against a snowy landscape.

Evening Grosbeak

FAMILY Fringillidae

SPECIES *Coccothraustes vespertinus*

LENGTH 8 in (20 cm)

HABITAT Woodland/backyards

CLUTCH SIZE 3–4

DISTRIBUTION Resident throughout southern Canada to Newfoundland and the western side of the United States. Winters east and south of this range.

THESE GROSBEAKS wander over a wide area, sometimes being common in one locality and then becoming scarce in the region over successive years, although their overall population is stable. Their movements tend to be the result of the changes in the availability of food. They will be attracted to backyard feeders, however, where their stout bills allow these birds to dehull sunflower seeds with ease. Evening Grosbeaks are conspicuous birds in woodland, as flocks are noisy by nature, with their calls drawing attention to their presence in an area. Pairs may nest close together too.

GENDER DIFFERENCES The cock is more brightly colored than the hen, whose plumage is a grayish-yellow shade.

Red Crossbill

FAMILY Fringillidae

SPECIES *Loxia curvirostra*

LENGTH 6¼ in (16 cm)

HABITAT Coniferous forest

CLUTCH SIZE 3–5

DISTRIBUTION Resident right across Canada, from southern Alaska to Newfoundland, and western parts down to Mexico. Eastward, generally not seen widely south of the Great Lakes.

THE MOST DISTINCTIVE feature of crossbills as a group is the way in which their bills are twisted over each other, rather than meeting at their tips. This modification means that they can extract seeds from pine cones more easily. Red Crossbills wander widely in search of suitable areas where pine cones are present. They can

COLORATION The sexes are easily distinguished: Only the cock bird (*left*) is red; hens are olive-gray.

be very common for a period, and then simply disappear as their food supply becomes exhausted and the birds move on. They may even be seen in parks if cones have matured on the conifers growing there.

White-winged Crossbill

FAMILY Fringillidae

SPECIES *Loxia leucoptera*

LENGTH 6½ in (17 cm)

HABITAT Coniferous forest

CLUTCH SIZE 3–4

DISTRIBUTION Resident throughout Canada, except for the far north. Winters in northern parts of the United States, from northeastern Montana and North Dakota eastward.

THE WHITE BARS running back from the shoulder region, and across the wing itself, help to identify this species. These areas of white plumage are smaller in immature birds, which otherwise resemble hens. On close examination, the bill of the White-winged Crossbill is relatively narrow compared with other crossbills, allowing it to feed more effectively on spruce rather than pine cones.

PLUMAGE This is a hen White-winged Crossbill. Cock birds have pinkish-red plumage, without any streaking on their bodies.

Pine Grosbeak

FAMILY Fringillidae

SPECIES *Pinicola enucleator*

LENGTH 9 in (23 cm)

HABITAT Coniferous/ deciduous woodland

CLUTCH SIZE 2–5

DISTRIBUTION Summer range from central Alaska eastward around Hudson Bay. Resident in the east to Idaho and some localities further south. Overwinters from eastern British Columbia eastward.

THESE RELATIVELY LARGE finches are usually seen in pine and spruce woodland areas, but particularly during the winter, they often wander further afield into deciduous woodland, and may be seen in parks and orchards. When breeding, a pair builds a bulky nest of twigs and other vegetation, with a softer lining for the spotted, greeny-blue eggs. The hen sits on her own, with incubation lasting for about 14 days. The young will then fledge after a period of approximately 21 days.

DISTINCTIVE FEATURE The red coloration of the Pine Grosbeak is reminiscent of a crossbill, but these birds can be easily distinguished by their respective bill shapes.

Common Redpoll

FAMILY Fringillidae
SPECIES *Carduelis flammea*
LENGTH 5¼ in (13 cm)
HABITAT Forest/tundra
CLUTCH SIZE 3–6

DISTRIBUTION Summer range extends across the far north, to Greenland. Resident to the south, from western Alaska to Newfoundland. Winter visitor south to the Great Lakes.

THE RED PLUMAGE on the top of the head is a characteristic feature of these hardy finches. Their range extends high up within the Arctic Circle, where they may shelter in mini-igloos of snow, created by the way in which it has drifted. Common Redpolls feed on seeds, as well as invertebrates, the latter are particularly important during the breeding season. Pairs nest on the ground, with young birds lacking the red markings of adults when they first leave the nest.

COLORATION The pink feathering on the breast indicates that this is a cock bird. Hens have white plumage here.

Hoary Redpoll

FAMILY Fringillidae
SPECIES *Carduelis hornemanni*
LENGTH 5½ in (14 cm)
HABITAT Tundra
CLUTCH SIZE 3–6

DISTRIBUTION Summer visitor to northwestern Greenland. Resident across the far north. Winters across Canada to the northeastern United States.

THIS REDPOLL may sometimes be seen in mixed flocks with Common Redpolls, although they do not interbreed. These species may be distinguished because, as its name suggests, the Hoary Redpoll has what can be described as a frosted appearance. Its plumage appears whiter overall, with little or no dark streaking apparent on the rump. Cocks have pinkish breast feathering.

SOCIAL When migrating, Hoary Redpolls are likely to be seen in large flocks, although these finches rarely travel as far south as the United States.

Pine Siskin

FAMILY Fringillidae
SPECIES *Carduelis pinus*
LENGTH 5 in (13 cm)
HABITAT Coniferous forest
CLUTCH SIZE 3–6

DISTRIBUTION Seen from southern Alaska across to Labrador in summer. Resident to the south and west, to Arizona and New Mexico. Overwinters through the United States.

THESE FINCHES occur in flocks, feeding together and sometimes combining with other species such as American Goldfinches. They eat a variety of foods, and are a frequent visitor to backyard bird feeders over the winter, when other food is scarce. Unusually, young birds in this case are more colorful than adults, with their streaked underparts being yellowish rather than white.

SOCIABLE BEHAVIOR Pine Siskins will even nest in groups, although the hen incubates the eggs alone. The cock will help to feed the chicks.

Lesser Goldfinch

FAMILY Fringillidae
SPECIES *Carduelis psaltria*
LENGTH 4½ in (11 cm)
HABITAT Fields/suburbs
CLUTCH SIZE 4–5

DISTRIBUTION Summer visitor seen across southern Canada, resident through most of the northern and central United States, to California in the west. Overwinters across the entire south.

THE COCK BIRD of the Lessser Goldfinch has a black crown, with bright yellow underparts and white patches on the wings and tail. They may be encountered not just in open areas, but also on the fringes of woodland. Lesser Goldfinches will eat various seeds, and may visit backyard feeders on a regular basis in suburban areas. Pairs nest in trees, or sometimes in bushes.

FEEDING Flocks of Lesser Goldfinches can be frequently observed in areas where thistles have seeded, as these plants are a favored source of food.

American Goldfinch

FAMILY Fringillidae
SPECIES *Carduelis tristis*
LENGTH 5 in (13 cm)
HABITAT Fields/suburbs
CLUTCH SIZE 3–6

DISTRIBUTION Summer visitor to southern Canada. Resident further south, down the west coast and in central and eastern parts. Present across the southern states in winter.

THE APPEARANCE of the male American Goldfinch changes markedly through the year, since they become much more brightly colored at the start of the breeding season. Hens are also transformed, with pale yellow plumage replacing the mainly gray-colored underparts leading up to this period. Males have cinnamon-brown upperparts in winter, appearing duller, with whitish plumage on the belly.

NESTING American Goldfinches build a cup-shaped nest from grass and other vegetation. Chicks are reared on invertebrates, as well as seeds.

House Finch

FAMILY Fringillidae
SPECIES *Carpodacus mexicanus*
LENGTH 6 in (15 cm)
HABITAT Open country/suburbs
CLUTCH SIZE 3–5

DISTRIBUTION Resident northward to southern British Columbia and other parts of southern Canada, down across the entire United States, although absent from southern Florida and southern Louisiana.

THESE FINCHES have expanded their range considerably over recent years, as they formerly only occurred in the west. Some House Finches were released in the vicinity of New York around 1940, and since then, they have prospered there, becoming widely established. Part of their adaptability stems from the fact that they will build their cup-shaped nest almost anywhere, even within buildings or hidden in the branches of trees. House Finches also eat a very varied diet, including invertebrates, seeds, and fruit.

PLUMAGE Red feathering on the head, extending to the breast, indicates that this is a cock bird. Hens have brownish, streaked plumage overall.

USEFUL BOOKS AND REFERENCES

Alderfer, Jonathan. *Complete Birds of North America*. National Geographic, 2006.

Alderton, David. *The Illustrated Encyclopedia of the Birds of the Americas*. Lorenz Books, 2004.

Alsop, Fred J. III. *Smithsonian Handbooks: Birds of North America—Eastern Region*. Dorling Kindersley, 2001.

Alsop, Fred J. III. *Smithsonian Handbooks: Birds of North America—Western Region*. Dorling Kindersley, 2001.

Alsop, Fred J. III. *Smithsonian Handbooks: Birds of the Mid-Atlantic*. Dorling Kindersley, 2002.

Alsop, Fred J. III. *Smithsonian Handbooks: Birds of New England*. Dorling Kindersley, 2002.

Brewer, David. *Wrens, Dippers and Thrashers*. Christopher Helm, 2001.

Brudenell-Bruce, P.G.C. *The Birds of New Providence and the Bahama Islands*. Collins, 1978.

Bull, John and John Farrand. *The Audubon Society Field Guide to North American Birds (Eastern Region)*. Knopf, 1977.

Byers, Clive, Olsson, Urban, and Jon Curson. *Buntings and Sparrows: A Guide to the Buntings and North American Sparrows*. Pica Press, 1995.

Cassidy, James (ed.). *Book of North American Birds*. Reader's Digest, 1990.

Dorst, Jean. *The Life of Birds*, two volumes. Weidenfeld & Nicolson, 1974.

Ferguson-Lees, James and David A. Christie. *Raptors of the World*. Christopher Helm, 2001.

Fjeldsa, Jon and Niels Krabbe. *Birds of the High Andes*. Zoological Museum, University of Copenhagen and Apollo Books, 1990.

Fry, C. Hilary, Fry, Kathie, and Alan Harris. *Kingfishers, Bee-eaters and Rollers*. Christopher Helm, 1992.

Gibbs, David, Barnes, Eustace, and John Cox. *Pigeons and Doves*. Pica Press, 2001.

Godfrey, Earl W. *Birds of Canada, NMC Bulletin 203*. National Museums of Canada, 1966.

Harrap, Simon and David Quinn. *Tits, Nuthatches and Treecreepers*. Christopher Helm, 1996.

Hayman, Peter, Marchant, John, and Tony Prater. *Shorebirds*. Christopher Helm, 1986.

Hilty, Steven L. and William L. Brown. *A Guide to the Birds of Colombia*. Princeton University Press, 1986.

Howell, Steve N. G. and Sophie Webb. *A Guide to the Birds of Mexico and Northern Central America*. Oxford University Press, 1985.

Hoyo, Josep del, Elliott, Andrew, and Jordi Sargatal (series' eds.). *Handbook of Birds of the World, Vols 1–12*. Lynx Edicions. 1992–2007.

Jaramillo, Alvaro and Peter Burke. *New World Blackbirds*. Christopher Helm, 1999.

Johnsgard, Paul A. *The Hummingbirds of North America*. Smithsonian Institution Press, 1983.

Land, D. *Birds of Guatemala*. Livingstone, 1970.

Madge, Steve and Hilary Burn. *Wildfowl*. Christopher Helm, 1988.

Madge, Steve and Phil McGowan. *Pheasants, Partridges and Grouse*. Christopher Helm, 2002.

Ogilvie, Malcolm and Carol. *Flamingos*. Alan Sutton Publishing, 1986.

Peterson, Roger T. *Peterson Field Guides: Western Birds*. Houghton Mifflin Co., 1961.

Peterson, Roger T. *Peterson Field Guides: Eastern Birds*. Houghton Mifflin Co., 1980.

Ridgely, Robert S. and J. Gwynee. *A Guide to the Birds of Panama*. Princeton University Press, 1989.

Ridgely, Robert S. and Paul J. Greenfield. *The Birds of Ecuador*. Christopher Helm, 2001.

Schauensee, Roldolphe M. de and William H. Phelps. *A Guide to the Birds of Venezuela*. Princeton University Press, 1978.

Sibley, David. *The North American Bird Guide*. Pica Press, 2000.

Sibley, David. *The Sibley Guide to Bird Life and Behavior*. Knopf, 2001.

Udvardy, Miklos D. F. *The Audubon Society Field Guide to North American Birds (Western Region)*. Knopf, 1977.

Wetmore, Alexander. *Song and Garden Birds of North America*. National Geographic Society, 1964.

GLOSSARY

B

Breeding plumage The typically more colorful plumage acquired in the case of some species by one or both members of a pair at the start of the breeding season.

C

Carrion Dead animals eaten by some birds, such as vultures.

Cob A male swan.

Cock Term for the male bird of a species.

Contour feathers The small feathers that cover the surface of the body.

Crown The top of the head.

Cryptic plumage Feathering that serves to disguise the outline of the bird, helping it to blend into its background.

D

Dabbling A term used for ducks which feed at the surface, rather than diving in search of food.

Distribution The typical area where a species occurs, although this may vary at different times of the year.

Diurnal A description applied to those birds of prey which are active during the day, in contrast to others, such as owls, that fly under cover of darkness.

Down The rather fluffy plumage of chicks, also present but less conspicuous in adult birds, serving primarily to insulate the body.

E

Ear coverts The feathers covering the ear orifices, behind the eyes.

Eclipse plumage The feathering that replaces the **breeding plumage**, with the result that over the winter, for example, it may not be possible to distinguish between the sexes in the case of waterfowl.

F

Flanks The sides of the body.

Flight feathers The long feathers running along the back of each wing that allow the bird to fly.

Frugivore A bird that feeds mainly on fruit.

H

Hen Term for the female bird of a species.

I

Insectivore A bird that feeds mainly on invertebrates.

L

Lek A communal display area where **cock** birds of certain species display at the start of the breeding period, in the hope of attracting a mate.

Lores The area between the bill and the eye, on each side of the face.

M

Mantle Area of the back and wings.

Melanistic A bird with darker plumage than normal, thanks to the increased presence of the dark pigment melanin.

Migration The way in which birds may fly from one area to another, depending on the season. Birds that undertake such journeys are called migrants.

Molt The process by which plumage is replaced, typically in the spring and then in the fall.

N

Nape The back of the neck.

Nidicolous A description of chicks, such as those of passerines, that hatch in a helpless state, and are totally reliant on adult birds for their wellbeing.

Nidifugous A description of chicks of waterfowl, for example, that hatch in an advanced state of development with their eyes open, and are able to move and swim almost immediately afterward.

Nuchal Refers to the neck.

O

Orbital The area of skin around the eye.

P

Passage The route flown by birds on **migration**, along which they may be spotted when resting or feeding.

Pectoral Relating to the breast.

Pen A female swan.

Precocial Equivalent to **nidifugous**.

R

Raptor A general name to describe a bird of prey.

Rump The lower back.

S

Seabird A general description of a species that ranges out over the ocean.

T

Territory An area occupied by one or more birds, which may be defended against potential intruders.

Torpid Inactive, a situation usually arising in birds from cold temperature combined with a shortage of suitable food.

U

Underparts The underside of the bird's body.

Upperparts The upper area of the bird's body.

V

Vagrant A bird that is present outside its usual area of distribution.

W

Wader A bird that frequents the shoreline.

Webbed feet The skin that links the toes of water birds, acting rather like a paddle and making it easier for them to swim.

Wing bar One or more stripe-like areas of different coloration running across the wing.

Wing coverts The feathers covering the wing.

INDEX OF COMMON NAMES

INDEX OF SCIENTIFIC NAMES

INDEX

ACKNOWLEDGMENTS

With thanks to the whole team at Studio Cactus, and also the late Stan Bayliss-Smith, author of *Wild Wings to the Northlands* for early inspiration, both as an ornithologist and as a teacher.

Studio Cactus would like to thank Sharon Rudd and Laura Watson for design work; Sharon Cluett for original styling; Jennifer Close and Jo Weeks for editorial work; Penelope Kent for indexing; Robert Walker for picture research; Anthony Duke for range maps; Claire Moore for introductory illustrations; Sharon Rudd for Order silhouettes.

PICTURE CREDITS

The publishers would like to thank the following for permission to reproduce copyright material:

Abbreviations: a = above, b = bottom, c = center, l = left, r = right, t = top

Carlos Arranz 17 (br); Bob Blanchard 384; Steve Byland 320–321; Richard H. Connors 245 (t); 277 (b); Corbis 220; Mike Danzenbaker 34; 35 (b); 36 (b); 203 (t); 236 (bl); 240 (t); 251 (b); 253 (b); 267 (t); easyshoot 18 (br); Karel Gallas 18 (blc); Getty Images 90 (t); 248–249; 260–261; 297; R.L. Hambley 380; Princess Lola 17 (cl); Robert A. Mansker 308–309; Maslowksi Productions 204 (t); 217; 284 (b); 340 (t); Charles W. Melton 364 (b); Erin Monn 18 (brc); Christian Musat 16 (b); pasphotography 18 (bl); Ed Phillips 18 (bc); Photolibrary Group 33 (t); 37 (t); 44 (t); 44 (b); 82; 153 (b); 183; 212 (b); 233 (b); 269 (t); 276 (b); 290–291; 347 (b); SouWest Photography 18 (crc); Brad Thompson 360–361; Graham Tomlin 192–193; Martin Trajkovski 336–337; H. Tuller 383; Jason Vandehey 18 (cc); Michael Woodruff 371; Workmans Photo 18 (cr); Robert Young 6; Andy Z 18 (clc). All other images © NHPA

Cover images all © NHPA except (from left to right) front cover bottom: Corbis (2); back cover top: Maslowski Productions (1)